A Face Drawn in Sand

A Face Drawn in Sand

Humanistic Inquiry and Foucault in the Present

Rey Chow

Columbia University Press / New York

Columbia University Press
Publishers Since 1893
New York   Chichester, West Sussex
cup.columbia.edu
Copyright © 2021 Columbia University Press
All rights reserved

Library of Congress Cataloging-in-Publication Data

Names: Chow, Rey, author.
Title: A face drawn in sand : humanistic inquiry and Foucault in the present / Rey Chow.
Description: New York : Columbia University Press, 2021. | Includes bibliographical references and index.
Identifiers: LCCN 2020039956 (print) | LCCN 2020039957 (ebook) | ISBN 9780231188364 (hardback) | ISBN 9780231188371 (trade paperback) | ISBN 9780231547796 (ebook)
Subjects: LCSH: Foucault, Michel, 1926–1984. | Humanism.
Classification: LCC B2430.F724 C495 2021 (print) | LCC B2430.F724 (ebook) | DDC 194—dc23
LC record available at https://lccn.loc.gov/2020039956
LC ebook record available at https://lccn.loc.gov/2020039957

Cover image: René Magritte, *The Human Condition II* (1935)
© 2020 C. Herscovici / Artists Rights Society (ARS), New York.
De Agostini Picture Library/ Bridgeman Images
Cover design: Lisa Hamm

The breakdown of philosophical subjectivity and its dispersion in a language that disposes it while multiplying it within the space created by its absence is [sic] probably one of the fundamental structures of contemporary thought.

—Michel Foucault, "A Preface to Transgression"

Contents

Part I. Humanistic Inquiry in the Era of the Moralist-Entrepreneur

    Introduction: Rearticulating "Outside" 3

Part II. Exercises in the Unthought

1. Literary Study's Biopolitics 39
2. "There Is a 'There Is' of Light"; or, Foucault's (In)visibilities 63
3. Thinking "Race" with Foucault 87
4. "Fragments at Once Random and Necessary": The *Énoncé* Revisited, Alongside Acousmatic Listening 113
5. From the Confessing Animal to the Smartself 139

    Coda: Intimations from a Series of Faces Drawn in Sand 165

Acknowledgments 167

Notes 169

Index 207

A Face Drawn in Sand

Part I

Humanistic Inquiry in the Era of the Moralist-Entrepreneur

Introduction
Rearticulating "Outside"

It seems to me that essentially there have been only two major models for the control of individuals in the West: one is . . . exclusion . . . and the other is . . . inclusion.

—Michel Foucault, *Abnormal*

An interesting article in the *New York Times* in the fall of 2017 describes how some of the richest businesspeople in the United States today are also among the most generous donors to charity. Some of these people, such as Facebook's Mark Zuckerberg and his wife, Priscilla Chan (founders of the Chan Zuckerberg Initiative), focus on medical science and disease-control research; others, such as George Soros, the founder of Open Society Foundations, contribute billions toward realizing the ideals of eliminating intolerance and promoting equality and democracy around the world. Still others, such as Bill and Melinda Gates, Warren Buffett, and Jeff Bezos, have been known to give away millions or billions to vital causes such as education (including education for children in less-developed parts of the world), global health, and climate-change research.[1] In her book *The New Prophets of Capital*, Nicole Aschoff summarizes this new phenomenon of philanthrocapitalism: "Unlike the traditional foundations (Rockefeller, Carnegie, Ford), philanthrocapitalists don't believe in old-fashioned charity. They have greater ambitions. Philanthrocapitalists want to harness the forces of capitalism that made them fabulously wealthy to help out the rest of the planet."[2]

As David Gelles, the author of the *New York Times* article, writes, "If a handful of billionaires want to spend their fortunes saving lives, why not simply applaud them? But as their ambitions grow, so too does their influence, meaning that for better or worse, a few billionaires are wielding considerable influence over everything from medical research to social policy to politics."[3] This new-age altruism is notable on several counts. The first is, as Gelles suggests, influence premised on ready cash: these megadonors' ideas and ideals have the power to shape everything from biomedical research to public policy, from education initiatives to political debates because of the spectacular quantities of money the donors have stockpiled. There is, in other words, an explicit causal relation between capital and benevolent giving in the form of one-way traffic, with benevolent giving being an effect of wealth accumulation rather than being the directive for wealth distribution and sharing. Second, such altruism fosters a public sphere in which certain types of issues tend to receive financial investment—the types that fit the "problem-solving mentality."[4] Issues that involve tangible material objects and procedures, such as equipment, trials, experiments, and iterative research, are usually the ones that succeed in obtaining funding. Such investment is, of course, far from purely financial even when the money is critical: it is also a signal that only some questions are worth exploring, and to be worth exploring, the questions must ultimately generate profits (thus providing an incentive for philanthrocapitalists to care in the first place). Third—and this is, I believe, the most notable aspect of new-age altruism—even something as seemingly nonnegotiable as the idea of social justice is under these circumstances eminently negotiable because the promulgation of social justice, not only in rhetoric but also in action, now seems a logical derivative from extreme corporate ownership, extreme income inequality, and extreme wealth hoarding. Social justice is being reinvented as a subsidiary of the capitalist enterprise, inextricable from the overall operative of generating profits. Hence, the popularity of "diversity" and "inclusion" as corporatist strategies and "best practices"—to appeal to the widest possible clientele.[5]

Humanistic inquiry, in contrast, cannot be further from such a problem-solving mentality. At its most radical, humanistic inquiry is about problems that do not have ready solutions, unlike the kind that can be delegated empirically in the form of lab space, high-tech equipment, retrofitted facilities, and iterative test procedures, with the prospects of patentable or saleable final products. If this fundamental difference of humanistic inquiry had been acknowledged, debates about the humanities in recent years might have taken a different turn whereby, instead of appending ever more purposeful-sounding modifiers to the word *humanities—environmental, medical, public, civic, neuro-, digital,* and *computational*—we could have allowed the modes of intellectual labor specific to humanistic inquiry to reassume center stage. This would not have to mean adopting a conservative or conservatively disciplinary stance toward the humanities. Rather, it would mean demonstrating the conceptual and practical manners in which humanistic inquiry handles intellectual problems without necessarily seeking to legitimize—or profitize—the relevance of its undertakings by way of social utility and consensus. The possibility of reimagining humanistic study in these terms is the basic assumption, orientation, and aspiration of this little book.

Michel Foucault's work has been a crucial threshold for my thinking, even though this book is not intended as a study exclusively of his writings. Foucault matters for a number of reasons. The tremendous impact his work has had on the humanities and interpretative social sciences internationally since the 1970s (despite continued resistance from some disciplinary sectors) suggests that a Foucauldian imprint is by now a familiar part of scholarly debates, from literature to political philosophy and theory, from science studies to queer and transgender theory, and from geography to cultural studies and visual studies. Meanwhile, the posthumous publication of the Collège de France lectures he delivered from the mid-1970s to 1984 and the slow but steady releases of other previously unpublished works have given us an updated and more expansive Foucault, who not only supplements the Foucault of classics such as *Discipline and Punish* and *The History of Sexuality* but also directs attention to timely topics such as security, territory, population, self-governance (especially as elaborated by authors of Greco-Roman antiquity), modern art, and visibilities. This host of topics makes it necessary to ask anew how Foucault's work continues substantially to enrich and, indeed, to mold humanistic and transhumanistic inquiry and how the challenging big questions he raised during his brief career—about the ordering and production of knowledge, the genealogy of human sexual practices, the state politics of population management, and the relations among pleasure, care, and self-governance, to name just a few—remain entirely current in the twenty-first century. The historically still-evolving nature of these questions is such that no adequate, let alone correct answers can ever be established without contention, and that is precisely the significance of Foucault's enduring legacy.

The Controversy Over Critique

At this juncture, a mode of thinking and writing associated with Foucault and his contemporary French philosophers of the mid–twentieth century, generally referred to as *critique*, warrants some reflection. An oft-cited challenge posed to critique is found in Bruno Latour's article "Why Has Critique Run Out of Steam? From Matters of Fact to Matters of Concern" (2004).[6] With his characteristically wicked humor, Latour raises a fundamental issue about the post-Kantian, post-structuralist direction of criticism as pursued by contemporary Western (largely Anglo-American) academic thought, a direction that, according to him, has witnessed its most impactful configurations in the popular trends of deconstruction, discourse analysis, and social constructivism. Latour begins his essay with this lament about wars:

> Wars. So many wars. Wars outside and wars inside. Cultural wars, science wars, and wars against terrorism. Wars against poverty and wars against the poor. Wars against ignorance and wars out of ignorance. My question is simple: Should we be at war, too, we, the scholars, the intellectuals? Is it really our duty to add fresh ruins to fields of ruins? Is it really the task of the humanities to add deconstruction to destruction? More iconoclasm to iconoclasm? What has become of the critical spirit? Has it run out of steam?   ("Why Has Critique," 225)

In the rest of the essay, Latour elaborates his questions with numerous memorable metaphors and caricatures, alluding to the collective practitioners of critique (himself included) as guilty of the following habits and tendencies: a refusal to suspend disbelief, a proclivity toward instant revisionism (often before the facts are settled), implicit or explicit attribution of conspiracy to others, and suspicion of ideological manipulation everywhere. Behind the mischievous jokes and at times mean-sounding portrayals of his predecessors and contemporaries, Latour delivers a priestly plea to rectify an intellectual climate in which things seem to have gone terribly wrong.[7] In a virtually confessional and seemingly contrite tone, Latour writes, "The mistake we made, the mistake I made, was to believe that there was no efficient way to criticize matters of fact except by moving away from them and directing one's attention toward the conditions that made them possible" ("Why Has Critique," 231). According to him, this movement has led ultimately to a decimation of "objects," which are either dismissed offhand as fetishes or distrusted as projections of some hidden dark intents.[8] "Is it so surprising, after all," Latour writes, "that with such positions given to the object, the humanities have lost the hearts of their fellow citizens, that they had to retreat year after year, entrenching themselves always further in the narrow barracks left to them by more and more stingy deans?" ("Why Has Critique," 239).

The mention of the "more and more stingy deans," of course, returns us squarely to the issue of monetary support: what kinds of questions are deemed worthy of funding at a time when resources are dwindling largely because of a historically unprecedented, exponential expansion of the university managerial class, dedicated to entrenching its own indispensability in what the political scientist Benjamin Ginsberg has called "the spread of administrative blight,"[9] often accompanied by a discourse of faculty supervision that other scholars have nicknamed "bullshit"?[10] As Bill Readings already wrote in the early 1990s, "The specificity of the modern University [sic] that the German Idealists founded was its status as the site of critique,"[11] but in the university as a transnational corporate bureaucracy things are quite different. In this setting, the administrator rather than the scholar-professor is the central figure. For the administrator, the university's tasks are figured "in terms of a generalized logic of 'accountability' in which the University must pursue 'excellence' in all aspects of its functioning."[12] As Chris Lorenz puts it, "The unstoppable rise of league tables—the ranking of citations, individual researchers, research groups, institutes, and whole universities—is an integral part of this development in the direction of audit cultures and an audit society."[13] His supposedly objective vision notwithstanding, Latour, in admonishing critique for the dire situation he depicts, does not touch upon this crucial aspect of bureaucratic obsession with accountability. To borrow from Foucault's comments on the history of sexuality, such a logic of accountability is "the internal discourse of the institution—the one it employ[s] to address itself, and which circulate[s] among those who [make] it function."[14] For Latour, accountability is rather a matter of reflecting on the etymological and philosophical connotations of the word *thing*—as parliament, forum, agora, congress, and court, as a gathering that involves society, association, and multifarious participants—that should be brought to bear on the investigation of academic objects. Instead of debunking (which he relegates to an activity of war, as indicated in his opening lines in "Why Has Critique Run Out of Steam?"), critics should, he urges in a manner that calls to mind his well-known "actor-network-theory,"[15] engage in gathering, assembling, and *adding to* (instead of subtracting from) reality.[16] ("Is it really possible to transform the critical urge in the ethos of someone who adds reality to matters of fact and not subtract reality?" ["Why Has Critique," 232].) As I discuss later, this viable point about adding may indeed be the crux of the matter, though not exactly in the way Latour envisages it.

What Latour has portrayed is a vivid picture of what I have elsewhere described as the ongoing practices and effects of "European theory in America," whereby intellectual investigations published in French in particular have acquired global attention through their translations into the English language.[17] My suggestion is in part corroborated by the list of French-language authors Latour calls out as villains, including Jean Baudrillard, Michel Foucault, and Pierre Bourdieu. (Michel Serres and Isabelle Stengers, in contrast, like the Anglos Alfred North Whitehead and Alan Turing, are for him the virtuous heroes.) And, as we know, the ideas of Immanuel Kant (the archvillain) and Martin Heidegger (a semi-archvillain with some redeeming qualities), though written in German, have also become more widely circulated through their offshore French agents who are then, as is often the case, translated into English.[18] Given the translational complications of this transgenerational, transatlantic scene, let me dwell a bit more on Latour's derisive sketch of the addiction to critique he has found on American campuses:

> Entire Ph.D. programs are still running to make sure that good American kids are learning the hard way that facts are made up, that there is no such thing as natural, unmediated, unbiased access to truth, that we are always prisoners of language, that we always speak from a particular standpoint, and so on, while dangerous extremists are using the very same argument of social construction to destroy hard-won evidence that could save our lives. ("Why Has Critique," 227)

Isn't it really worth going to graduate school to study critique? "Enter here, you poor folks. After arduous years of reading turgid prose, you will be always right, you will never be taken in any more; no one, no matter how powerful, will be able to accuse you of naiveté, that supreme sin, any longer? Better equipped than Zeus himself you rule alone, striking from above with the salvo of antifetishism in one hand and the solid causality of objectivity in the other." ("Why Has Critique," 239)

Once Kant and his followers crossed the Atlantic, or so according to Latour's sketch, their philosophical probing into the limits of reason seems to have metastasized so aggressively as to envelope "entire Ph.D. programs" and put us all on the road to perdition. Which Ph.D. programs might these be? Are they really attended only by "good American kids"? Clearly, the point of these generalizations is to offer a caricature, a stereotype, so we should probably overlook the anonymity of the Ph.D. programs and the exclusion of other kinds of kids in said programs. Rather, what is more disturbing is Latour's elision of some basic, practical questions: How do European philosophy and theory typically transition into North American academe, and how does such a transitioning produce the unfortunate consequences, the mayhem, he dramatizes? Should we blame the producers of philosophy and theory (those clever and vile Europeans) or the audience (those gullible and opportunistic Americans)? Or is there something about the material circumstances of transatlantic transitioning that deserves closer scrutiny because it is bound up with a transnational university entrepreneurialism to which the very currency of Latour's work—the fact that it is being published by top venues, read, taught, debated, circulated, and thus has acquired influence in North America and elsewhere—is not an exception? Is not such currency in alignment with the success of those "automated reflex-action deconstructors" ("Why Has Critique," 243) that he disparages? To invoke Latourian terminology, what are the actors or actants involved in this academic network?

To be fair, higher education should indeed, to use Latour's titular phrase, be a matter of concern. His proposed ideal of "gathering" and "adding," however, seems a somewhat weak fix to the problems he presents, not least because the claims to sharing, cooperation, collaboration, and togetherness (as he suggests) are, as we have seen with the philanthrocapitalists mentioned earlier, a hallmark of global entrepreneurialism. In the research university setting, these altruistic claims translate readily into the mantra "interdisciplinarity." (Even the "more and more stingy deans" tend, by default, to be enthusiastic about interdisciplinarity these days.) To that extent, Latour's plea for "a multifarious inquiry launched with the tools of anthropology, philosophy, metaphysics, history, sociology to detect how many participants are gathered in a thing to make it exist and to maintain its existence" ("Why Has Critique," 246) is, if not already a reality, a concept firmly condoned by elite administrative culture, often with provisions of support of one kind or another. Although Latour equates critique with a taking-away (a subtraction from reality) and advocates in its stead an adding-to, the reverse can also be argued—namely, that one effect critique has had on knowledge production in academe is precisely the imperative to renegotiate disciplinary boundaries with the input of other kinds of actors and that a consciously pluralistic perspective has been well under way in the nameless Ph.D. programs he ridicules.

Latour's analysis is offered from the standpoint of science studies, but his displeasure at critique is shared by many working in the humanities as well. In what some have called a backlash against critique that is often traced to Paul Ricoeur's suggestion, in 1970, of a hermeneutics of suspicion instigated by Marx, Nietzsche, and Freud,[19] various scholars have provided reappraisals of critique's emergence in the historical context of modern European religious and secular intellectual practices as well as accounts of how critique has evolved in such ways as to become associated with the arts, literature, and the literary humanities in general.[20] Other scholars describe critique as a thought style that slices across differences of field and discipline, a genre, an ethos, a method, a sensibility, a critical mood, a spirit of incessant interrogation, an affective instance that orients us in certain ways, and a reflex negativity.[21] Critique, it is said, can be "like an upscale detox facility" or "like Baskin Robbins ice cream ... in various flavors."[22] All in all, as a contagious yet charismatic mode of "skepticism as dogma,"[23] critique has, over the past few decades, banalized gestures of demystification and impoverished the study of literature and art. Still other scholars, arguing the continued relevance of Marx, Nietzsche, and Freud, dispute the view that a more fashionable "surface reading" can serve as an antidote to the symptomatic reading associated with critique, which may be defined as "the practice that endeavors to think what we cannot know in advance."[24]

An interlocutor whose intervention has exerted an influence perhaps as broad as if not broader than Latour's, albeit among a somewhat different audience, is Eve Kosofsky Sedgwick. In her renowned essay "Paranoid Reading and Reparative Reading, or, You're so Paranoid, You Probably Think This Essay Is About You" (1997),[25] Sedgwick, without referring to critique as such, invokes the psychoanalytic category of paranoia in her analysis of the methodological assumptions that undergird what has, for her, become a monopolistic intellectual program of suspicion and exposure. She sums up these methodological assumptions in this manner: "Subversive and demystifying parody, suspicious archaeologies of the present, the detection of hidden patterns of violence and their exposure:... these infinitely doable and teachable protocols of unveiling have become the common currency of cultural and historicist studies" ("Paranoid Reading," 143). Although, unlike Latour, Sedgwick is writing from the standpoint of literary studies and queer theory (citing scholars such as D. A. Miller and Judith Butler, among others), she obviously likewise deems it necessary to find comic relief in what she characterizes as "the broad consensual sweep of such methodological assumptions, the current near professionwide agreement about what constitutes narrative or explanation or adequate historicization" ("Paranoid Reading," 143–44). This pedagogical situation seems to her increasingly shallow and unviable:

> A disturbingly large amount of theory seems explicitly to undertake the proliferation of only one affect, or maybe two, of whatever kind.... It's like the old joke: "Comes the revolution, Comrade, everyone gets to eat roast beef every day." "But Comrade, I don't like roast beef." "Comes the

revolution, Comrade, you'll like roast beef." Comes the revolution, Comrade, you'll be tickled pink by those deconstructive jokes; you'll faint from ennui every minute you're not smashing the state apparatus; you'll definitely want hot sex twenty to thirty times a day. You'll be mournful *and* militant. You'll never want to tell Deleuze and Guattari, "Not tonight, dears, I have a headache."   ("Paranoid Reading," 146, Sedgwick's emphasis)

In the midst of both hilarity, as indicated by the tone of this quote, and a sobering sense of realism—marked by the mention in the essay of her own advanced breast cancer and the deadly ailments afflicting her close friends—Sedgwick suggests that we consider as an alternative to paranoia the merits of "reparative reading." With reference to the psychoanalytic work of Melanie Klein and Silvan Tomkins as well as to the writings of Marcel Proust, she describes how the reparative mode sets itself apart from both the anticipatory and the nostalgic temporalities of the paranoid mode. Instead of aiming to unmask, reveal, demystify, and expose the shortcomings of a particular text, a reparative reading would rather energize (readers) by highlighting epiphanic experiences that give pleasures in ways that are aesthetic or ameliorative or both. And with a stress strikingly in tune with Latour's, Sedgwick speaks of adding, of assembling, and of conferring plenitude on an object: "The desire of a reparative impulse . . . is additive and accretive. Its fear, a realistic one, is that the culture surrounding it is inadequate or inimical to its nurture; it wants to assemble and confer plenitude on an object that will then have resources to offer to an inchoate self" ("Paranoid Reading," 149).

Relations of Exteriority, Logics of Reparation

These debates around critique and paranoid reading are without question intelligent, stimulating, and instructive. Marked as they are by a commendable reflexivity on the perceived affects—what may be described as knee-jerk attitudes of denigration and antagonism toward objects of study—purportedly triggered by the widespread dissemination of post-structuralist theory, these debates are in many ways part of a collective's periodic stocktaking and self-evaluation. As Ashley Barnwell points out in a judicious analysis of Latour's and Sedgwick's discussions, however, "The move to leverage new methods *against* critical methods risks recuperating a partition between verifiable and felt truths, or facts and values."[26] Noting the ambiguities in the two theorists' narratives—ambiguities that mark tensions, struggles, and entanglements between subjective impressions and objective realities—Barnwell suggests that the points of differentiation between critique and postcritique methods are actually quite mutable. Propelled by *concern* and based on *experience* (according to the authors' autobiographical statements), Latour's and Sedgwick's *critiques* of critique seem in many ways robust participants in the hermeneutics of suspicion they scorn.

That being said, what seems noticeably absent from these heated debates is a reflection on the global rather than the strictly national or regional ramifications of such knee-jerk attitudes (the kind of combative group "mentality" or style that forms the butt of Latour's, Sedgwick's, and other critics' jokes). If an outcome of critique *popularized* is an active imagining of relations of exteriority—of possibilities that lie outside established structures of meaning production—how might such democratic imagining be evaluated in light of what Latour, Sedgwick, and others have observed as (what seem to be) increasingly cynical and formulaic enactments of the critical impulse in Western academe? Above all, how can we go about considering such globality or transnationality without resorting immediately to a geographical extension or an epidermal spread—that is, by simply equating such words (*globality, transnationality*) with mere *countable* additions (more countries, more skin tones, more languages, more cultures, etc.)?

To help elucidate what is at stake, let me, for the moment, borrow some basic terms from the familiar vocabulary of structuralism. In one way, we can say that a groundbreaking step introduced by critique is the simple yet profound dislocation of the sign—the rifting apart, that is, of the signifier and the signified, the binary constituents supposed to be held together by convention to produce stable meanings. If critique may be condensed in this manner, with what events of humanistic knowledge production has this breakup of the sign been coeval (contemporaneous), events that may be described as global or transnational?

If the signifier is, say, the work of Jane Austen, what does the rift between that signifier and the signified (some general, abstract notion of Jane Austen) suggest? A similar series of questions has been posed regarding other familiar signifiers such as *Europe, man, history, world, family, woman, English,* and so forth.[27] If each of these signifiers used to be anchored in safely integrated registers, that anchoring can no longer be assumed in contemporary academic inquiry; it is often not even feasible. This ever-widening chasm between the familiar bearers of presumed stable meanings, on the one hand, and the shifting plurality of possible significations nudging such bearers, on the other, is perhaps the signature, irreversible contribution that critique has made in humanistic learning of the past several decades. *This is the nudging of what may be called an "outside"* (a thematic that runs throughout Foucault's work). The knee-jerk negative attitudes that critique has purportedly helped bring about, in other words, may be understood in terms of a heightened awareness of this proliferation of significations that can no longer be comfortably contained under/within (their once assumed) signifieds or cinched to (once accepted) universals. The slippages between ever-multiplying, possible objects of study and these objects' supposedly corresponding but often rapidly changing meanings have instead come to dominate contemporary intellectual horizons, oftentimes to the exclusion of substantive contents.

Still, how exactly are such relations of exteriority played out in the day-to-day institutional context? This crucial question somehow escapes Latour's and Sedgwick's attention even as they portray the attitudes of enmity adopted by "entire Ph.D. programs" and "a disturbingly large amount of theory" or endorsed "near professionwide." A similar negligence of this question characterizes many other accounts decrying critique's folly. Although abundant in impassioned judgments, such accounts typically offer little evidence of how critique functions with a collectively accepted rationality in an actual pedagogical environment. Let us attempt a response by adhering to the convenient example of Jane Austen.

A fictional work by Austen can be studied by drawing on literature, history, and economics, including the subfields within these disciplines—English literature of the nineteenth century, the social history of conduct and etiquette, the history of women writers, imperial economics of the rising British Empire, domestic economics of the middle and upper-middle classes in Britain, and so on. An awareness of relations of exteriority in this case would be a matter, to use Latour's and Sedgwick's suggestions, of *adding to* an existing object and in that manner opening the established borders of specialized knowledge terrains in an approach that has come to be named *interdisciplinarity*. If this additive opening of disciplinary borders is, strictly speaking, a work in progress—because knowledge expansions and revisions are potentially limitless—it has meanwhile crisscrossed another phenomenon in the contemporary Western university. A class on Jane Austen, under the rubric of English, is nowadays placed on more or less equivalent footing in terms of course scheduling to classes on, say, Asian cinema, queer theory, Wittgenstein's theory of language, African American fiction, existentialism, Marxist cultural theory, film philosophy, Hegel, Althusser, science fiction, Lacanian psychoanalysis, Walter Benjamin, introduction to Latinx studies, Holocaust films, brain cultures, and social movements in the age of social media. Such mindboggling heterogeneity of epistemic encounters in many a college curriculum has seldom been addressed, even though it is, I believe, as much an outcome of the globalizing consequences of critique as it is a feature of interdisciplinarity.

In the North American context, at least, knowledge pursued under a more traditional discipline such as literature is nowadays made to cohabit not only with knowledge from comparably traditional disciplines (such as philosophy and history) but also with knowledge pursued under the rubrics of area studies (involving East Asia, South Asia, the Middle East, Latin America, and sub-Saharan Africa) and identity studies (pertaining to women, gender and sexuality, LGBT, transgender, black, Latinx, postcoloniality, and disability issues). Bearing the claims and demands of another kind of "outside," the objects, rationalities, and practices of these other studies are quite differently conceptualized.[28] Unlike the *haut-bourgeois* Enlightenment ideal of disinterestedness, these other studies are typically established and pursued with explicit group interests and purposes. In the case of area studies, for instance, the pursuit of non-Western languages and cultures has for so long been entangled with and aided by the U.S. State Department's foreign-policy agendas and initiatives that the end of the cold war has led to a decline in funding for such studies.[29] Identity studies, meanwhile, emerged from the U.S. civil rights movement of the 1960s and its mission to advance minoritized subjects and populations such as women and peoples of color, and it continues to expand its reach to those involved in updated or newly visible politicized struggles.[30]

Despite these ongoing histories, seldom do we stop to ponder the incongruence of the latter—what some have called *intersectional—*studies' institutional cohabitation with the more formal disciplines.[31] That cohabitation intimates equivalent standing and comparable value, but the disjuncture between the epistemic underpinnings of, say, early modern English and social media studies, between analytic philosophy and disability studies, or between classics and Asian American history is simply too acute not to be heeded. Although their juxtaposition in an institutional setting advances the administrative ideal of letting plural forms of learning flourish alongside one another, the arguably discordant effects produced by such juxtapositions are far from having been confronted, let alone resolved. It would not be much of an exaggeration to say that the humanities curriculum across many colleges and universities today resembles Borges's imaginary Chinese encyclopedia, famously invoked by Foucault at the beginning of *The*

Order of Things to underscore the vertiginous collapse of conventional European classificatory reasoning (a collapse that Foucault likens to an aphasiac's linguistic dysfunction).[32] As though to corroborate Foucault's point, a comparative literature conference in 2009 listed the following possible topic areas in its call for papers: comparative literary history; literature and the languages; world literature, translation, and globalization; colonial and postcolonial literatures; deconstruction and its legacies; hermeneutics; gender, sexuality, and eroticism; drama, theater, and performance; the history of the discipline; philosophy and religion; psychoanalysis, trauma, and testimony; visual arts and architecture; technology, media, audio-visual culture; sociology, anthropology, and political economy; history and historiography; geography, geology, and ecology.[33]

In a manner that speaks uncannily to the progressivist entrepreneurial spirit of our time, this liberally diversified and inclusive curriculum also resembles cable television, a marketplace where each channel must aggressively promote its own brand of programming (replete with attention-grabbing course titles and synopses, syllabi previews, advertising flyers, and trackable previous consumers' ratings) in order to compete for subscribers. The language of "shopping" so matter-of-factly adopted by students on U.S. campuses during the first two weeks of a semester or quarter, when they make decisions about which courses to take, is perhaps only a handy demonstration of this widely accepted, commercial-business ambience of higher learning. In this ambience, the hodgepodge of disciplinary knowledge, area-based knowledge, and identity-based knowledge seems collaboratively to fulfill a troubling because consensually instrumentalized function: this, I believe, is the juncture at which the knee-jerk denigration and antagonism attributed to critique need to be heard as being in sync with *a specific kind of refrain about the "global" or "transnational."* How so?

If, for the knee-jerk denigrators and antagonists, Western knowledge must be disparaged as deficient because it is Eurocentric, racist, sexist, homophobic, and so forth, area-based or identity-based knowledge easily comes in as a form of risk management or damage control for this perceived deficiency, a corrective measure that would help adjust the biases inherent in our institutional structures. Let us make way for a black theme or a transgender emphasis here and there; let us add a sampling of women, colored folks, and people of different sexual or religious orientations just so we can meet the requirements (whose requirements?) for diversity and inclusiveness![34] Contrary to the basis of disinterestedness that underpins classical humanistic inquiry,[35] area-based and identity-based knowledge (and their representatives) are, within the corporate university milieu, thus aligned with an implicit *solution* to the problems that supposedly beset the conventional pursuits of Western knowledge. This problem-solving and, I would add, *reparative* logic whereby some kinds of knowledge carry the service function of delivering (or at least bringing us closer to) social justice and whose presence supposedly attests to a neoliberal academy's compassion, atonement, and capacity for "self-culpabilization"[36] mean that a certain kind of purpose—not so much the financial imperative of providing jobs as the moralistic imperative of providing rehabilitation for the soul (whose soul?)—is systemically yoked to a part of humanistic inquiry in an attempt to rescue all of it. Obviously, my use of the notion of "reparative" in a material sense—pertaining to reparations, indemnities, compensations, and similar demands imposed on defeated parties during warfare—differs from Sedgwick's use of the term in the psychoanalytic sense of therapy.[37]

This curricular solutionism is a leading factor in why humanistic inquiry has found it so difficult, if not virtually impossible, to refashion itself with credibility in the early twenty-first century. The predominant idea of moral repair—together with the variables of remedy, redress, uplift, rebirth, and remodeling—means that transcendental signifieds are once again activated but this time affixed to area-based and identity-based signifiers (be they peoples, practices, languages, histories, or cultures). This bungling of the disciplinary, geopolitical, and identitarian valences of "outside" through the logic of reparation has led to a distinctively *compensatory* atmosphere in the current higher-education institution. On the one hand, formal disciplines of knowledge such as philosophy, history, religion, and literature (that is, English and classics) continue to be the mainstays of humanistic inquiry; on the other hand, we are also told that we *should* foster the other kinds of learning based in diverse areas and identities. Set against the formal disciplines, nonetheless, the rationales of knowledge brought along by designated betterment projects from Asian studies to women's studies and ethnic studies inevitably seem improper simply because their formations are differently articulated and their objectives far from disinterested. Although in one respect they are performing the task of what Jacques Derrida calls the "dangerous supplement" (an addition that, once introduced, tends to unsettle the entirety of the preceding chains of signification),[38] these other forms of knowledge are in effect made to shoulder what might be called *the white academy's burden* (of filth and guilt). For precisely that reason, within the knowledge economy of the university they are often perceived as lacking the prestige and respectability of the classical disciplines. After all, they have been brought in as a kind of cleaning service, and engaging with them remains, in the eyes of many colleagues, tantamount to intellectual slumming.

Limits, Caesuras, Heterotopias, Predeterminisms

This is the point at which a return to the notion of "outside" as it repeatedly occurs in Foucault's work seems opportune, even as ambivalences and tensions are likely to persist. Simply put, is "outside" an antagonistic excess, capable of destroying the limits of extant discourse (as in what Foucault calls *déraison* in his study of madness), or is "outside" a matter of the delimiting constraints that sustain discursive formation (in what Foucault theorizes as the archaeology of knowledge)? As Austin Sarfan asks in a nuanced study, "Is the outside an ahistorical or historical phenomenon?"[39]

In his engagement with Maurice Blanchot's thought, Foucault reads "the outside" (*le dehors*) as a force of intensity stemming from language's dispersal or canceling-out of itself. Rather than being a site of geographical certitude, the outside in Blanchot's work has to do with "the anonymity of language liberated and opened to its own boundlessness." In this context, Foucault describes the outside as an open (or openness) to which one cannot gain access because, he writes, "the outside never yields its essence. The outside cannot offer itself as a positive presence."[40] Although his philosophical observations about Blanchot and other writers (Sade, Hölderlin, Nietzsche, Mallarmé, Bataille, Artaud, and Klossowski) would eventually give way to more sociologically oriented investigations of disciplinary and biopolitical society's systemic segregations—of those who are diagnosed as mentally ill, behaviorally criminal, sexually perverse, and politically dangerous—Foucault is clearly invested throughout his career in "outside" as a way to grapple with the limits of European reason in their multidiscursive, multi-institutional iterations. As he demonstrates in so many different analyses and discussions, these limits need to be historicized not simply by way of empirical additions but also, more importantly, through a disassembling of the relations of forces that bind them together in the first place.[41]

Such a disassembling is possible only if we keep in mind a point Foucault underscores in the first preface to *The History of Madness*: "What is originary," he writes, "is the caesura that establishes the distance between reason and non-reason."[42] Etymologically, the word *caesura* means "a cut"; in the same paragraph, Foucault also refers to the "cutting gesture." He has written elsewhere that "knowledge is not made for understanding; it is made for cutting."[43] Addressing "outside" can then be seen as an endeavor to examine the caesuras or cuts that for one reason or another have become hegemonic (that is, dominant and entrenched yet invisible). Although recognizing that such hegemony might have taken on the appearance of being irreducible during a particular historical period (say, several hundred years), Foucault suggests that thinking "outside" is simultaneously a matter of asking how other cutting gestures, not necessarily these, not necessarily in this manner, *might* have been possible. This is what Foucault proposes "as a very first definition of critique": "a way of thinking" that is also "the art of not being governed like that and at that cost."[44]

Does not Foucault have the caesura in mind when he talks about *heterotopia*, foregrounding the relations of seriality, proximity, segmentation, and juxtaposition (as opposed to hierarchy) that, according to him, define conceptions of space in modern times?[45] How might Foucault's vision of other or different spaces help revitalize humanistic inquiry without becoming recuperated under a reparative regime, the kind that governs by calibrating, indeed litigating, social relations in terms of debts, credits, damages, indemnities, audits, and other monetized settlements?[46] Perhaps only when critical practice refrains from rushing in to fill "outside" with a set of predeterminisms about the objects under investigation—when critical practice, rather than automatically bypassing or foreclosing hard questions, allows such questions to unfold intensively from within the disparities of these objects (including, in particular, their self-contradictions)?

Although these suggestions are by no means new, a problem we face in the contemporary university setting is that of an implicit selection process whereby only some objects tend to receive this kind of intensive critical attention,[47] while other objects typically receive only—and are frequently endorsed by—treatment of a predetermined kind. What does such predetermined treatment look like or sound like? The knee-jerk denigration and antagonism pointed out by Latour and Sedgwick, for instance, would mean that a text by a white author is subject to dispute because it is, by default, considered symptomatic of Western imperialism and exploitation. By the same token, a non-Western author, text, artifact, artwork, film, or happening is often assumed in an a priori manner to be oppositional and emancipatory. That is to say, irrespective of content, the non-Western X is often preassigned a politicized status and fixed in an externally imposed role—as the witting or unwitting harbinger of repair and purification to

Western thought. Along similar lines, it would be inconceivable these days for an author of a nonheteronormative sexual orientation to speak or write in any other manner than a presumed resistance, silent or staged. In all these cases, a tacit pact of already-known meaning has been made in advance, independent of the author's speech, the historical circumstances of production, or the work itself.

"Outside" Normed; or, the Repressive Hypothesis as Consensus

When Foucault coins the phrase "the repressive hypothesis" in *The History of Sexuality*, he challenges precisely an instance of such predeterminism in the generation of discourse across modern Western society (*HS*, 1:15–49). "In the course of recent centuries," Foucault writes, the phenomenon of sex has been "multiplied in an explosion of distinct discursivities which took form in demography, biology, medicine, psychiatry, psychology, ethics, pedagogy, and political criticism" (*HS*, 1:33). As is characteristic of Foucault's mode of inquiry, it is not exactly the object per se—in this case the widely held belief in sexual repression—that he is trying to cast in doubt.[48] Of much greater concern to him is the question of how such a *consensus*, such a mass submission to that belief is possible—how it becomes a pivotal force in social organization, directing and cohering entire modes of conduct and the discursive circuits around them. With what mechanisms in the state management and control of populations, what prescriptions for copulation and biological reproduction within the nuclear family, and what incitements to discourse in different sectors of everyday life is this event of a collective *un*questioning accomplished? Raising such issues is, we might say (echoing Latour), Foucault's way of *adding to an object*, of restoring to the object its multiple layers of historicity, intensity, and still-dormant potentiality.

For these reasons, more consideration needs to be given to the little word *hypothesis*. Foucault's point is that the consensus about our being repressed may be just that, a hypothesis, a supposition. We may go so far as to say that this *hypo*-thesis, this "iffy" space that, etymologically speaking, is below the stronghold of a thesis, is for Foucault something of an epistemic leeway. Although this leeway, this flexible fringe area, undoubtedly signals the possibility of a heterotopos, it is also exactly where a norm, so to speak, tends to gather momentum—typically by experimenting with various distinctions, such as the distinctions between what is permissible and what must be forbidden, what is good and what is bad, what is valuable and what is disposable, what can be talked about and what must be hushed up, and so forth. As Foucault writes in *Discipline and Punish*, the art of punishing in the regime of disciplinary power "brings five quite distinct operations into play. . . . The perpetual penalty that traverses all points and supervises every instant in the disciplinary institutions compares, differentiates, hierarchizes, homogenizes, excludes. In short, it *normalizes*."[49] Only when such distinctions or distinctive operations are pursued through repeated courses of action over time does a norm become solidified—become *normed*, as it were. And what is becoming-normed if not precisely the process in which, beyond the positivity of everyday happenings, a transcendental import comes somehow to be conferred on select beliefs and practices, which henceforth proceed with the mythical aura of an exception? As Foucault writes, "What is peculiar to modern societies . . . is not that they consigned sex to a shadow existence, but that they dedicated themselves to speaking of it *ad infinitum*, while exploiting it as *the secret*" (*HS*, 1:35, Foucault's emphasis).

In an essay titled "Towards a Natural History of Norms," Pierre Macherey proposes that we approach Foucault's understanding of norms in terms of *immanence*, a notion central to Spinoza's philosophy.[50] As Macherey reads him, even as Foucault remains intrigued by the concept of the norm, he is careful to avoid any recourse to a transcendental sense of origination (one that could anticipate or predetermine what it would produce). Rather, Macherey argues, Foucault consistently directs attention to how the norm comes into existence only through its action. A few excerpts from Macherey's discerning comments go as follows:

In order to escape the myth of origins ... [i]t would also be necessary to understand that there is no norm in itself, there is no pure law, which could be affirmed as such in its formal relationship with itself, ... and could proceed out of itself only to mark its effects negatively by limiting them, or delimiting them. What we learn from the history of sexuality is that *there is nothing behind the curtain.*

In other words, sexuality is nothing more than the ensemble of historical and social experiences of sexuality, and in order to explain these experiences there is no need for them to be confronted with the reality of a thing in itself, whether this be situated in the law or in the subject to which it is applied, reality which would also be the truth of these experiences. *This is the nature of Foucault's positivism: there is no truth other than the phenomenal* and there is no need for reference to be made to any law which would anticipate the reality of the facts to which it is applied.

If the norm is not exterior to its field of application, this is not only because ... it produces it but because *it produces itself in it* as it produces it. Just as it cannot be said that it acts on a content existing independently of and outside the norm, so too *the norm is not in itself independent of its action ... It is in this sense that it is necessary to talk about the immanence of the norm*, in relation to what it produces and the process by which it produces it: *that which "norms" the norm is its action.*[51]

Reading with Macherey, we can say that for Foucault in the context of *The History of Sexuality*, volume 1, what has become normed is not so much sexual repression as the collective conviction that such repression's status is unquestionable—that is, that it precludes dissent. The norming course of action in the modern West has been such that "being repressed" has taken on the import of something that goes without saying: a kind of predeterminism that has proven exceedingly generative—anticipating, regulating, suspecting, forbidding, judging, penalizing, and valorizing innumerable elements that it keeps circulating and reproducing in a potent discourse.

Notably, a key feature of this discourse is a certain relation of exteriority, conjured in the form of a revolution that would liberate sex from the oppressive constraints that once kept it in check (such constraints are the negative parts, the kinks, so to speak, that the norm needs to work through in order to come into being). In light of Macherey's point about the immanence of the norm, however, Foucault's well-known concluding remarks in the first volume of *The History of Sexuality* are nothing short of a wake-up call: "We must not think that by saying yes to sex, one says no to power" (157). The "outside" projected by the liberation of sex—in denigrating and antagonistic relations to our putative condition of being repressed—is, for Foucault, eminently co-optable within the agency already granted the repressive hypothesis by our society. It is by soliciting such an outside as a transcendental promise ("have sex and you [or your value] will be redeemed") that the norm—to wit, the consensus about our repression—pulsates and replenishes itself. And it is in this specific sense that Foucault invokes the phrase "the speaker's benefit" to describe those who speak against repression as though they were, by performing such a "transgressive" speech act, outside the reach of power.[52]

The manners in which non-Western X's are typically empowered to speak in Western academe today are inextricably entangled with these manners in which sex was liberated in recent history—that is, through the steady, iterative fleshing-out of a certain repressive hypothesis.[53] The discursive place occupied by sexual repression is in this instance filled with references to negative encounters of a geopolitical or cross-cultural kind—imperialism, colonialism, racism, discrimination, and so forth—while a parallel evocation of a condition of subjugation—of being oppressed, disrespected, wounded, or violated—fuels a palpably norming, morally self-righteous discourse in action.[54] This discourse includes, in particular, the creation of distinctions that in turn become hierarchical selections: what kinds of generalizations are all right to declare in public versus what kinds are not; whom it would be safe to denounce in public and who must be shielded or revered; where it would be permissible to direct verbal aggression unchecked and where caution and reservation must be exercised. It is exactly the proliferative potency of this norming work, itself always a work in progress, that arguably gives rise to some of the pedagogical scenarios that so alarm scholars such as Latour and Sedgwick. As is the case with successful instances of norming, institutional—that is, material—benefits tend to accrue: audience attention, funding opportunities, career advancement, and the power to mobilize publics are some of them. Like Foucault's repressed sexuality, then—and in intimate kinship to those whom Latour censures as addicts to critique and those whom Sedgwick diagnoses as paranoiacs—the guilt-tripping figure of a non-Western or nonheteronormative *complainant* coming forward, alleging past crimes, injuries, and grievances seems fast becoming a newly normed paradigm of discourse incitement and dissemination in the humanities.[55]

What Latour and Sedgwick have left out in their accounts of the contemporary university, in other words, is a delicate and thorny issue that nonetheless needs to be spotlighted in order for the picture they present to come into sharper focus. In corporatized higher education, how do the knee-jerk tendencies of suspicion they so provocatively depict become ironically complicit with neoliberal bureaucratic tactics of embracing diversity and inclusiveness? How do these knee-jerk tendencies help aggrandize university managers, in particular, through a procedurally normed, and norming, politicized stance toward area-based and identity-based knowledge objects as well as minority subjects?[56] This ubiquitous scene of complicity, readily recognizable though it might well be, is the telltale missing piece in the prevailing puzzles on the pros and cons of critique.

Put somewhat differently, when the dislocated sign, propelled by critique, encounters the curricular panoply of formal disciplines, area studies, and identity studies in the globalized university, a function of "outside" tends to be routinely if not automatically imputed to specific forms of knowledge production, the most visible of which have been those associated with non-Western cultures and diversified sexual/life practices. Is it any surprise that these forms of knowledge, regularly normed through the twin mechanisms of moral reparation and entrepreneurial instrumentality, are so often performed by their practitioners as minefields where Western rationality by necessity trips, founders, and implodes? Even though these moralizing and entrepreneurial initiatives have granted marginal populations and representations a token share of visibility and recognition, they have also, by the sheer force of their norming impetus, precluded serious critical engagement with such populations and representations in ways that are on a par with their counterparts in the formal disciplines. Not only are such populations and representations left to multiply in the spirit of "anything goes" (as in cable television), but they are also presumed to be always-already oppositional and emancipatory in their acts of enunciation. From an evaluation of constraints, limits, and finite conditions of possibility (as in the Kantian sense of critique), critique has under these circumstances transformed into a verb, a modus operandi that preemptively invalidates what is deemed politically disagreeable—and by so invalidating seizes everything from professional attention to professional opportunity and advantage. Reading with Macherey on Foucault, we can venture that this is exactly how norms *congeal*—not at all metaphysically, but rather through a quotidian course of action routinely and repeatedly implemented. In this case, such congelation happens when "outside" has become enmeshed, since the second half of the twentieth century, with the corporate university's neoliberal strategies of governance and self-governance.

Foucault's Challenge: Thinking "Outside" Without Transcendental Guarantees

My discussion so far has concentrated on some of the more problematic consequences that have arisen not necessarily from critique per se, as some of critique's detractors might argue, but rather from the manner critique is institutionally situated between humanistic inquiry, on the one hand, and an entrepreneurial ethos that has become normed in the globalized university, on the other. This entrepreneurial ethos may be glimpsed from the daily bureaucratic communications with which faculty members everywhere are accustomed. Above all, as Bill Readings, Chris Lorenz, and others remind us, it is the rationale of accounting—not only in the sense of bookkeeping but also in the sense of performance indicators such as "output," "impact," and "recognition," self-assessment metrics, national and international rankings, career-advancement incentives and benchmarks, cost–benefit analyses, and their like—that nowadays underwrites the corporate university's understanding of its social responsibility, its role in higher education.[57] Under these conditions, a type of study dedicated to questions that have no calculable answers or marketable solutions would naturally seem out of place—and, in the eyes of some, altogether disposable. The justifications proposed for the humanities in recent years through different varieties of technological or moral appendages, including the very processes in which the notion of "outside" is normed through the service burdens attached to area-based and identity-based knowledge, are indexes to much larger and more precarious epistemic transitions in our time.

How does Foucault's work matter in the age of postcritique humanistic inquiry? In part II, I address topics from a number of fields and subfields as ways of responding to this question. Foucault's relevance, it seems to me, continues to revolve around the big question of "outside," and the challenge he offers is formidable. Thinking "outside" is for Foucault an exercise in pressing against the limits of a particular order of things, without, however, resorting to what I would call transcendental guarantees—those projections of a futuristic beyond in relation to which present limits are viewed simply as impediments, bad things to be overcome, like debt, poverty, illness, deformity, and mortality. Is the overcoming of limits necessarily a good thing? Or is such a "good" not part and parcel of a genealogy of morals in flux, a contingent assemblage of morphing states that, as always, is in the process of hardening into some comforting norm? These questions are among the most trenchant that Foucault leaves to his readers.

Here, the structuralist vocabulary of the sign (divided into signifier and signified) may no longer be adequate for the critical tasks before us. The sheer proliferation of material objects to be studied (interdisciplinarily, intermedially, and intersectionally), though ostensibly a joyous event in and of itself, is ever steadily giving way to a rebooted process of selection (and categorization) in which, as is usually the case, distinctions have to be made, followed by the hierarchization of values. Even as signifiers (and significations) multiply with the breakup of the sign, this pluralization wrought by sheer addition can have ramifications that are less than democratic. As the conceptual space once fortified by a magical alliance between signifier and signified stands evacuated, the sign also becomes a virtual backdoor through which transcendent continuities (in different versions of a newly invented, futuristic beyond) can creep back in. This is perhaps why for Foucault the operative interval—the decisive caesura or cut—is not exactly the slash between signifier and signified but rather, as he already signals in an early work such as *The Order of Things*, the interstice between (two or more) material entities, sites, series, or actions—for instance, between words and things or between speaking and seeing. One could further speculate that Foucault, perhaps because of his lifelong interest in history, including natural history that evolved into biological science, has the prescience to refrain from taking his analytic cues from the Saussurean sign, a structure that, despite its binarist (that is, split rather than unified) architectonics, is nonetheless subsumed under an overarching definition of linguistic signification as *incorporeal*. "In language there are only differences *without positive terms*".[58] in hindsight, this radical gist of Saussure's semiotics seems to assure a return of the transcendental even—and perhaps especially—when the sign disintegrates, when meanings begin to slip and slide.[59] In a resolutely immanent approach to "outside," Foucault insists, instead, on tackling different worldly phenomena (including language) in their material confrontations with one another.

There are a great many books about Foucault on the English-language academic market, but few, to my knowledge, use his work to reflect on the dead ends and potentialities of humanistic inquiry in the current Western academy. The rest of this book comprises a loosely linked series of microarguments aimed at foregrounding Foucault's germaneness for a nonutilitarian, nonconsensual approach to humanistic inquiry. By juxtaposing debates about literary study, visibilities and invisibilities, race and racism, sound/voice/listening, and self-governance and self-entrepreneurship in a constellation against what I am polemicizing as the moralistic-entrepreneurial norming of knowledge production, these microarguments are intended as renewed stresses on some of the basic issues facing humanistic study: How to process, analyze, and evaluate different types of texts? How to form and sustain arguments? How to reconceptualize familiar problems through lesser-known as well as very well-known sources and figures? Above all, *how not to have the answers before the questions are asked?*

A Brief Overview of Part II

Instead of seeing literary study as the reflector of a biopolitical reality, chapter 1 approaches the crisis of literary study (often invoked as a synonym for the crisis of the humanities) in terms of a biopolitical struggle. Returning to Foucault's analysis of the historical transformations of Western language usage over recent centuries and the emergence of differentiated disciplinary (or specialized) languages in modern times, explicated in *The Order of Things*, I discuss the crisis of literary study by tracing the vicissitudes of language *theorization* in the Western academy from the various attempts to reanimate the functions of language (such as those by I. A. Richards, T. S. Eliot, and Martin Heidegger) to the more recent efforts to change the object of literary study altogether, as found in Franco Moretti's controversial proposal of "distant reading." The interest of Moretti's project lies in his attempt at a methodological exteriorization, whereby a new object of literary study can be produced computationally by correlating data embedded—or stored linguistically—in those archives known as novels. In particular, I draw attention to an important factor that is left unexplored in Moretti's otherwise thought-provoking project: the status of visualization, as evidenced in the graphs, maps, and trees with which he calls for a rethinking—and salvaging—of literary learning. The discussion of this factor segues logically into the next chapter.

Chapter 2 examines Foucault's approach to visualization through a reading of some of his unfinished work on modernist art. With a focus on his writings on Édouard Manet and René Magritte, I take up the question of visibility and invisibility that underlies all of Foucault's work, a question that has not, to my mind, been sufficiently addressed even by Foucault scholars other than a few notable exceptions. What makes Foucault's approach vital is the fact that he does not assume visibility to be about transparency; instead, he treats visibility as an objectified presence whose emergence needs to be understood as historical rather than natural. By exploring his analyses of a number of artworks, from Manet's *Olympia* and *Luncheon on the Grass*, with passing references to *The Balcony* and other titles, to Magritte's *La Décalcomanie* and *This Is Not a Pipe*, I intend not to replicate Foucault's inimitable discussions but rather to use his self-described "amateurish" engagement with painting to underscore his distinctive conceptual method. This is a method in which space carries singular import—not only in the empirical sense of places, terrains, landscapes, and enclosures but also, perhaps more crucially, in the geometric and aesthetic sense of *place taking* that is synonymous with the unfolding of thought. (This is how Michel Serres, for instance, understands Foucault's project on madness.) As I demonstrate, Foucault's discussions of the details of these artworks offer fascinating clues to the ways in which he grapples with "outside."

When it comes to Foucault and questions of race, the critical challenge is presented by the ready charge of Eurocentrism—that is to say, the charge that Foucault's perspectives, bound as they are to European cultures and societies, are negligent of that "outside" that is the other parts of the world. In chapter 3, I propose ways of coming to terms with Foucault's significance for race studies without following the predictable (because geopolitically overdetermined) direction of this line of criticism. Among other things, I focus on Foucault's question "What in fact is racism?" As he writes in *"Society Must be Defended,"* racism "is primarily a way of introducing a break into the domain of life that is under power's control: the break between what must live and what must die."[60] Rather than understanding racism by way of differentiations based on anatomy or geopolitical location, Foucault characteristically returns it to relations of power (and, we might add, the discourses that revolve around such relations). For Foucault, such an approach clarifies racism first and foremost as a class struggle, whereby society is divided in a warlike manner between those who are privileged to live and those who must die (that is, those who are banished to some expendable "outside"). This struggle, always involving temporal and spatial particulars yet pertaining to the universals of life and death, has intimate links to Foucault's work on the history of sexuality in the West as well as to his numerous discussions of pastoral power, governmentality, police, populations, and post–Second World War neoliberalism.

Chapter 4 considers voice, sound, and listening, topics for which Foucault is not ostensibly known. This chapter seeks to establish a new point of departure for the (hitherto seldom studied) encounter between post-structuralist theory, including Foucault's work, and contemporary sound theory. Since the 1960s, the music theorists Pierre Schaeffer and Michel Chion have written about sound in terms that seem, in retrospect, entirely resonant with the exercises in critique. How can we resituate the theorization of sound alongside such exercises? I approach this question through a discussion of the theoretical and historical ramifications of listening, with reference to Jacques Derrida, Roland Barthes, Jean-Luc Nancy, and Mikhail Bakhtin, among others. By implication, this chapter conveys my skepticism about some of the work in contemporary media theory that has adopted the notion of an archaeology of knowledge from Foucault's early work without, however, coming to terms with the force of "outside" that is fundamental to Foucault's thinking. Instead of a Foucauldian vocabulary of interstitial ruptures and seismic shifts, contemporary "media archaeology" seems to lean more readily on a machine-centered rationalism—lodged in computational models, algorithmic permutations, and actively excavated technological objects—as the way to chart the infinity of knowledge. In this eminently positivistic, numerically oriented approach, the critical dynamism characteristic of Foucault's archaeological methods—even as such methods metamorphose into what he calls genealogy—seems readily bypassed. By engaging with some of the appropriate works by the aforementioned authors and in particular with the elusive notion of the *énoncé*, I suggest ways of gauging the potency of thinking about voice, sound, and listening *with* Foucault and his interlocutors.

Chapter 5 explores the trajectories of selfhood through the historical shift portrayed by Foucault from a Western society dominated by religious belief and monarchical rule to one dominated by neoliberal modes of self-governance. Foucault's scathing criticism of Christian pastoral power and its demand for permanent obedience can be understood in tandem with his description (in *The History of Sexuality*, volume 1) of Western man as the "confessing animal." At the same time, through the variegated mechanisms of neoliberal self-governance, the practice of confessing (which in the context of Christianity amounts to a verbal form of self-flagellation) seems to have devolved into a noticeably different kind of imperative: the imperative to actively self-mobilize, self-advocate, self-enhance, indeed self-*entrepreneurialize* (as Foucault asserts, for instance, in *The Birth of Biopolitics*). Rather than simply being the site of a repressed sexuality or a rampant consumerism, then, the neoliberal self is, from a Foucauldian perspective, the site of a proactive politicizing-cum-commodifying enterprise. The strategic move of *going public*—both in the socially activist sense of "coming out" regarding one's sexual orientation and/or past injuries and in the corporatist sense of a company's stock option becoming available on the market—fuels this entrepreneurialization of subject formation, which is anchored not only in the advancement of self-interests but also in the systemic striving for public validation, legitimation, exhibition, and performativity.

Foucault's approach to the neoliberal self can clearly be linked to Max Weber's classic argument of the ideological mutuality between capitalism and Protestantism. Going considerably beyond Weber, however, this neoliberal self is activated today through a proliferating range of therapeutic *self-care* technologies, which call on people to augment their selves not only in the form of ever renewable electronic screens, gadgets, and devices but also in the form of self-enhancement programs such as professionalized skills, dietary regimens, physical and spiritual exercises, investment portfolios, ecological consciousness-raising practices, and side-hustling ventures. The self as an endless, versatile *busy*ness project comes with its own critical vocabulary—one that is couched less in an acknowledgment of human limits (as in the older language of the sacred) than in the demand for choice and consent (that is, contractual deal making). Foucault's provocation here is profound and unsettling: With such thriving of the operations of the entrepreneurial self everywhere, is the notion of "outside" still of relevance in humanistic study? How?

Paul Veyne, Foucault's close friend and ally, summarizes his work in this pithy statement: "Here is a philosophy without a happy end. Not that it ends badly: nothing can 'end,' since there is no end point any more than there is an origin. Foucault's originality among the great thinkers of our century lay in *his refusal to convert our finitude into the basis for new certainties*."[61] Readers will remember that two remarkable images bookend *The Order of Things*. Beginning with Diego Velázquez's painting *Las Meninas* (1656), an artistic monument whose details Foucault explicates with bold historical strokes and painstaking visual finesse, he concludes his book by analogizing "man," whom he has described as an empirico-transcendental doublet, to a figure on the verge of disappearance—a face drawn in sand at the edge of the sea. Although Foucault's analysis of the first image has given rise to wide-ranging, animated debates, scholars have said much less about the mundane second image. Is not this casual sketch of a face in effect a caesura, a cut through the events of human finitude that Foucault has so eruditely narrated? The fugitive visage emblematizes the possibilities and uncertainties as well as the limits of being human as a historical condition, as expressed through the phenomena of bodies, accidents, and passions; the fragile and increasingly abstract rationalizations that tend to self-perpetuate alongside temporary victories;[62] and the imminent expiration of all these ephemeral happenings—that is, imminent transmutation and dispersion. As Mark Cousins and Athar Hussain comment, "[Foucault's] own contribution to hastening the demise of the figure of Man does not take the form of denunciation, polemic or the presentation of formal alternatives. It consists in patient descriptions of the internal relations of the human sciences. But by describing them in their internal necessities he powerfully diminishes their grip, and increases the possibility of thinking otherwise."[63]

The face drawn in sand, about to be washed over by the sea, is a reminder of and an invitation to this "possibility of thinking otherwise."

Part II

Exercises in the Unthought

1
Literary Study's Biopolitics

The decline of literature as a subject of academic study is indisputable in today's world, but seldom is this decline approached as a form of biopolitics. In contemporary literary and cultural studies, the term *biopolitics* (traceable to the Swedish political scientist Johan Rudolf Kjellén, who also coined the term *geopolitics*) is usually associated with Michel Foucault's efforts to politicize the institutional management of human life as it enters history in modern times. As invoked by Foucault in works such as *The History of Sexuality*, volume 1, *"Society Must Be Defended,"* and *The Birth of Biopolitics*,[1] biopolitics has to do with historically evolving systems of sovereignty, discipline and control (including surveillance, pathologization, and penalization), and knowledge production. Above all, the discussions in these works reiterate Foucault's stated interest in the governance of human populations—a relatively new historical entity—through the abstract permutations of a quantity-driven scientific field such as statistics.

My use of the term *biopolitics*, though also closely tied to Foucault, follows a somewhat different trajectory. First, in an old-fashioned humanistic manner I associate "life" as much with processes of mentation involving semiotic systems as with the physical dimensions of human existence as defined within the frames of biodiversity and ecology. Because language plays a crucial role in the creation of imaginary worlds that are indispensable to human life, language and literature should, to my mind, be acknowledged as part of biopolitics (even if such acknowledgment may not be currently fashionable). Second, perhaps more importantly, the emergence of literature as an object of interest in modernity has a history that is coextensive with the politics of discourse formation. This history is part institutional, part practical, part national-geographical, and always language oriented. In the Foucauldian sense of discourse, such a history is animated and mediated not only through literature's internal dynamics but also through its coevolution and competition with other histories of discursive ruptures. From this perspective, it is Foucault's book *The Order of Things*,[2] with its analyses of modern discourses' developments both from their historical predecessors and in their contemporaneous relations with one another, that foreshadows his subsequent discussions of the politics of life. For are not the academic and social pathways of biology, political economy, and literature—the three mutually affecting disciplines of knowledge production featured in *The Order of Things*, corresponding to the contents of life, labor, and language—inherent to the organization of modern life in ways that are replete with struggles for legitimacy, dominance, and survival? This biopolitics—the contentious strife for the governance of life through discourse rationalization (and its attendant modes of objectification)—is what I'd like to foreground as literary study's special contribution.

More typically, of course, when biopolitics is invoked in relation to literature, the tendency is rather to treat biopolitics as an empirical reality, one that is then said to be reflected or represented in the medium of literary writing. To the extent that biopolitics is regarded as some kind of extratextual happening, it is interchangeable with an entire series of thematics in literary study, from the proletarian struggle against capitalism in the days of Marx and Engels to the rise of the nation-state, working-class lives, domestic and nondomestic forms of desires, anticolonial and antislavery insurgence, postcolonial Anglobalization, and environmental issues in the age of the Anthropocene, among others. For reasons just mentioned, my aim in this chapter is to pursue an alternative line of inquiry. Instead of treating literature as a type of reflective or expressive activity (however complex), and instead of attributing to this activity a mysterious capacity for resisting or contesting the reality around it (in a type of academic speech act that has become rather predictable and banal), I would like to pose the following, biopolitical questions. How does literary study live and die in the vast historical shifts from a world that once upon a time seemed organized, indeed dominated, by language to one in which language no longer enjoys the privilege of being the exclusive or primary key to knowledge? What are some of the modern and contemporary efforts to justify, to save literary study? What kind of picture of the future emerges when literary study is situated within the institutional struggles for power and legitimacy in the ongoing realignments of discourse networks in the global corporate university?

Evicting Language

> This evictive state naturally corresponds to a plenitude of virtualities: it is an absence of meaning full of all the meanings.
> —Roland Barthes, "The Rhetoric of the Image"

The contemporary world, we are often told, is characterized by postmodern motifs such as an incredulity toward metanarratives; incommensurability among different forms of knowledge; the commodity- and nostalgia-driven cultural logic of late capitalism; play with artistic forms from collage and pastiche to repetition and citation; and a pervasive sense of cultural relativism. For those working in the literary humanities, these motifs also necessitate a reflection on the status of language. How are we to describe postmodernity's inheritance, if it may be so called, of modernity's fraught relation to language? What is the nature of that fraught relation?

In the Anglo-American context, T. S. Eliot's well-known experiments with language in his early poetic work, experiments that are as morally pessimistic as they are stylistically innovative, are characteristic of high modernism's twin (and one might say schizophrenic) approach. In the famous poem "The Love Song of J. Alfred Prufrock,"[3] for instance, the relationship of the poet to language is implicitly homologized to a balding middle-aged man haunted by his own sexual impotence. If this anxiety about an age-old medium that seems increasingly unreliable and untrustworthy shapes literary modernism's classic sense of its own verbal predicament ("It is impossible to say just what I mean!"[4]), the lack of fit, the ever-widening gap, between words and things (what Samuel Beckett's tragicomic plays dramatize as a prevailing condition of unhappiness) also proves to be a source of immense artistic productivity, as modernist writings in different genres—by canonical authors such as James Joyce, Virginia Woolf, Gertrude Stein, William Faulkner, and innumerable others—have shown. From modernity's perspective, then, the incontrovertible epistemic issue seems to be the sense of a definitive transformation of language's status in relation to representation. As Foucault writes with reference to Georges Bataille in the French-language context, "This 'difficulty with words' ... defines the space given over to an experience in which the speaking subject, instead of expressing himself, is exposed, goes to encounter his finitude and, under each of his words, is brought back to the reality of his own death"—a death that Foucault, in a manner resonating with Eliot, associates with sexuality, which protrudes as a fundamental problem of knowledge in the void left by the disappearance of God.[5]

Not surprisingly, this transformation in language's status is commonly conceived of and narrativized or lyricized as a loss, perhaps even a fall: language, once like a polished windowpane in possession of a sovereign overview of the world, is now said to have become opaque, impenetrable, and unwilling or unable to communicate. (In today's biomedical terms, we could say that this is a story of language's becoming *autistic*—that is, experiencing insurmountable difficulty communicating with the outside world; talking to that world has now become a fundamental challenge.) This nostalgic imagining of language's bygone potency (or state of eloquence) can be included among the metanarratives whose increasing untenability has, according to Jean-François Lyotard, come to define the postmodern condition.[6] Even though we cannot verify whether language was ever really the master of representation, the collective mournful belief—one that has powerfully influenced Western philosophical and artistic thinking about the modern world—is that it has somehow slipped and fallen from this magical, originary status.

In response to language's putative demise, scholars of the literary humanities of earlier generations have typically attempted to defend language's relevance by portraying an antagonism and incompatibility between humanistic learning, on the one hand, and science and technology, on the other. Martin Heidegger, for instance, is an outstanding example of a philosopher who tries to reanimate language—to bring it back to life—in this manner. For Heidegger, speaking about poetry, language not only is the dwelling of Being but also is equipped with the mystical power to interpellate, to invite and bid things to come forth by being named. Poetic language is a calling-out in which presence is sheltered in absence, and what is brought near remains still at a distance. Select passages from Heidegger's discussion (in a chapter titled "Language" in *Poetry, Language, Thought*) of the poem "A Winter Evening" ("Ein Winterabend") by Georg Trakl offer a sense of his approach:

> Language *speaks*.... The speaking names the winter evening time. What is this naming?... This naming does not hand out titles, it does not apply terms, but it calls into the word. The naming calls. Calling brings closer what it calls.... Thus it brings the presence of what was previously uncalled into a nearness. But the call, in calling it here, has already called out to what it calls. Where to? Into the distance in which what is called remains, still absent....
>
> Mortal speech is a calling that names, a bidding which ... bids thing and world to come. What is purely bidden in mortal speech is what is

spoken in the poem. Poetry proper is never merely a higher mode (*melos*) of everyday language. It is rather the reverse: everyday language is a forgotten and therefore used-up poem, from which there hardly resounds a call any longer. . . .

Man speaks in that he responds to language. This responding is a hearing. It hears because it listens to the command of stillness.

It is not a matter here of stating a new view of language. What is important is learning to live in the speaking of language.[7]

Similarly turning to poetic language as a way to reclaim humanistic learning's universal significance, the Anglo-American New Critics—Allen Tate, I. A. Richards, William Empson, Cleanth Brooks, W. K. Wimsatt, J. C. Ransom, Monroe Beardsley—exemplify the poem appreciated in isolation as an organic whole, one whose reality is deemed independent of history and authorial intention. "A poem should not mean / But be": in this well-known assertion from Archibald MacLeish's "Ars Poetica,"[8] one detects a purist desire for the artistic or literary work to be (understood as) ontologically self-sufficient, as though any swerve into meaning would amount to a detraction or contamination. Once ontological self-sufficiency has been elevated to the status of a humanistic and moral virtue, literary form, often taken as an analogue to personhood, assumes the aura of an ideal to which everyone aspires.[9] The postmodern trends in multiplying narratives, in particular narratives about the self, could in this light be seen as a continuation of the ongoing revitalization and reinvention of (the idiocy of) poetic language. The label *postmodern* (rather than *modern*) simply means that anyone should now be entitled to such poetic rebirth and renewal: however trivial or eccentric, every human being's life story ought to be given a chance to be told and actualized afresh as an organically complete poem, with a value in and of itself. To this end, the celebration of multicultural diversity and of multiethnic literatures in North American academic institutions is historically speaking both a symptom and an extension of the unfinished New Critical literary project.

In *The Order of Things*, Foucault, too, offers a memorable analysis of this story of language's dislocation in the West based on changes in linguistic and grammatical features over time.[10] When juxtaposed against Heidegger's and the Anglo-American New Critics' analyses, however, Foucault's point of departure is notably different in that he does not approach language by way of a mystical function (such as naming cum calling forth) or by way of a putatively organic entity (such as a poem). Using Jorge Luis Borges's fantastic Chinese encyclopedia as an entrance into his account of how language divides, multiplies, and arranges the universe differently in another civilization, he prepares the stage for a historicizing of the story of language's transformation, making us realize that the lingual properties to which Western civilization has long been accustomed may be just local flora and fauna. Because of this self-consciously comparative method based in historical shifts and relative values, and because Foucault refrains from demonizing science and technology in the manner characteristic of many of his literary contemporaries and forbears, his discussion of the mutations of language in modernity remains highly instructive. As the book's original title indicates, *Les mots et les choses* is about the emergence of a certain epistemic void—that is to say, an increasing rift— since early modern times in the relationship, the assumed linkage, between words and things. Although Foucault admittedly partakes of the prevalent modernist tendency to project a linguistic plenitude retrospectively onto former time periods, his treatment of the plenitude's disappearance is remarkably divergent. According to Foucault, language's decline from the happy, intimate condition of being continuous with the world—in what he calls language's demotion to the mere status of an object—has led to three types of compensation in three main areas of knowledge production.[11] In what we call the humanities and the interpretative social sciences (*les sciences humaines*), Foucault writes, techniques of exegesis specializing in the discovery and disturbance of buried, muted, or unconscious meanings become key to scholarly undertakings. The works of Marx, Nietzsche, Russell, and Freud are exemplary of this specialization. In the realm of literature, in contrast, a type of avant-garde creative writing looms on the horizon, deriving its power paradoxically from language's awareness of its own newly historical uselessness. Rather than being in communication or communion with the world in a seamless fashion, this type of creative writing radically withdraws into itself, taking on an unintelligibility that becomes, in turn, the hallmark of an artful, self-referential quality, a quality that henceforth distinguishes "literary" language as such. An excerpt from Foucault's eloquent description goes as follows:

> The word [*literature*] is of recent date, as is also, in our culture, the isolation of a particular language whose peculiar mode of being is "literary." ... Literature is the contestation of philology (of which it is nevertheless the twin figure): it leads language back from grammar to the naked power of speech, and there it encounters the untamed, imperious being of words. From the Romantic revolt against a discourse frozen in its own ritual pomp, to the Mallarméan discovery of the word in its impotent power, ... literature becomes progressively more differentiated from the discourse of ideas, and encloses itself within a radical intransitivity; it becomes detached from all the values that were able to keep it in general circulation during the Classical age (taste, pleasure, naturalness, truth), and creates within its own space everything that will ensure a ludic denial of them (the scandalous, the ugly, the impossible); it ... becomes merely a manifestation of a language which has no other law than that of affirming—in opposition to all other forms of discourse—its own precipitous existence; and so there is nothing for it to do but to curve back in a perpetual return upon itself, as if its discourse could have no other content than the expression of its own form; ... [as if] it has nothing to say but itself, nothing to do but shine in the brightness of its being.[12]

Although Foucault's examples are French, his description of literature in these terms is reminiscent of the Anglo-American New Critics' notion that a poem should not mean but be. To this extent, he corroborates a largely western European and North American diagnosis of literary writing's becoming an autistically closed-off world—in what, biopolitically speaking, might be called episodes of *discourse mutation and differentiation*—in the course of modernity.[13] When reconsidered in light of the two other sets of power realignments portrayed in *The Order of Things* (political economy and biology), Foucault's depiction of the emergence of modern literature (in France and western Europe) suggests that the story of literary writing is one about *speciation* and *specialization* as well as about processes of (dis)empowerment understood in close relation to these biologically inflected terms. The estranged—and sacralized—state in which, according to Foucault, literature finds itself in the modern, liberal West—the state that he names *impotent power* in the quoted excerpt—is where we continue to find the proliferation of avant-garde and experimental arts around the world today. Notably, Foucault associates such estrangement and sacralization with institutional validation—that is, with the university. "No one has really analyzed how, out of the mass of things said, out of the totality of actual discourse, a number of these discourses (literary discourse, philosophical discourse) are given a particular sacralization and function," he says during an interview in 1975. He goes on: "On the one hand, we shall have to ask ourselves what exactly is this activity that consists in circulating fiction, poems, stories ... in a society. We should also analyze a second operation: among all the narratives, why is it that a number of them are sacralized, made to function as 'literature'? They are immediately taken up with an institution that was originally very different: the university institution. Now it is beginning to be identified with the literary institution."[14]

In the area of knowledge production that may be broadly labeled scientific, Foucault argues in *The Order of Things*, the newly emergent, deepening abyss between words and things has led instead to the construction of a neutralized language, one that would be so thoroughly stripped of accidents and alien elements that "it could become the exact reflection, the perfect double, the unmisted mirror of *a nonverbal knowledge*." If language in the other knowledge domains has become conjectural and speculative, requiring ever more nuanced interpretation to the point of rendering all claims to certitude relative or provisional, in the scientific domain language remains bound to the optimism of "a search for a logic independent of grammars, vocabularies, synthetic forms, and words." This search materializes in symbolic logic, a discipline intent on "representing the forms and connections of thought *outside all language*."[15]

Rather than dismissing science on the basis of the ills of instrumentalism and mercantilism, then, Foucault makes the refreshing move of showing science as participating in language's historical mutation process, albeit taking up a different kind of niche. As a type of discourse, science continues to dream of, indeed to strive toward, being a language that corresponds to reality—a language, in other words, that is somehow able to keep itself pure and free of the chaos, derangement, and ambiguity in which other forms of knowledge production increasingly find themselves. While also confronted with modernity's language crisis, scientific discourse takes the form, or so according to Foucault's description, of a mode of enunciation or signification whose most fundamental attribute is its aspiration to speak and write *without words*, without the metaphoric clutter, noise, and messiness of linguistic mediation. Scientific discourse rigorously adopts the ideal and practice of *objectivity* that, as Lorraine Daston and Peter Galison argue, arose in the mid–nineteenth century as a radical epistemological therapy against the fear of subjective errors, against the threat of subjectivity as errancy. "Objectivity is to epistemology what extreme asceticism is to morality," they write.[16]

Dreaming Denotation

In an interesting parallel to—or perhaps as a result of?—this scientific vision of a zero degree of representation and, by implication, an ideal of transcribing thought directly without language, multiple attempts to make use of scientific-looking graphs and diagrams can be found in the theoretical writings of well-known thinkers in the literary humanities and interpretative social sciences. For a preliminary list, recall the figures used by Ferdinand de Saussure to discuss the relation between the linguistic signifier and signified and Martin Heidegger's crossing-out of Being, which subsequently transmutes into Jacques Derrida's line-across that puts words and concepts (and the metaphysics of presence they conjure) "under erasure." Worth noting also is the interesting prominence of the mathematical and the geometrical in some of Heidegger's unique observations—as in, for instance, the jug that holds in the form of a void.[17] Heidegger's fondness for etymologies, accordingly, may be understood as a fondness for organizing words that visibly and vocally correspond to one another as though they belong in a sequence or series. (What are etymologies if not graphic and sonic *sets*?) Such work on language can thus be analogized to archaeology, with the aim of establishing connections among buried, broken fragments of meaning. (Although Foucault did not continue to pursue this connection between language and archaeology, it was clearly behind his musings in *The Archaeology of Knowledge*.) There are also Claude Lévi-Strauss's structures of myth and mathematical charting of kinship relations; Roland Barthes's staggered rectangles for explaining the semiotic workings of ideology or myth; Jacques Lacan's bars, diagrams, and knots for signaling the absences that constitute the subject; A. J. Greimas's and Fredric Jameson's semiotic squares for describing the behavior and circulation of linguistic, cultural, and ideological data; Foucault's references to lists, tables, and calligrams; Gilles Deleuze's folds, vectors, and rhizomes; . . . the list goes on. How can we begin to understand these remarkable but rarely discussed pictorial occurrences in the theoretical writings so intimately linked to literary study?

One possible explanation is that such graphs and diagrams lend the study of human language and culture respectability through the fashionable aura of systematicity (resulting from optical consistency). Be that as it may, what remains intriguing from the stance of a postmodern world inundated with virtual images seems something of a different order (if only because "respectability" tilts the issue a little too hastily in the direction of an acquiescence to institutional power, of what might be called STEM, science-technology-engineering-math, envy). Indeed, can we not venture a speculation along the historical lines I am describing—namely, that even for theoretical thinkers whose bread and butter come from language (the language of myth, philosophy, fiction, and history), graphs and diagrams offer the allure of instantaneous transmission and illumination, a type of perceptual immediacy that seems impossible with cumbersome words?

To see this allure, let us consider the enthusiasm for a contemporary technology such as PowerPoint. What this technology provides, of course, is the convenience of a standardized format for public presentation by way of projectable visual arrangements of contents. While doing so, it announces something else—namely, the suggestion that what is written in language *can* become accessible in visibly capturable modules of information (summary points). This accessibility is often presented in the form of a cutting-up of prose narrative's forward movement, but this cutting-up, or rendering into parts, does not materialize through reduction but rather through addition. Supplementary items such as bullet points, paragraph spaces, enlarged fonts, colors, charts, and so on are visually *added* to the contents through computer software, even though the point, ostensibly, is to minimize language's elaborateness, to help extract what is imagined as the gist, core, or essence of a narrative or an argument (as if this were indeed possible through such visual manipulations). The gist, core, or essence, so to speak, is thus literally grafted onto writing as a prosthesis, an extra collection of settings that henceforth competes for attention as the (putatively) more precise and more intelligible version of what is being presented.

As this rather crude example indicates, even in the simplest of cases the appearance of diagrammatic icons and alignments serves a function other than that of direct communication. For if such icons and alignments distinguish themselves visibly from the procession of the printed words, such a distinction also carries with it the implication of what Roland Barthes, in his analysis of the rhetoric of the image, refers to as "denotation." Defining *denotation* in contrast to *connotation* as "a message by eviction, constituted by what is left in the image when the signs of connotation are mentally deleted," Barthes calls this evictive (or evicted) state of intelligibility the "utopian character of denotation."[18] Going along the structural linguistic grain of his argument, we can say that denotation amounts to the supposition of an assured arrival at the destination of meaning, as opposed to the errancy, the drifting and digressing, that linguistic connotation is all about. (For T. S. Eliot, such drifting and digressing find their fitting personification in "the women [who] come and go / Talking of Michelangelo."[19]) Denotation is about putting a stop to these errant movements once and for all so that we can, as it were, grab hold of something.

In the context of theoretical discourse, the use of graphs and diagrams gives to denotation, an abstract ideal, a palpably objectified material shape. Often referred to as "illustrations," such graphs and diagrams are visual aids, devices intended to help us understand what is happening in (spite of) the verbal text. But practical experience tells a different story: more often than not the illustrations are a source of puzzlement and confusion. The question that is seldom asked is the one posed succinctly by Barthes: "What is the signifying structure of 'illustration'? Does the image duplicate certain of the informations [*sic*] in the text by a phenomenon of redundancy or does the text add a fresh information to the image?"[20] In a similar vein, when discussing Lacan's interest in topology—"with its progressively more and more mind-boggling objects, from the Moebius strip, the Klein's bottle and the torus to cross-cap, the Borromean knot and the whole theory of knots, all of which take off from Lacan's early and ample use of schemata and graphs"—Mladen Dolar points to the heart of the matter:

> It would seem that the topological objects were meant to serve the purpose of giving an "illustration" or a spatial demonstration of [Lacan's] theoretical propositions. This purpose immediately entailed a reversal, I

suppose not unintended, for *what was designed to facilitate understanding (or was it ever?) was far more difficult to grasp than the thing it was supposed to render intelligible and, rather, served as an impediment, itself in need of explanation.* Gradually the topological objects and paradoxes, and particularly the knots, lost their status of illustrating something and became the thing itself, the focus of interest and elaboration in itself, the very way that theory should proceed, embodying something that cannot be rendered in any other way.[21]

As it assumes the form of nonverbal knowing, of a thinking outside of language, what begins as a seemingly scientific, because denotative, act, in spite—or perhaps because—of its ambition to discern and record (thought) objectively, ends up rejoining the literary and artistic forces of modernity to become an exercise in esoterism, in which objectivity seems indistinguishable from solipsism, from the arcaneness of intransitive (because self-referential) speech. Offering the semblance of positivity and universality, the graphs and diagrams are simultaneously cryptic and enigmatic, their readily visible forms impenetrable even to sophisticated readers, who are typically at a loss as to what they mean without detailed explanations, without a careful reconsideration of the words.[22]

The coexistence of such polarities of meaning making suggests that diagrammatic denotation—or, more precisely, the diagram as denotation—needs to be rethought as an epistemic conundrum, one in which the ongoing modernist sense of a crisis of language continues to play itself out in the form of a collective fantasy. This is the fantasy that language is somehow disposable, that if we could simply find a way to get to the bottom of things—geometrically, algebraically, statistically, or however—we ought to be able to arrive at that utopian, evicted state of not needing language altogether. Beyond the dots, the lines, the curves, the circles, the squares, the numbers, and other figures on the page, there persist a wish and a demand that bestow on diagrammatic denotation the import of something excessive, something obscene.

To put it differently, when graphs and diagrams are used in theoretical writings in the literary humanities and interpretative social sciences, they serve in effect as little theaters where the unresolved relationship between words and things repeatedly stages itself as a spectacle, calling attention to what Franco Moretti calls a "total *heterogeneity of problem and solution*."[23] Side by side with the words, the diagrams appear as something like a language, albeit one that dreams of being without language; something like writing, albeit one that dreams of doing without writing. In their proximity to words, the graphs and diagrams yearn, as though with a kind of mimetic desire, to take language's place, to usurp writing's hold on abstraction by becoming the preferred native informants of thought.

Is not our contemporary nanotechnology—with its infinite imaging capabilities, set into motion with simple manipulations such as keystrokes, clicks, taps, finger swipes, as well as text-messaging operations limited to 140 characters and discharged with abbreviated spellings and emoticons—part of the same dream, the same ecstasy? Perhaps this entangled relationship between the verbal and the graphic in the aftermath of the historical emergence of objectivity needs to be made part of our reevaluation of the coexistence, however fraught, of the humanities and the sciences? If the postmodern condition is indeed about the end of (the possibility of) metanarratives, it is high time we abandoned the metanarrative of the antagonism and incompatibility between these two areas of knowledge production to make way for an alternative view of their uneven coevolution in the age of informatics. In particular, what does and can this coevolution mean for the study of literature?

Rescuing Literary Study

From the abode of noise and impropriety, where nobody was in their right place, to the asshole gringos handing him bullshit about

> sovereignty, democracy, and human rights. This is what comparative literature could be, if it took itself seriously as *world literature*, on the one hand, and as *comparative morphology*, on the other.
>
> —Franco Moretti, *Graphs, Maps, Trees*

Within the Anglo-American university, the turn of the twenty-first century has seen serious attempts to reanimate the study of literature. Under the rubrics of postcolonial, Anglophone, Francophone, world, planetary, neurological, medical, environmental, computational, and other similarly timely connections, scholars seek to restore to literature its due relevance in a relentlessly chimerical world. In particular, geopolitical considerations have emerged as a compelling form of reasoning, wherein movements of peoples, languages, and cultures have led to creatively new ways of reading texts (for instance, by way of issues of migration, deterritorialization, and translation). As literary critics and historians hunker down in their increasingly specialized pursuits, however, relatively little has been said about how literature continues to be produced, with or without changes, as an object of study in an age when numbers, formulas, and algorithms dominate. *Exactly how are we to think about the literary object in the era of mass quantification? What is this object? By what processes is it constituted and objectified? By what processes might it be reconceptualized and remade?* This cluster of questions seems to bypass scholars even as they scrutinize writings produced under different historical circumstances. Yet if we follow Foucault's lead in *The Order of Things* and take seriously the coevolution of languages or disciplinary discourses—so that practices of language study, for instance, can be shown to be epistemically coextensive with theorizations of biological systems or economic models—we might have some means of grappling with these eminently interdisciplinary and, as I contend, biopolitical questions.

The groundbreaking work of Franco Moretti, who argues for changing the object of literary study by way of "operationalizing" quantifiable data, offers some provocative suggestions.[24] With a critique of close reading as his strategic point of departure, Moretti takes aim at the method that for decades has helped constitute the literary object in the Anglo-American context,[25] where the New Critical approach to literary study achieved ascendency in the postwar American college (a quintessential middle-class institution) by way of assistance from foundation funding.[26] A practice of concentration based on the contemplation of words, a skill cum drill supposed to deliver the truth of a text regardless of the author's intentions, biographical details, and other extraneous circumstances surrounding the text's production: once the point is underscored that what constitutes literary study and its objects is simply the repeated intensive examination of a few canonical texts by a select group of people—in what Moretti calls "a theological exercise"[27]—close reading, like the Christian church, is desacralized. This challenge to the doxa sets the euphoric tone of the debates to come precisely because it carries the equivalent of both a blasphemous charge and a reformist aspiration. However radical close reading might have been in its heyday as a tactical intervention in the study of literature, the realization that such focus on the text is possible only when both the volume and variety of texts involved are restricted and, indeed, suppressed means that close reading needs to be historicized and, as it were, put in its place. Although close reading of a play by William Shakespeare, a poem by William Wordsworth, or a novel by Jane Austen used to be an activity taken for granted in a university setting where the English department is usually the largest unit of the literary humanities, in the aftermath of civil rights and multiculturalism repeated close readings of these select authors have come to seem, in the eyes of some, parochial and unacceptable. Even in the context of English as an evolving field, there needs to be room nowadays for more exotic contemporary authors such as J. M. Coetzee, V. S. Naipaul, Kazuo Ishiguro, Michael Ondaatje, Jamaica Kincaid, Timothy Mo, Amitav Ghosh, and Zadie Smith. And things are more complicated once other languages and canons enter the picture. Alongside the multiplicity of a single text, a single passage, or a single word, which close reading is so adept at deciphering, other forms of multiplicity—such as demographics, together with the existential and political demands they bring—loom with justifiably persuasive influence.

Against the time-honored method of close reading, Moretti introduces what he calls "abstract models" for literary history; specifically, he shows how a use of graphs, maps, and trees enables one to foreground interconnections among textual elements (that is, generic, geographical or locational, and stylistic variations) that are otherwise inaccessible through conventional habits of reading. In contrast to the intensive pondering of a small number of individual texts, Moretti's visual models allow for a wide range of literatures to be *scanned* in a comparative manner, frequently in association with historical developments in different parts of the world. Among other merits, the use of graphics avoids the pitfalls of a trendy, moral instrumentalization of so-called world literature that, not unlike traditional close reading, is often based on selective or eclectic analyses of very few sample texts.

At this juncture, a difficulty arises that typically results from an endeavor to overturn accepted custom: the questioning of such custom is indubitably valid, but the alternatives proposed are far from satisfactory. "Distant reading," Moretti's ambitious antidote to close reading, is a fascinating case in point not least because of Moretti's admirable intellectual vision: "Problems without a solution are exactly what we need in a field like ours, where we are used to asking only those questions for which we already have an answer." In the book *Graphs, Maps, Trees*, he advances the titular trio of artificial constructs as examples of distant reading, in which "the reality of the text undergoes a process of deliberate reduction and abstraction," whereby distance is "not an obstacle, but a *specific form of knowledge.*" The aim of this new method, he suggests, is "a more rational literary history."[28]

When viewed in light of the aforementioned paradoxes of diagrammatic denotation, Moretti's overall project appears to partake—albeit on a much grander and more replicable scale—of the fantasy shared among some of our foremost literary and cultural theorists: the fantasy of being unencumbered by language. As a well-intentioned attempt to update, indeed to rescue, literary study by broadening its geopolitical reach, distant reading seems the latest rejoinder to those graphs and diagrams whose "utopian" character, as Barthes points out, consists in the wish for an eviction—that is, for a language that has been vacated and preferably can be left on the side. The irony of this wishful thinking does not escape Moretti. An expert and experienced reader of literature in multiple languages, Moretti is the first to call attention to the fundamental problem with such an eviction—the fact that the abstract visual figures he proposes cannot stand alone without the help of words: "To make sense of quantitative data, I had to abandon the quantitative universe, and turn to morphology: evoke form, in order to explain figures."[29] Rather than reducing the text, as Moretti seems to believe,[30] the abstract visual figures have actually added another dimension, a numerical or mathematical frame, to the literary texts in question. What this means is that when studying novels, readers will henceforth need to contend not only with the novels' verbal significations but also with the graphs, maps, and trees Moretti has introduced.

In this construction of a new object for literary study, what is the status of the visual material? If, as a speculative program, distant reading is meant to explore "the true nature of the historical process"[31] by charting the links among textual elements that are otherwise not apprehended, what is the relation between the graphs, maps, and trees, on the one hand, and Moretti's own verbal explanatory accounts, on the other? As he writes more recently in the introduction to the volume documenting the efforts of the Stanford Literary Lab, "Images, first of all: time plots, histograms, trees, networks, diagrams, scatterplots.... Images come first... because—by visualizing empirical findings—they constitute *the specific object of study of computational criticism*; they are our 'text'; the counterpart to what a well-defined excerpt is to close reading."[32] Next, and only next, come the captions.

Where the visualized data are explained, in other words, it is in terms of a new or novelized knowledge to be acquired, however tentatively. Visualization is hailed as a method of structuration that sharpens correlations by making them readily perceptible and graspable. In a manner not unlike the enigmatic visual figures adopted by theorists from Lacan to Deleuze, Greimas, and Jameson, there seems in Moretti's discussions an implicit equation of visualization (in its apparently positivistic mode) with recognizability, accessibility, and knowability—an equation that belongs, as I have been suggesting, in the collective fantasy of diagram as denotation. Although there is in fact nothing transparent about the graphs, maps, trees, and other similar optical figures, all of which are coded data—no such representation can signify, can "mean," without verbal explanation—they are nonetheless treated and presented as though they were code free. To borrow the words of Dennis Tenen, "The visualization belies a mathematical model, a metaphor, which should not be confused for the thing it is meant to represent. The graphic is subject to the usual pitfalls of interpretation: it is at once overdetermined and necessarily reductive; it leads to an excess of signification."[33] In the type of study sponsored by Moretti, however, the rationale for one type of significatory excess, language, has been superseded by or subsumed under the rationale for another type of significatory excess, computation.

The disjuncture between, on the one hand, close reading, which specializes in metaphorical depth, the inner dynamics of language, and most of all a select repertoire of texts, and, on the other, distant reading, which favors geographical expanse, comparative interactions among diverse literary productions and lineages, and the prospects of an extensive, de facto limitless global archive, is symptomatic of the problems confronting most practitioners of literary study today. And once it is realized that such study cannot with any good reason be confined to a particular language as used strictly by one group of readers, writers, and speakers, comparativism ineluctably follows, only henceforth to be dogged by metacomparative questions, not least of which would be those regarding the often incommensurate assumptions about comparison per se as a practice (often implicit) across genres, forms, languages, time periods, and cultural traditions. Different languages' renderings of a similar-seeming word, for instance, may cause apparently straightforward quantitative findings to become dubious and unreliable. As Moretti puts it in a conversation, "The problem is when you start to zoom in." Moreover, though open-ended by design, the quantitative approach has ironically led to a "reprovincialization" of literary study because computational research on different literatures tends to be conducted routinely, if not exclusively, in the national languages in which the literatures are written. By the same token, the overwhelming bulk of the work done in the so-called digital humanities has been on English and American corpora.[34]

The problems are clear, but the solutions, whenever proposed, seem only to generate other problems—hence, Moretti's astute observation that there is a total heterogeneity of problem and solution. The numerous calls in recent years to reconceptualize literary study—in terms of circulation, republicanism, literary worldedness, untranslatability, colonial philology, modern capitalist world-systems theory, postcoloniality, normativity, and non-Anglophonic cultural pluralism—as well as the erudite debates for and against world literature by authors such as David Damrosch, Pascale Casanova, Eric Hayot, Emily Apter, Siraj Ahmed, the Warwick Research Collective, Pheng Cheah, Simon Gikandi, and Aamir Mufti[35] are part and parcel of this, what I propose to call the "biopolitics of literary study." In this biopolitics, played out in academic institutions across the globe, it is a savvy navigation of vast distances in both time and space, as opposed to a contemplative groping in the dark labyrinths of language, that, I suspect, will gain increasing currency. Distant reading (and an affiliate such as surface reading), whereby the utopian promise of language's eviction goes hand in hand with the fund-raising potential of data mining and with denotative diagramming—and whereby, as Moretti writes, "the unprecedented empirical power of digital tools and archives offer[s] a unique chance to rethink the categories of literary study"[36]—is likely the materially generative biopolitical niche in which literary study will be able to have some kind of future life in the corporatized university setting.

These institutional efforts to salvage literary study—of which database compilation is simply one prominent example—can also and perhaps unavoidably seem subjective and random precisely because they are democratizing (that is, pluralizing) exercises. Once opened up and diversified, literary study's raw materials and epistemic boundaries tend to become infinitely (re)negotiable: such materials and boundaries may be as easily disparaged and dismantled as they are assembled in ways that resemble some creative installation art exhibits. For instance, if the comings and goings in a village in a nineteenth-century French or English novel can be graphically calculated to reveal economic or sociological patterns, what about happenings in a town setting in a twentieth-century African or Russian novel? Or, if biblical allusions can be systematically charted in the linguistic styles of some European fiction, why not chart Zen Buddhist allusions in the linguistic styles of some East Asian fiction? If *this* is trackable and measurable, . . . why not *that*? And so on. Where would such a list of possible computational projects begin and end? Who should decide how far artificial intelligence and Big Data should go in helping refashion the literary object, for whom, and why?

Meanwhile, as higher education morphs into a transnational business enterprise, replete with name-brand monitors, investment-portfolio managers, designated content deliverers (the instructors), and worldwide customers (students and their parents), initiatives to streamline and market literary study as a tangible product are well under way. Witness the hefty literary histories, companion volumes, and handbooks, each costing U.S.$100 or more, commissioned by publishers such as Harvard, Oxford, Cambridge, Wiley-Blackwell, Routledge, Palgrave, and their competitors and aimed mainly if not exclusively at libraries as buyers. Assorting literary writings by way of national languages, geographical regions, genders, ethnicities, sexual orientations, and other popular thematics, these doorstoplike "books" are usually manufactured through entrepreneurial teamwork in a relay from volume editors (the forepersons and content managers) to authors (the assembly-line laborers recruited to churn out the goods in accordance with preset formats)[37] and then to an entourage of copyediting, indexing, production, and marketing personnel behind the scene.

The biopolitics of literary study is the politics of finding—or, just as easily, losing—one's way in these large, impersonal loops and circuits of our time. On one side lies a dazzling abundance of fiction-making talent: novels, short stories, plays, and poems in different languages and formats, serialized television dramas, and film scripts—all in addition to the canonical classics composed in different languages and made available in different translations. As in ages past, there is no shortage of excellent creative writing, whose richness and ubiquity defy even the most diligent efforts at perusal and classification. On the other side, meanwhile, proliferate the utilitarian strategies of institutional control and monetary capture, to which the twenty-first-century university has become a proactive partner and collaborator. As Richard Grusin puts it, "Even while neoliberal market logic has led to the decimation of mainstream humanities, this same logic has encouraged foundations, corporations, and university administrations to devote new resources to the digital humanities,"[38] hailed as the next bright horizon precisely at a time when the neoliberalization and corporatization of higher education, together with the precaritization of labor both inside the university and beyond it, have intensified. As academics, we face the bureaucratization (that is, the regimentation) of every aspect of teaching and learning even as we are bombarded by incessant appeals to "free" and "enhance" our habits, including the tools and instruments we use to read, write, and communicate, through commodified technologization.

These mutually reinforcing dynamics suggest that the biopolitics of literary study cannot be effectively challenged by social activism and its sponsorship of particular populations—such as workers, women, LGBT groups, subalterns, and disabled people—each with its variant of literary output. Such identity-based productions of resistance, collectively signaling "the end of the reign of literary culture as the organizing discipline of the University's cultural mission,"[39] are by now quite normativized constituents of the politicization of global culture. This biopolitics instead stands to remind us that literary study, too, needs to be rethought as a mutating life form, whose existence hitherto does not have to mean that its continued existence is inevitable or guaranteed. In the corporatized university setting in particular, literary study's seasoned capacity for engaging with age-old humanistic issues—pain, suffering, deceit, error, illusion, dissent, hatred, conflict, and failure—in deeply reflective and empathetic ways seems today as much a potential for the discipline's progressive institutional diminution as it is a potential (as some colleagues will no doubt want to argue) for its continued survival. This is simply because engagements with such humanistic issues have been steadily and effectively appropriated by the academic sectors with "problem-solving" missions grounded in empirically verifiable research and/or morally righteous causes. Alongside philanthropic fields and subfields such as global health, public policy, environmental ethics, international relations, and social justice—with their ameliorative rationalizations and expert metrics—how can the non-problem-solving work of language and literature be (again) of import? Can it? The challenge facing literary study's practitioners seems nothing less than making way for their object's evolvement into a viable new biopolitical niche: to change, indeed to reinvent, the literary itself qua object.

2
"There Is a 'There Is' of Light"; or, Foucault's (In)visibilities

In the Collège de France lectures Michel Foucault delivered in 1978–1979 on the topic of the birth of biopolitics, he provides, in the midst of his eloquent discussions of the workings of (neo) liberalist politicoeconomics, a strikingly perverse reading of the famous "invisible hand" in Adam Smith's *The Wealth of Nations* (1776). Most readers of Smith's classic are familiar with the association of the hand with a form of agency, Foucault writes. Be it providence, direction, or a force of unity, the hand has long been imagined as a player that steers or sways the market in a certain direction—specifically toward a state of equilibrium to the benefit of all. Foucault, however, urges us to be more imaginative and to think instead of Smith's reference to the invisible:

> The collective good must not be an objective . . . because it cannot be calculated, at least, not within an economic strategy. *Here we are at the heart of a principle of invisibility.* In other words, what is usually stressed in Smith's famous theory of the invisible hand is, if you like, the "hand," that is to say, the existence of something like providence which would tie together all the dispersed threads. But I think the other element, invisibility, is at least as important. Invisibility is not just a fact arising from the imperfect nature of human intelligence which prevents people from

realizing that there is a hand behind them which arranges or connects everything that each individual does on their own account. Invisibility is absolutely indispensable. It is an invisibility which means that no economic agent should or can pursue the collective good.

But we must no doubt go further than economic agents; not only no economic agent, but also no political agent.[1]

For those invested in reading Foucault by way of a safely condonable progressive politics about human agency, this passage stands as a good reminder of the mercurially unconventional nature of his thinking. He is often not where we expect him to be. If there is a radicality in his intriguing statements in this instance, it is much less a matter of a ready call to political activism than an insistence on a certain unknowability—an invisibility, he says—as an ineluctable component to collective life, however fastidiously regulated and proceduralized collective life might be. For Foucault, the fact that the sovereign (that is, whoever is in charge of the political state) as much as the market can be in a state of not-knowing is what paradoxically enables (neo)liberalism to function effectively as a form of governance; this unknowing sovereign or—to spell out Foucault's logic—this condition of a *sovereign unknowing* is what allows the system to do its work. Between those who govern and those who are governed, there persists a gap—a vacuum left in the very analysis of labor by classical economics—that cannot be quite filled.[2] This gap, which makes it possible for *homo economicus* to say to the sovereign who wants complete power over him, "You must not," is crucial. "You must not because you cannot," Foucault continues. "And you cannot... because you do not know, and you do not know because you cannot know."[3] Foucault's interest in invisibility is an interest in this "cannot know." For him, such not-knowing stands less as a negation of a known quantity than as an open form of potentiality.

In a similar vein, he offers a succinct explanation of the relation between the essentially unknowable or uncontrollable nature of economic rationality, on the one hand, and the atomistic behavior of *homo economicus*, whom he calls an "island," on the other, adding that the latter is the only manageable unit in an otherwise uncontrollable environment:

> Economic rationality is not only surrounded by, but founded on the unknowability of the totality of the process. *Homo economicus* is the one island of rationality possible within an economic process whose uncontrollable nature does not challenge, but instead founds the rationality of the atomistic behavior of *homo economicus*. Thus the economic world is naturally opaque and naturally non-totalizable. It is originally and definitively constituted from a multiplicity of points of view which is all the more irreducible as this same multiplicity assures their ultimate and spontaneous convergence.[4]

This unique reading of one of the founding texts of liberalism by way of invisibility and unknowability bears an intimate relation to Foucault's other writings, even when those writings are not ostensibly about sovereignty, governmentality, or biopolitics. To explore this point, I draw on the insights of Gilles Deleuze, John Rajchman, Gary Shapiro, Joseph J. Tanke, Catherine M. Soussloff, and others who have provided nuanced critical accounts of the ways Foucault approaches the relations between the visible and the invisible.[5] These scholars' copiously informed discussions make it possible to raise a set of questions seldom addressed by most Foucault scholars. How might a turn to Foucault's unfinished work on modern art shed light on politics, collectivity, and the good (all invoked in the earlier quote about the invisible hand)? How do the forces that modern painting renders perceptible help us understand the ongoing flux of knowledge and the transformation—or what might be called the neoliberalization—of social relations? Above all, how do Foucault's visual-reading tactics, frequently embedded in or extended from his analytic approach to architectural, clinical, carceral, work, pedagogical, and familial spaces, contribute to a theory of social and political change? My goal, an immodest one that obviously exceeds the parameters of the present chapter, is to argue that a dynamic theorization of visibilities and invisibilities runs through Foucault's work, so much so that to sidestep or ignore that theorization is to risk impoverishing the quality of *any* attempt to come to terms with his signature contributions and their enduring, transdisciplinary impact on humanistic study.

Foucault and the (In)visible: Some Brief Reminders

In *The History of Madness* and *The Birth of the Clinic*, visibility is in play in the ways humans are spatially constituted on an elaborate, rationalist construction of *what* can be seen—both through the designs and divisions of architecture and through the instruments and procedures of biomedicine. The former render some groups of humans identifiable through their sequestration from other groups, while the latter render the individual human body legible through processes of examination, measurement, vivisection, and observation. "The eye becomes the depositary and source of clarity," Foucault writes in *The Birth of the Clinic*, foregrounding the rationale that promoted visibility's ascendency in the modern period. The eye "has the power to bring a truth to light that it receives only to the extent that it has brought it to light; as it opens, the eye first opens the truth: a flexion that marks the transition from the world of classical clarity—from the 'enlightenment'—to the nineteenth century." Since that transition, Foucault tells us, the empirical gaze, as it were, has been endowed with a new "sovereign power."[6] As exercised through the biomedical research lab, the clinic, and the hospital as well as through closely related institutions such as the insane asylum, light and visibility provide a literalization of the ideality of progress and become the de facto ruling standard against which everything is judged.

In *The Order of Things*, as Foucault narrates the parallel constellations of knowledge production that have been occurring among different disciplines and discourses since the eighteenth century, invisibility—in the sense of unverifiable or unavailable causal explanations—structures relations among the constellations like an ever-widening abyss. If Foucault manages eruditely to elucidate the historical mutualities, the shared rationalities, among grammar, political economy, and biology (together with their respective mutating objects of language, labor, and life), he nonetheless concludes the book with the face of man, the subject cum object of these evolving knowledges, on the verge of disappearing, of becoming invisible. In *Discipline and Punish*, the reform routines imposed on prison inmates—embodied offenders housed in atomized cells and trained to internalize the Panopticist gaze of the authorities (who do not need to be physically present)—exemplify surveillance as the mechanism par excellence for modern soul or conscience fabrication.

In each of these major studies, be the stress biomedical, scientific, archaeological, epistemic, sociological, or criminological, Foucault alerts us to the entanglement between visibility and *divisibility*: what can be divided (separated, partitioned, distributed, shared—in the multiple valences of the French word *partage*[7]), insofar as such division brings with it intelligibility and legibility, becomes a potential snare. Hence, Foucault's memorable statement in *Discipline and Punish* that "visibility is a trap."[8]

These divergent but interrelated instances, which I have recalled here in a rather schematic fashion, suggest that a more seriously coordinated look at visibilities and invisibilities in Foucault's work is in order. Is the invisible simply the opposite of the visible—that is, a negative, with the potential of evacuating power relations constituted by visibility as the modern sovereign and ruling standard? Or is the invisible something more than a force of negation? To respond to these questions, it is important to note in Foucault's investment in the invisible the remnant of a phenomenologically inflected descriptor. What is most absorbing in his account of the evolution of modern political economy, for instance, is much less the advocacy of any kind of revolutionary utopianism than the residue of a philosophical language, traceable to the influential work of Maurice Merleau-Ponty (such as *Phenomenology of Perception* [1945] and *The Visible and the Invisible* [1968]), which theorizes knowledge by way of the staging of human perception and the interactive social relations entangled with perceptual processes (seeing and being seen, touching and being touched, and so forth).[9] Like his fellow "structuralists," however, Foucault rejects the synthesis that is bestowed on the phenomena of vision, gesture, movement, and intentionality—a synthesis that, for Merleau-Ponty at least, remains centered in the idea of the *integrated* human being.[10] Far more critical for Foucault and his contemporaries is the endeavor to scramble the synthesized elements and dismantle the proclaimed coherence and unity of "man" himself. As he observed in an interview late in his life, "Everything that took place in the sixties arose from a dissatisfaction with the phenomenological theory of the subject, and involved different escapades, subterfuges, breakthroughs, according to whether we use a negative or a positive term, in the direction of linguistics, psychoanalysis or Nietzsche."[11]

At this juncture, a brief comparison with the figure of bareness, signifying a reality of no-thing-ness, might be helpful. Giorgio Agamben's notion of bare life, drawn from a philosophical lineage beginning with the ancient Greeks' distinction between *zoe* and *bios*,[12] is perhaps only a culmination of a long rhetorical tradition of deploying *destitution*—personified by those who are deprived, homeless, oppressed, downtrodden, victimized, and so forth—as a way to articulate an originary or ultimate desolate condition. In contemporary media and cultural studies, this popular deployment of destitution now includes the innovative talk of the screen or the image itself as wretched and poor rather than simply a reflection of wretchedness and poverty.[13] Although admittedly partaking of a similar fascination with what might be called the void,[14] Foucault's invisible is, I believe, not exactly an attempt to articulate originariness or ultimateness in this more familiar sense. More pertinent here is Michel Serres's comparison of Foucault's thinking to geometry in its earliest form, when it (thinking/geometry) is *suspended between different states*: "at the precise moment when it is still aesthetic and already formalized, when its form of expression is still concrete but already highly rigorous, when its density is presented in a conceptual quasi-emptiness."[15] The invisible in Foucault's work should therefore not be too hastily assimilated to some essentially bare, naked, or poor truth (such as no-thing-ness) that has been covered over (by culture, hypocrisy, cruelty, capitalist commodification, and the like) and awaits uncovering and restoration to its pristine originary condition.[16] Rather, Foucault, I propose, associates invisibility with a passing condition, a temporality whereby lines, shapes, gestures, and motions come into being only to constitute the makings of a situation in flux—a situation in which knowledge emerges only to become inextricably enmeshed with the possibility, perhaps the inevitability, of its dissolution.

How does Foucault perform such intangible tasks—that is, return lines, shapes, gestures, and motions to invisibility as *a force of flight*[17]— even while rendering them visible, mentionable, and perceptible? His work on painting offers some provocatively instructive demonstrations. As I would like to show with the help of select examples, Foucault's manner of reading painting departs significantly from the more customary, indeed venerable, conventions of investing the eye (and with it sight and light) with deep, religious-cum-psychoanalytic connotations. As is well known from his discussion of Diego Velázquez's *Las Meninas* (1656) at the beginning of *The Order of Things*, he approaches sight and light neither in a transcendent and theological sense, as an allusion to the divine, nor in a secular humanistic sense, as a symptom of what Otto Fenichel, after Freud, calls "scoptophilia."[18] The profound powers usually attributed to the eye, such as threat, malice, horror, and lust—in adjectives such as *penetrating, probing, piercing, sadistic, phallic, devouring*, and so forth—are strategically put aside for a newer way of coming to grips with vision as a material practice and project characterized above all by *noncoincidence* and *nonrecognition*, by the breaking-up of the dyad seeing/being seen.

In his brief discussions of the paintings by René Magritte and Édouard Manet,[19] for instance, Foucault, reading with the pleasure and modesty of an amateur (referring to himself as a "layman"[20]), raises the fundamental issue of how modern art participates in the material as well as conceptual generation of perception and knowledge. Notably, he does not ask, as might a philosopher, what *is* modern art? Instead, he shows the art in action or as a form of action.[21] In his readings, we see the comforting recognizability of labels such as *impressionism* and *the avant-garde* becoming moot, giving way to surprising forms, or nonforms, in the operative interval between seeing and speaking. These readings allow us to apprehend imagistic shapes and linguistic references in processes of being made and unmade, sutured together and torn asunder. Sight and light come across in these processes as nontransparent, enigmatic surfaces with a materiality all their own. Foucault's notion of visibilities, then, hinges on *sight and light becoming objects of reflexivity*, or what he in an evocative manner calls "picture-objects." He defines the term *picture-object* this way: "the picture as materiality, the picture as something coloured which *clarifies an external light* and in front of which, or about which, the viewer revolves. This invention of the picture-object, this reinsertion of the materiality of the canvas in that which is represented, this I believe is at the heart of the great change wrought by Manet to painting."[22]

As Gilles Deleuze states in his perceptive discussion of Foucault, his friend and ally, "*Visibilities are not defined by sight* but are complexes of actions and passions, actions and reactions, multisensorial complexes, which emerge into the light of day."[23] For this reason, it is possible to say, with John Rajchman, that "what makes the visual intelligible is itself unseen."[24] Accordingly, for Deleuze, in Foucault's work "there is [always] a 'there is' of light."[25]

The Light That Strikes, Extremities, a Silhouette Series, the Unraveled Calligram: Some Examples of Foucault's Approach to (In)visibilities in Painting

Although it is impossible to recapitulate Foucault's readings in detail, I would like to bring attention to a few instances that exemplify his skill, acuity, and finesse as a reader,[26] beginning with an example of bareness: Manet's *Olympia* (1863, figure 2.1).[27] Addressing the most controversial part of the painting—Manet's parody of the classical genre of reclining Venuses (especially Titian's *Venus of Urbino*, 1538) in the substitution of a bald-faced prostitute in the place of the divine—Foucault suggests that the naked female body on display is the effect of an invisible movement and action, which he names *"a very violent light which strikes"*:

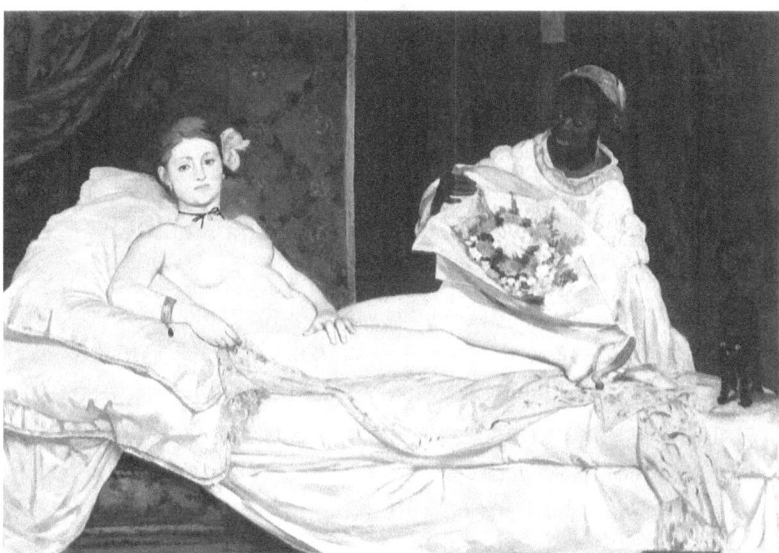

Figure 2.1 Édouard Manet, *Olympia*, 1863.
Source: © Musée d'Orsay, Paris.

If Manet's *Olympia* is visible it is because a light strikes her. This light is certainly not a soft and discreet lateral light, it is a very violent light which strikes her here, full shot.... [T]his luminous source, where is it, if not here, precisely where we are?... [T]here is [rather] nudity and us, we who are in the very place of lighting: in other words, it is our gaze which, in opening itself upon the nudity of *Olympia*, illuminates her. It is we who render it visible ... we are responsible for the visibility and for the nudity of *Olympia*.[28]

Several things are remarkable about this passage. Insofar as Foucault connects the center of the picture with the space of the spectator, the passage calls to mind the manner he reads Velázquez's *Las Meninas*. In the latter case, as is well known, he formulates that connection by way of a depiction of the historical reconfiguration of sovereign power that was traditionally rooted in monarchs. In the place of the monarchs, who are now a faint mirror reflection at the back of the room, arises the invisible spectator, whose gaze from outside the picture—from the very spot where the king and queen are supposedly seated—seems to rival the royal subjects as the very object of the painter's attention. Indeed, being by logic present yet withheld from sight, the royal subjects are positioned (or demoted) in such a manner as to become virtual equals with the spectator, with whom they now share the vanishing point of the painting's organization. As Joseph J. Tanke writes, "Henceforth, it will be the viewer who, in a sovereign act, fixes the relationships between the tableau's various elements."[29] In *Olympia*, this updated relation between sovereignty and spectatorship takes the form of the scandalous spread of a naked prostitute staring at us in a businesslike manner, but what seizes Foucault's attention is, once again, the invisible yet active gaze of someone or something looking in *from the outside*, a gaze that is at once the "luminous source" and "violent light" that structures the painting. He tells us that it is "we" who are responsible, through our gazing, for the spectacle of this socially debased female. In a liberal society in which the market rather than the sovereign reigns, this "we" *responsibly generates the (commodity of) nudity that it consumes*. In ways that resonate with the British art historian John Berger's well-known Marxist critique,[30] Foucault's articulation of the trajectory that moves from Olympia's nudity to luminosity, to light, and finally to the spectator's gaze politicizes sight and light as nontranscendent relations of coercion. It is tempting to see the figure of the black woman, presumably a servant, holding a bouquet beside the prostitute as part and parcel of these relations, even though Foucault makes no mention of this point.

If, as Deleuze reminds us, "Foucault is uniquely akin to contemporary film,"[31] might not we venture further and think of the light that strikes Olympia as a precursor to the blows that are dealt the character Marion Crane, another pretty woman in pursuit of money, in the famous shower scene in Alfred Hitchcock's film *Psycho* (1960)? There, too, what illuminates the crime against the naked female body is the action of an invisible violence *series* (seriality being a key concept in Foucault's readings of art): not only the knife-wielding, disguised, male psychopath, Norman Bates, but also the director's camera's exposing lens and the worldwide audience's voyeuristic participatory gaze.[32]

Both Foucault's sensitivity to the places within a picture frame on which light falls and his effort to track light in the form of movements or routes are evident in the numerous comments he makes on one interesting type of detail: extremities. In reading the human figures in Manet and Magritte, he regularly zooms in on the hands (or gloves), the feet (or shoes), the knees, the fingers, the eyes, and the front or back of faces turned at different angles. Linking these human figures to their surroundings, these end-body organs are, strictly speaking, *indexes* and *vectors*, position and direction markers that carve out spaces in transit, spaces on their way to becoming something else.[33] This analytical approach, consisting in a methodical serializing of space—by cutting up or multiplying space into folds, layers, or levels—is especially clear in Foucault's reading of Manet's *Luncheon on the Grass* (1863, figure 2.2).

Foucault divides the frame into two systems of lighting, one operating in the depths of the picture and the other in front, centered on

Exercises in the Unthought

Figure 2.2 Édouard Manet, *Luncheon on the Grass*, 1863.
Source: © Musée d'Orsay, Paris.

the naked woman looking at us. These two systems, he suggests, are joined together at the place where a fold line is possible, signaling a repetition, a series in progress.[34] Though invisible, this fold line is conjured by the hand extended by the man sitting on the right and placed near the center of the picture. Foucault's perspicacious remarks are worth quoting at length:

> These two systems of representation, or rather these two systems of manifesting light inside a picture, are juxtaposed here in this very canvas, are in a juxtaposition which gives this picture its slightly discordant character, its *internal heterogeneity*; an internal heterogeneity which Manet tried in a way to reduce or perhaps rather to underline—I don't know—by this hand which is here, this clear hand which is in the

middle of the picture ... so here you have this hand with its two fingers, one finger which points in this direction; or this direction, which is precisely the direction of the interior light, of this light which comes from above and from elsewhere. And on the contrary the finger is bent, bent towards the outside, on the axis of the picture, and it indicates the origin of the light which strikes here, in such a way that you have in this hand-play the fundamental axes of the picture and the principle—at once of linking and of heterogeneity—of this *Luncheon on the Grass*.[35]

Clearly, what captivates Foucault about this man's hand—what he calls "hand-play"—is how it keeps two systems of light in suspension alongside each other. One classical and deep, the other contemporary and flat, the two systems are disparate while continuous, separate while conjoined. Pointing both in the direction of the interior light, seemingly from above and elsewhere, *and* in the direction of the light that strikes here and now, the hand emblematizes a principle that Foucault defines as "at once of linking and of heterogeneity." Materially inscribed into the picture's composition, this principle marks Manet's visibilities as precisely movements and routes, *light in transport*. By concisely teasing out the concrete pictorial details and pinpointing the abstract theoretical significations they carry, Foucault makes a powerful case for Manet's work not only as innovative art but also, more critically, as an epistemic threshold that brings about a "deep rupture" or "rupture in depth."[36] In Foucault's vivid, *painterly descriptions*,[37] Manet's work emerges as an event: light and space lose their classical interiority and mystery, intensify as shifting lines of verticality and horizontality, and finally (re)appear as surface phenomena and heterotopic possibilities.

In a comparable manner, in his reading of René Magritte's piece *La Décalcomanie* (1966, figure 2.3), the serialization of spaces takes the form of a visual doubling, an iteration that turns out to be both a hollowing-out and the generation of an extra. Reading from left to right, we first see the silhouette of a man, standing in front of a curtain, looking out to a distant horizon with clouds. This silhouette

Exercises in the Unthought

Figure 2.3 René Magritte, *La Décalcomanie*, 1966.
Source: © 2020 C. Herscovici / Artists Rights Society (ARS), New York.

then becomes evacuated—as though a section of the curtain into which the man was enfolded has been snipped away. Through the hole, a partial view of the sky, the sea, and the beach is exposed. The spaces occupied by the two silhouettes are at once similar and different, filled and emptied, adjacent and apart, realistic and surreal. What would more variables of these silhouettes look like, and what if we were to read them from right to left? Would letting the spaces proliferate indefinitely or reading them in the reverse direction change anything? As Foucault comments, referring to the complex play of ideas embodied in Magritte's title *Décalcomanie*, "Transference? Doubtless. But from what to what? From where to where?"[38] In Magritte's use of similitude, "the similar [as opposed to resemblance] develops in series that have neither beginning nor end, that can be followed in one direction as easily as in another, that obey no hierarchy, but propagate themselves from small differences among small differences." By the same logic, "'Right is left, left is right; the hidden here is visible there; the sunken is in relief; flatness extends into depth,' say the similitudes of *Décalcomanie*."[39]

Although Foucault is dealing with art, his approach is unmistakably not aesthetic in a narrow or strictly disciplinary sense. He reflects on the details of painterly composition with the same kind of analytical rigor that he applies to historical subjects. As is evident in this picture of the two silhouettes, paintings simply allow him a handy set of visible objects with which to address the abstract or invisible yet decidedly political ramifications of space organization, a recurrent topic in his work. Amid the technical considerations of position, sequence, priority, hierarchy, relief, and directionality, a parallel vocabulary of government—of representation, sovereignty, and monarchy—adroitly makes its appearance in his conceptualization of these picture-objects. When commenting on Magritte's painting *Représentation* (1962), for instance, he writes: "What 'represents' what? Even as the exactness of the image functioned as a finger pointing to a model, to a sovereign, unique, and exterior 'pattern,' the series of similitudes (and two are enough to establish a series) abolishes this simultaneously real and ideal monarchy. Henceforth the simulacrum, in a sense always reversible, ranges across the surface."[40] Albeit compressed and incomplete, these writings on art encapsulate some of the key interventional strategies that we have come to associate with Foucault's extended sociohistorical and philosophical studies.

When discussing Magritte, Foucault is particularly drawn to the way the artist plays with, and in doing so unravels, the intelligibility of the calligram, an operation made famous by Guillaume Apollinaire in which the meanings of words and an image are held together—that is, made to reciprocate and reinforce each other. (Put differently, the calligram is a construction in which the visible shape of the image and the alphabetical letters spread along the image's contours share a common ground as both refer to the same thing.)

Figure 2.4 René Magritte, *The Treachery of Images / This Is Not a Pipe*, 1929.
Source: © 2020 C. Herscovici / Artists Rights Society (ARS), New York.

According to Foucault, in the painting *The Treachery of Images/ This Is Not a Pipe* (1929, figure 2.4),[41] Magritte breaks up precisely the presumed inevitability of this common ground, this mutual corroboration between plastic form and linguistic reference. Magritte dissociates them first by placing the words below the image (of a pipe), so that the words literally become a legend. But he does something more: he also inserts a negative, "not," in the declarative, naming statement of the legend. The positivity of the pipe image now floats above a denial, a negation of the pipe expressed in another register. Foucault:

> Now, compared to the traditional function of the legend, Magritte's text is doubly paradoxical. It sets out to name something that evidently does not need to be named (the form is too well known, the label too familiar). And at the moment when he should reveal the name, Magritte does so by denying that the object is what it is. *Whence comes this strange*

game, if not from the calligram? From the calligram that says things twice (when once would doubtless do); from the calligram that shuffles what it says over what it shows to hide them from each other.[42]

Even as the two registers, language and image, seem to have become independent after Magritte's unraveling experiment, Foucault introduces yet a further level of complexity—we could say of *enfoldment*—by drawing attention to the deictic expression "This" ("*Ceci*"). (In doing so, he reminds us of the nimble manners in which he talks about the fingers, hands, and feet in Manet.) The linguistic equivalent of a pointing finger, the little word "This" brings with it the force of indexicality. Depending on where within the picture frame this is located and directed—up (above), down (below), left, or right—and with what elements it is combined, a hitherto suppressed multiplicity of referents, supposedly related yet also autonomous and all vying for validity and legitimacy, now surges forth, resulting in the suspension once and for all of any certain, secure, or permanent connection.[43] In good humor, Foucault marshals a vocabulary of the battlefield to convey the tensions of the situation. The word *this*, he writes, complicates things with "a whole series of intersections—or rather attacks launched by one against the other, arrows shot at the enemy target, enterprises of subversion and destruction, lance blows and wounds, a battle."[44] As "this" unleashes significations in numerous possible dimensions and directions, not only is the calligram unraveled, but also whatever stable referent it used to hold in place has vanished: "Magritte reopened the trap the calligram had sprung on the thing it described. But in the act, the object itself escaped."[45]

By telling the story of how Magritte's art breaks up the naturalized resemblance, the presumed neutralized zone, between words and images into disparate series that can, henceforth, never lie together in peace again, Foucault acquaints his readers with what might be called an interventionist experimental analytics, which he would elaborate with extensive and at times arcane archival resources in his major works. His engagement with Magritte—in particular with how

Magritte disassembles the calligram with its order of stabilized meaning and peaceful coexistence—makes way, I believe, for *a special theory of intersemiotic or intermedial unbecoming* that is simultaneously a practice of gauging change through the most minute of visual and formal details. As he argues in *The Order of Things*, if words and things once coexisted in a relation of integration and mutuality, they now live in a state of disconnect, their former transparent linkages overshadowed by increasingly opaque objects, held in trajectories that may seem parallel to yet are resolutely estranged from one another. Adopting Foucault's militaristic rhetoric, Tanke comments: "The essay on Magritte should be viewed as an extension of Foucault's archaeology of the mobile relationship between seeing and saying.... Stripping them of that common place where they peacefully coexisted, Magritte revives the conflict between plastic and discursive signs. With the demilitarized zone rendered volatile, they launch incursions into one another, covert operations that subtly undermine the principle by which these elements maintained their separation."[46]

The sight and light that Foucault brings to Magritte are, to wit, not a sight and light from an external or transcendent source. To be precise, they occur through a method of opening things up from within the frame—a method of moving things around, redistributing and realigning them, and marking the interstices in between. Rather than making visible what is hidden in depth, this sight and light make visible what is already visible, reminding us that the visibility that is taken for granted, that is supposedly there for all to see, can be torn down, taken apart, and reassembled. Foucault's whimsical remarks about the practice of captioning "illustrations" in books provide an excellent instance of his imaginative reading–visualizing practice: "On the page of an illustrated book, we seldom pay attention to the small space running above the words and below the drawings, forever serving them as a common frontier. It is there, on these few millimeters of white, the calm sand of the page, that are established all the relations of designation, nomination, description, classification. The calligram absorbed that interstice; but once opened, it does not restore it."[47]

On an everyday level, Foucault's work on Magritte may also be understood as a clarification of something that has become the unstated norm for most contemporary practices of viewing art: the divorce, or the removal of an essential continuity, between an image/object and its caption. We have all had the experience of standing in the midst of an exhibit, trying to figure out what a particular artwork is all about. Looking at the colors, lines, and shapes in a picture frame (or in the form of an art piece on display) and reading the caption beside it constitute two separate, often discordant exercises, even though by the convention of their sheer juxtaposition we might still assume their integration and believe that the caption names (or describes the meaning of) the image/object. It is hard not to recall here what Foucault has written about "objects" (and we can certainly add "art objects" and "art *as* an object"): that they can be defined only by relation "to the body of rules that enable them to form as objects of a discourse and thus constitute the conditions of their historical appearance."[48] After Foucault, a different kind of question will become necessary. First: From where does the inevitability of connection between two things (such as an image/object and a caption) arise? What and whose assumptions make possible that connection, that order of coherence? But also: *Hasn't the two things' separation or disjuncture, too, become a common/place that seems just as readily exploited, commodified, and consumed?* If "there is a 'there is' of light," how might we pursue this other conceptual series by probing the "there is" of separation, disjuncture, and other nonrelational (in)visibilities today?

Where Gazes Do Not Meet

In the final lecture on Manet, Foucault draws attention to another type of disconnect—this time not so much between words and things as between human figures caught in different social situations. Noticeably, this interpersonal void assumes the form of noncorrespondent gazes: people in paintings who are looking intensely at something beyond that we, the viewers, cannot see or people whose gazes somehow do not meet and thus annul one another within the picture frame. Examples of such gazes abound in the paintings Foucault selects for his lecture: *In the Greenhouse* (1879), *Argenteuil* (1874), *The Waitress* (1879), *St.-Lazare Station* (1873), *The Balcony* (1868–1869), and *A Bar at the Folies-Bergère* (1882). Both Gary Shapiro and Joseph Tanke have offered incisive comments on this compositional peculiarity in Manet that captivates Foucault. Shapiro writes, in reference to the painting *St.-Lazare Station*, "If painting no longer evokes a theater of light, neither does it reveal a coherent relation between the looks that are internal to it and their objects. Persons in Manet's works look out beyond the canvas, or to the side, but in any case we typically know nothing about the target of their gaze.... Foucault suggests that Manet tempts us to go around the canvas, to change our position, in order to see what the observer in the painting sees. The work forces a sense of invisibility upon us."[49]

Tanke's comments, specifically on the painting *The Balcony*—which Foucault dramatically announces as "a picture which is nothing other than *the brilliance of invisibility* itself"[50]—may be borrowed for a general description of this recurrent aspect of Manet's work: "To indicate this surge of invisibility opening up within the representation, Manet's characters each point the viewer in a different direction, suggesting that there is something taking place outside of the representative space. This game by which the direction of each character's glance annuls those of the others leaves the viewer in an uncertain position. What are these figures looking at? How should one approach this scene?"[51]

In reflecting on Foucault's way of reading these eyes that veer toward elsewhere and nowhere, it seems reasonable to recall a famous but very different approach to eyes—the Sartrean notion of "regard" in all its negative connotations. The memorable affect associated with the eye in the work of Jean-Paul Sartre is that of a menace: nonreciprocity and noncommunication are effects of a fundamental aggression and hostility toward the other. In contrast, Foucault's attraction to noncoincident gazes (as in his readings of Manet) is more akin to his fascination with the invisible as part of a pure exteriority, an economy of no returns, and a creativity through loss, dispersion, and limit experiences—themes that he is well known to have admired in Georges Bataille's work, in which the eyes, when they do appear, tend to be rolled back in ecstasy.[52]

Where gazes do not meet in a straight or unified line is where a blank, an ellipsis, occurs within a frame that is otherwise filled with visible objects and characters.[53] Foucault does not jump in to fill this ellipsis with meaning. Nor does he lament the failure of a smooth match-up of sights in the form of "Alas, traditional social ties have broken down; people no longer even see each other. How sad! How much better connected they used to be and can be!" Eschewing such banal, mournful moralization of noncorrespondence, Foucault invites us to ponder instead a different kind of event unfolding through the gazes that do not meet. For are not these sights that miss one another only to head toward unknown destinations saying something precise about a social situation that is becoming exponentially impersonal and abstract? Such impersonality and abstractness are the effects of what might be called the infinitization, the limitless extendability and optimizability, of data produced by finite systems (individual human bodies with their various physical capacities and activities—looking, sitting, walking, drinking, eating, gesturing, talking, dancing, swimming). Although the finite elements are eminently perceptible and, in hands of a talented painter, portrayable, what escapes even the most skilled and lifelike portraiture is the elusive notion of *a totality* (a class, a society, a nation, a population, a species, and so forth). As Foucault defines it, such a totality (he is referring specifically to a population) is "a new body, a multiple body, a body with so many heads that, while they might not be infinite in number, cannot necessarily be counted."[54] And yet this conception of human sociality *as* a totality, which is a modern way of imagining—indeed, of imaging—the world, is exactly the kind of epistemic shift to which a groundbreaking discursive field such as is instituted by Manet cannot not be receptive—even when the artist knew full well that he could not actually paint it.⁵⁵ The rhizomatic sightlines—we might also say viewpoints or perspectives—that keep shooting or swerving off in different directions are thus, it could be argued, the artist's way of gesturing toward the increasingly *unpaintable* aggregate of proliferating itineraries and nontotalizable objects that is modern industrialized life.⁵⁶

The mathematical science that Foucault repeatedly invokes in his work on biopolitics and governmentality in (neo)liberal society is that of statistics. As is usually the case, he is careful to describe not a timeless type of knowledge but rather a historically evolving technology and apparatus of computation. The art of government, he writes, based as it was in the premodern West on the family as the economic model, gave way in the eighteenth century to a political science, *a science of the state*, that aims its tactics instead at the theme of population:

> Whereas statistics had previously worked within the administrative frame and thus in terms of the functioning of sovereignty, it now gradually reveals that population has its own regularities, its own rate of deaths and diseases, its cycles of scarcity, and so on; statistics shows also that the domain of population involves a range of intrinsic, aggregate effects, phenomena that are irreducible to those of the family, such as epidemics, endemic levels of mortality, ascending spirals of labor and wealth; finally, it shows that, through its shifts, customs, activities, and so on, population has specific economic effects. Statistics [makes] it possible to quantify these specific phenomena of population.⁵⁷

Along with quantification comes the important technique of correlation (as we have seen, in the previous chapter, with respect to Franco Moretti's ambitious proposal for "distant reading" of novels from different parts of the world in the realm of literary study). This technique enables the discrete, large-scale kinds of data Foucault mentions in the passage just quoted to be consolidated and converted into newfound units or repositories of decipherability, predictability, and manageability. Through the ever more sophisticated mechanisms of chartable (or visualizable) representations and projections, *homo economicus* becomes an eminently measurable, knowable, and governable entity. To this extent, I concur with Shapiro's astute observation that Foucault's unfinished work on Manet should be read as a pair with the book *Discipline and Punish*: "Both the book and the lectures treat highly powerful and influential diagrams of the visible, one directed at positioning individuals as objects of surveillance and self-surveillance, the other at transforming painting from an art of the illusory viewing of an imaginative space into an organon for the contemplation of surfaces without depth, opening onto nothing but themselves. In this respect the art that follows Manet's innovations can be construed as a form of resistance to the society of surveillance." Going a bit further along the same lines, Shapiro remarks: "In the Panopticon the gaze is mobilized and fixed on each individual; it is a floating or functional gaze that need not appear as the look of anyone in particular. In Manet looks meet no object, no person, even though we see their source. *What we see, then, is an eye disconnected from a content of vision.*"[58]

If statistics has irrevocably systematized the impersonal, abstract spaces between the finite and the infinite by turning them into permutable, visible data-objects, in the experimental terrains of modern painting, or so Foucault suggests through his riveting readings, such spaces are holding on in the empty form of blanks, chasms, fissures, and nonintegrated flight paths. Around these elliptical passages captured momentarily on the canvas, perhaps the potentiality of utopia and anarchy—literally of nonplace and nongovernment—can still be dreamt? We should insist on at least asking such a question. In an era of computer-algorithm-assisted facial-recognition systems, when law enforcement officers are equipped, we are told, with capabilities to create perpetual line-ups of suspects, people can now be identified not only by their facial features such as their brow, nose, cheeks, lips, and chin but also by their irises. Just as long as their eyes are in use—just as long as they are looking, that is—they can be tracked without their knowing, their gazes met, matched, and *completed* in the loop of an inhuman surveillance network. As such surveillance networks become normativized with state-of-the-art technologies around the globe, Foucault's untimely meditations on the gazes that do not meet begin to assume a refreshing sense of poignancy. Veering off in different directions into invisibility, these uncaught gazes are, or so he seems to say, vectors to an open that will remain unknowable and nontotalizable because it is unclosable.

3
Thinking "Race" with Foucault

It is generally recognized today that no scientific definition of race is possible.

—W. E. B. Du Bois, *The Negro*

If racial essentialism and its recent history foster a conception of racism that is imperative to combat, it has also spawned resistance—intellectual and activist, known as identity politics. The two tendencies arise from a similar impulse and share certain assumptions about race and racism.

—Roxann Wheeler, *The Complexion of Race*

Racial categories have to be denatured. We have to see ... how ... whiteness is assembled and brought to actual and virtual life. What are its historical, economic and social conditions of existence? How does it become articulated to juridical, scientific, medical, aesthetic, military and technological forms of expertise?

—George Yancy and Paul Gilroy, "What 'Black Lives' Means in Britain"

What in fact is racism? It is primarily a way of introducing a break into the domain of life that is under power's control: the break between what must live and what must die.

—Michel Foucault, *"Society Must Be Defended"*

When it comes to Foucault and questions of race, the critical challenge to date is the ready reproach of Eurocentrism—the charge that Foucault's perspectives, derived as they are from close studies of European cultures and histories, are negligent of other parts of the modern world. In particular, the disciplinary institutions in Europe that he analyzes with such brilliance were, chronologically speaking, evolving during the same time period when European nations aggressively pursued their imperial and colonial enterprises overseas, but Foucault does not offer any analysis of such enterprises. Even as he helped popularize the important concept of heterotopia (discussed in greater detail in chapter 5), he has been generally found guilty of not being heterotopic enough. The present chapter is an attempt to argue the relevance of Foucault's work to the study of race in a different direction from this justified, though in my view not necessarily intellectually productive, approach.

Foucauldian Discourse and Its Postcolonial Inflection

In his critique of European imperialism, Edward Said, greatly influenced by Foucault's early work on discourse, performs the trend-setting task of mapping the systemic and structural correlations between textual formations and economic-political formations. In the classic study *Orientalism*, Said argues that these correlations constitute a kind of material history based as much on representational traditions as it is on physical invasions and annexations. "The things to look at are style, figures of speech, setting, narrative devices, historical and social circumstances, *not* the correctness of the representation nor its fidelity to some great original. The exteriority of the representation is always governed by some version of the truism that if the Orient could represent itself, it would; since it cannot, the representation does the job, for the West, and *faute de mieux*, for the poor Orient," Said writes,[1] laying down the methodological blueprint for critiquing a history that, according to him, has contributed to the concerted Western construction of the Orient as a distinct and inferior entity. Even so, from the standpoint of race, Foucault's imprints on Said's seminal work are perhaps less a matter of the empirical objects of study chosen (the texts and artworks that make condescending references to oriental identities and cultures) than of a new, reflexive method of conceptualizing the colonial situation and its aftermath. By positioning the East and the West as clusters of discourses rather than as ontological fixities, and by showing that the East as such is constituted through the collaborative criss-crossings of different branches of Western knowledge (such as history, art, literature, philosophy, geography, economics, politics, and so forth), Said inaugurated a secular theoretical model of scholarship that has proven resiliently adoptable and adaptable and that remains current in many academic and journalistic investigations of (post)colonial histories and cultures.

Similarly, in his book *Time and the Other: How Anthropology Makes Its Object*, Johannes Fabian interrogates the philosophical, theological, and historical foundations of Western anthropological thinking along the lines introduced by Foucault in his early work such as *The Order of Things*. Writing in the wake of Said's antiorientalist critique, Fabian goes further (than Foucault) in underscoring a basic unevenness embedded in ethnographic practice—that is, in the communication loop through which Western anthropologists routinely report their observations and findings about non-Western cultures back to audiences in the West. In an ingenious stroke, Fabian defines this unevenness in terms of a geopolitics of time: whereas Western researchers write about other cultures to Western readers in the forward-looking present, the cultures being studied are, or so his argument goes, typically objectified in such ways as to seem frozen in some other temporality, one that is, moreover, implicitly deemed primitive, backward, and unchanging.[2] In Fabian's account, as in Said's, using the Foucauldian notion of discourse—an ever-shifting, textual-cum-social grid of articulations spread over the course of time—means foregrounding not only an open-ended multiplicity of constituents and players but also a persistent relation of closure, of inequality between cultures. If Western researchers' work is predicated on mobility and freedom, their habits and privileges of travel being constitutive of their techniques of producing knowledge, the peoples they study, by contrast, are epistemologically confined in a standstill to their culture gardens.[3]

As in the case of the transatlantic slave trade in the context of the United States, the political and economic aspects of European empire building of the past few centuries have definitively molded the understanding of race in the global postcolonial context, in which race is more or less irrevocably marked by this relation of inequality and its egregious consequences. As Roxann Wheeler puts it, "Too often race has been treated only as a subset of slavery and colonialism, an emphasis that has reinforced the fallacious belief that race is primarily about blackness or African origins." Drawing on a scrupulous study of the more elastically articulated categories of human variety in eighteenth-century British culture, Wheeler observes that most contemporary colonial and critical theorists tend to "silently base their assumptions about race on the mid-nineteenth-century heritage of biological racism," which is predominantly characterized by "an anxiety about cultural and racial purity, pervasive white supremacism, the white man's burden of civilizing native populations, and an interventionary political rule."[4] Wheeler's observations corroborate Foucault's in *Discipline and Punish*. In discussing the emergence of delinquency as a punishable personality trait, Foucault describes the early nineteenth century as "a time when the perception of another form of life was being articulated upon that of another class and another human species. A zoology of social sub-species and an ethnology of the civilizations of malefactors, with their own rites and language, was [*sic*] beginning to emerge in a parody form."[5]

Given the powerful influence of this nineteenth-century heritage, in what Nikolas Rose has termed "a concerted biologization of race,"[6] we can see how, even when not explicitly invoked, the infrastructural relations between colonizer and colonized—much like the infrastructural relations between slave traders/owners and slaves—have largely determined the stakes in contemporary debates about race and modern Western thought.[7] In these debates, race remains understood mainly in terms of the immutability of skin color and other biomedically deterministic (molar) rather than probabilistic (molecular) classifications,[8] and racism is understood as practices of exploitation and discrimination by those historically on the side of the victors (associated with political success and economic privilege) against those historically on the side of the victims (deemed linguistically, culturally, and institutionally inferior and unfairly deprived of opportunities for social mobility and advancement).[9]

In the ready (and understandable) reification of race and racism in these anachronic terms, an important and arguably more critical contribution made by Foucault is often elided. The Foucauldian notion of discourse has exerted such an impact through its Saidian inflection, it would seem, not necessarily simply because of Said's pioneering, paradigm-setting politicization of Western representations of the East. In a manner that is quite worthy of Foucauldian analytics are, we should note, Said's own rhetorical moves: not only has Said brought what are actually divergent (and usually discontinuous) series of historical events into coherent alignment with one another, but he has also strategically halted their multidirectional, uncoordinated movements by conjoining them at a particular nexus. That is to say, if there are no intrinsic or essential connections between colonial territorial conquests, military occupations, and economic exploitations, on the one hand, *and* linguistic, textual, and visual representations, on the other, Said's deployment of discourse, together with the postcolonial studies that follows its lead, has powerfully interpellated audiences by insisting and reiterating that such connections are an incontrovertible certitude.

In some ways, the controversies of race as they continue to be generated in the Anglo-American academy today are an outcome of such strategic halting and binding—one might say essentializing—of the fluid transitions among contingent events into a continuous, subterranean master narrative. This is one reason some scholars have, for instance, disputed the origins (or causes) of orientalism as advanced by Said and his followers, citing the major counterexample of German orientalism, in which the seeming contiguity between empire and orientalist textual studies is not necessarily self-evident or consistent and in which older religious, spiritual, and philosophical preoccupations rather than chronologically more recent political-economic conquests assumed a pivotal role in modern Europe's encounters with the East.[10] Although this point will need to be substantiated by a consideration of the vertiginously multilingual deliberations of different orientalist traditions, my point is simply that in the context of contemporary critical race studies Foucault's contribution to the politics of discourse demands to be carefully revisited and reevaluated. If our current understanding of race—in particular within the English-speaking academy—has been preemptively shaped by postcolonial studies' articulation of the dialectic between colonizer and colonized, it behooves us to ask, after Foucault: What are the factors that make that preemptive shaping possible? Could it have been otherwise? Were there other evental series in operation that could have led to different configurations of race and racism?

Race Studies' Repressive Hypothesis?

The suturing of race to the hierarchical colonizer–colonized relation has been so institutionally generative that any attempt to conceptualize race differently would seem counterintuitive. To this extent, post-Saidian postcolonial studies has been instrumental in enabling, indeed empowering, representations of those who are historically disadvantaged, peripheralized, or silenced, even as cautionary reflections of what it means to let the subaltern speak have long been present.[11] As an increasingly hegemonic trend in spotlighting victimhood reproduces itself across the studies of intergroup and intercultural encounters, postcolonial studies' more positivistic and less-elastic version of race can seem at times to resonate a little too neatly with the popularized Freudian paradigm of sexual repression. Along these lines, race is commonly equated with oppression based on anatomy (that is, skin complexion), which is in turn deemed intractable rather than as one factor among a range of factors.[12] Such intractability is then further discoursed in terms of loss, grief, melancholia, precarity, and other naturalized—that is to say, normativized—psychoanalytic coordinates.

Foucault's critique of popularized Freudian repression is too well known to warrant repeating in full, though the salient aspects of his argument remain noteworthy. As a mechanism that animates discourse, repression functions not merely as a means to articulate sexual differentiations from within an individual but also, according to Foucault, as the motor of an entire regime of thought, rendering our sense of self in the binarized states of imprisonment and liberation (or secrecy and transparency or darkness and light). This collaboration between a negative referent, repressed (that is, injured and obstructed) sexuality, and the positive significatory potency of discourse is what Foucault intends by the phrase "the repressive hypothesis." Unlike Freud, Foucault is not exactly interested in asking why or how we are repressed, but rather in how we *come to believe* that we are. His oft-cited remarks to this effect go as follows in *The History of Sexuality*, volume 1: "The question I would like to pose is not, Why are we repressed? But rather, Why do we say, with so much passion and so much resentment against our most recent past, against our present, and against ourselves, that we are repressed? By what spiral did we come to affirm that sex is negated? What led us to show, ostentatiously, that sex is something we hide, to say it is something we silence?"[13]

For Foucault, writing in the mid–twentieth century, sexuality is not exactly "a stubborn drive, by nature alien and of necessity disobedient to a power which exhausts itself trying to subdue it and often fails to control it entirely." Instead of this romanticist approach, he proposes thinking of sexuality as "an especially dense transfer point for relations of power"—one that is, moreover, "endowed with the greatest instrumentality" (*HS*, 1:103).

If Foucault's critique succeeds in challenging the ingrained beliefs in injury and obstruction that underpin the popular narratives of sexual repression, it meanwhile acknowledges how effectively the repressive hypothesis works as an incitement to discourse. Indeed, Foucault's notion of discourse's power is in part based on his grasp of how incessant *talk* about sexual repression—as instigated and encouraged by Freudian clinical custom and its commercial, mass-media, and self-help industry spinoffs—has activated an explosion of discourses and practices.

Might not Foucault's critique of the repressive hypothesis also be instructive for thinking about race?

Consider the monumental figure of Frantz Fanon, whose work speaks to colonial oppression *as* psychic repression. For Fanon, writing in the 1940s as a colonial émigré from French Martinique educated in the metropole, race connotes above all the psychic wounding that the black subject endures at the hands of his white oppressors. As identification with the white oppressor is both required and impossible, self-alienation or psychic disability becomes the defining limit for black identity formation. According to Fanon, such internal fragmentation is reinforced by denigrating interactions in the metropolis, in which the black subject is regularly reduced to his skin color and hailed as resolutely other, so much so that the fragmentation tends to gravitate outward, creating psychic schisms within the colonized population as a whole. Notably, the unforgettable street scene of racial hailing as described by Fanon is no less constitutive of the self-identification of the white child who cries out, "Look! A Negro!," at the sight of the black man.[14] For this child, race means subjecting the other to exoticism, a type of recognition based in the aesthetics of shock and wonderment as well as in stigmatization.

In Fanon's descriptions, not only is race soldered to the entanglement between colonizer and colonized, but it is also theorized in (Freudian) Oedipal terms. The white man occupies the position of the authoritative father who must be removed in order for his reign of tyranny to end and for the angry son, the black man, to gain a positive sense of his own identity. Injury seems counterable only with injury, as violent overthrow is the only means by which the black man can externally compensate for his internal bereavement, repossess what was taken from him, and assume a renewed sense of wholeness. Race (which in this instance equals racism), as experienced by the black male subject, seems symptomatic of the repressive logic that characterizes the paternalistic functioning of power. Above all, race (or racism) heralds the sign of damage, a perpetually internalized state of negation that can be ameliorated only through periodic eruptions of revolutionary violence.[15]

The Entry of Life Into History

Foucault's leftist political sympathies notwithstanding, his take on race and racism is quite different from the classic argument of repressive violence as advanced by Fanon, not least because Foucault was guided by his lifelong interest in critiquing modern Western political reason. To begin to explore Foucault's vision of race, which is inextricable from the sustained project of that critique, we need to turn to part 5 of *The History of Sexuality*, volume 1—"Right of Death and Power Over Life"—which during a conversation he named the "fundamental part" of that book.[16]

In the sections preceding part 5, Foucault offers a riveting account of the history of sexuality in modern Europe as a history of the will to knowledge. The abnormalities and perversions discussed by Freud—more or less ahistorically—as variants of a polymorphous sexuality, Foucault rewrites as Western society's way since the eighteenth century of monitoring human populations by regulation and surveillance, mechanisms that were implemented through medicine, law, education, the family, and statistics (the science of government).[17] In particular, he discusses four types of institutional practices that together form the "strategic unities" in enforcing "normal" sexuality: a hysterization of women's bodies, a pedagogization of children's sex, a socialization of procreative behavior, and a psychiatrization of perverse pleasure (*HS*, 1:104–5). Foucault's passionate depiction of the regimentations and penalizations of sexual behaviors suggests something crucial: that although his work proceeds in accordance with Freud's argument that the sexual instinct is nonessential in character, he has chosen quite deliberately to sidestep that argument in order to theorize sexuality in a new way, as a *rational deployment of bodies and institutions* through steadily expanding apparatuses of measurement, calibration, and supervision. Rather than a matter of "instincts and their vicissitudes," as Freud calls them, which require ever more sophisticated efforts at classification and interpretation,[18] sexuality for Foucault is a vast, heterogeneous network of modern knowledge production that includes legal, moral, scientific, architectural, philosophical, and administrative discourses, all of which evolve with shifting boundaries as well as with effects of exclusion and homogenization.

Foucault's remarks on race in "Right of Death and Power Over Life" should be read in tandem with sexuality understood in the terms of this historically emergent power nexus of the will to knowledge. Both sexuality and race, that is, have to do with what he calls *the entry of life into history*—"the entry of phenomena peculiar to the life of the human species into the order of knowledge and power, into the sphere of political techniques" (*HS*, 1:141–42).[19] This formulation of life's significance as a historical threshold is already evident in *The Order of Things* (published ten years before *The History of Sexuality*, volume 1), in which Foucault elaborates on the developments of political economy, biology, and language as coevolving new modes of knowledge production since the early nineteenth century.[20] Of the three, it is biology after the naturalist and zoologist Georges Cuvier, regarded by Foucault as the key transitional figure in the modern European conceptualization of life, that seems to have most instructed Foucault's own thinking:

In short, throughout the Classical age, life was the province of an ontology which dealt in the same way with all material beings, all of which were subject to extension, weight, and movement; and it was in this sense that all the sciences of nature, and especially that of living beings, had a profound mechanistic vocation; *from Cuvier onward, living beings escape, in the first instance at least, the general laws of extensive being; biological being becomes regional and autonomous; life, on the confines of being, is what is exterior to it and also, at the same time, what manipulates itself within it.*[21]

Life's historicity, in other words, has to do with the confrontation in modernity between the will to knowledge and life's newly theorized, Janus-faced status (as something both exterior and internal to biological being, beckoning both with the possibility of the living and with the inevitability of death). For Foucault, despite such a will's attempt to tame life for the sake of human survival, life remains (as he writes in the extended quote at the end of this paragraph) an "untamed ontology" whose "mute and invisible violence" is "devouring [things and beings] in the darkness." For precisely this reason, Foucault tells us, this untamed, destructive ontology stands as "a critique of knowledge." His eloquent exposition needs to be quoted at length:

For life—and this is why it has a radical value in nineteenth-century thought—is at the same time the nucleus of being and of non-being: there is being only because there is life, and in that fundamental movement that dooms them to death, the scattered beings, stable for an instant, are formed, halt, hold life immobile—and in a sense kill it—but are then in turn destroyed by that inexhaustible force. The experience of life is thus posited as the most general law of beings, the revelation of that primitive force on the basis of which they are; it functions as *an untamed ontology*, one trying to express the indissociable being and non-being of all beings. But this ontology discloses not so much what gives beings their foundation as what bears them for an instant towards a precarious form and yet is already secretly sapping them from within in order to destroy them. In relation to life, beings are no more than transitory figures, and the being that they maintain, during the brief period of their existence, is no more than their presumption, their will to survive. And so, for knowledge, the being of things is an illusion, a veil that must be torn aside in order to reveal *the mute and invisible violence that is devouring them in the darkness. The ontology of the annihilation of beings assumes therefore validity as a critique of knowledge*: but it is not so much a question of giving the phenomenon a foundation, of expressing both its limit and its law, of relating it to the finitude that renders it possible, as of *dissipating it and destroying it in the same way as life itself destroys beings*: for its whole being is mere appearance.   (*OT*, 278–79, emphases added)

In his study *Life: A Modern Invention*, which begins with Foucauldian ruminations about life's new conceptual status in modernity, Davide Tarizzo uses the phrase "epistemological indicator" to underscore Foucault's interdiscursive vision of life as emblematic of the struggles of the will to knowledge, struggles that, according to Tarizzo, can be traced to a philosophical lineage from Kant, Schelling, and Herder to Schopenhauer, Nietzsche, Freud, and others.[22] Foucault's most important point in *The Order of Things*, however, is that these struggles have brought about forms of knowledge that, although profoundly interrelated, are increasingly incommensurate or incompatible with one another. Speaking of political economy and biology, for instance, Foucault writes: "Where one mode of thought predicts the end of history, the other proclaims the infinity of life; where one recognizes the real production of things by labour, the other dissipates the chimeras of consciousness; where one affirms, with the limits of the individual, the exigencies of his life, the other masks them beneath the murmuring of death" (*OT*, 279). This kind of discursive incommensurateness implies that "from the nineteenth century the field of knowledge can no longer provide the ground for a reflection that will be homogeneous and uniform at all points" (*OT*, 279). Instead, it seems increasingly the case, or so Foucault suggests, that each form of knowledge will need to be rationalized with a philosophy that specifically suits it (*OT*, 279).

In other words, rather than taking race through the route of the repressive hypothesis and equating it—as is often the case in the fields of knowledge driven by contemporary identity politics—with racism, which is understood as an injurious subjective experience, Foucault approaches race primarily as an outcome of the intensified, compulsory objectification, bureaucratization, and normalization of life, whose rise to epistemic power, as he tells us in *The Order of Things*, was signaled in part by a shift from the classical field of knowledge known as natural history to the modern science of life known as biology. If plants and animals used to be classified in natural history by their common visible traits, they are henceforth conceived synthetically as deep structures based in invisible relations of subordination and organization. Foucault's vivacious narration of this epistemic shift, which, according to him, enabled biological segments to become *correlated* as parts of a (nontransparent) structure across an ensemble of species or genera, may be glimpsed in extended passages such as the following:

> When we consider the organ in relation to its function, we see, therefore, the emergence of "resemblances" where there is no "identical" element; a resemblance that is constituted by the transition of the function into evident invisibility. It matters little, after all, that gills and lungs may have a few variables of form, magnitude, or number in common: they resemble one another because they are two varieties of that nonexistent, abstract, unreal, unassignable organ, absent from all describable species, yet present in the animal kingdom in its entirety, which serves for *respiration in general*. Thus there is a return in the analysis of living beings to Aristotelian analogies: the gills are to respiration in water what lungs are to respiration in air. True, such relations were perfectly well known in the Classical age; but they were used only to determine functions; they were not used to establish the order of things within the space of nature. From Cuvier onward, function, defined

according to its non-perceptible form as an effect to be attained, is to serve as a constant middle term and to make it possible to relate together totalities of elements without the slightest visible identity. What to classical eyes were merely differences juxtaposed with identities must now be ordered and conceived on the basis of a functional homogeneity which is their hidden foundation. When the Same and the Other both belong to a single space, there is *natural history*; something like *biology* becomes possible when this unity of level begins to break up, and when differences stand out against the background of an identity that is deeper and, as it were, more serious than that unity.[23]   (*OT*, 264–65, Foucault's emphases)

As living things were increasingly understood as constituted by hidden animating principles—that is, by vital functions *shared invisibly* across species and organisms—a transcendental notion of life steadily assumed center stage in scientific and other discourses. Jeffrey T. Nealon's elucidating account of this profound epistemic shift may be borrowed here as a summation of this point: "In the birth of biology the question of life unhinges itself from a practice of representation (the discourse is freed from what Foucault calls the 'pure tabulation of things' [*OT*, 131] in natural history's grids) and attaches itself instead to a mode of speculation about this murky thing called life—now understood *not* as a visible manifestation of similitude but as the darkly hidden secret that connects living things."[24] It is precisely in examining the "mode of speculation about this murky thing called life" that, as Foucault writes, "it became possible to replace natural history with a 'history' of nature" (*OT*, 275).

Because of this overarching emphasis on life as a historically mutating discourse threshold, race in Foucault's work, like sexuality, requires a different kind of amplification. Foucault does not exactly conceptualize race as something with essential or positive features (epidermis, anatomical traits, individual or group markers, or geographical regions). Nor does he view the antagonisms around racialization simply in terms of repressive violence. Rather, in keeping with his interrogations of the will to knowledge in modern times, he writes about race as an epistemic fault line that erupts *alongside* major historical transitions—such as the transition from a society governed by the symbolics of blood and sovereignty as invested in the monarch to one administered through disciplinary institutions and finally to one managed through biopolitical networks. This is how he describes the historical emergence of Nazi racism, for instance:

> Beginning in the second half of the nineteenth century, the thematics of blood was sometimes called on to lend its entire historical weight toward revitalizing the type of political power that was exercised through the devices of sexuality. Racism took shape at this point (racism in its modern, "biologizing," statist form): it was then that a whole politics of settlement (*peuplement*), family, marriage, education, social hierarchization, and property, accompanied by a long series of permanent interventions at the level of the body, conduct, health, and everyday life, received their color and their justification from the mythical concern with protecting the purity of the blood and ensuring the triumph of the race. Nazism was doubtless the most cunning and the most naïve (and the former because of the latter) combination of the fantasies of blood and the paroxysms of a disciplinary power. (*HS*, 1:149)

As Foucault underscores on another occasion, "What is new in the nineteenth century is the appearance of a racist biology, entirely centred around the concept of degeneracy."[25] Modern antisemitism, he adds, began in that ideological form, whereby it was imperative to rid society of those elements that were deemed degenerate, unclean, and unhealthy. But Foucault goes further with a more provocative point about Nazi racism: for all their seemingly old-fashioned talk about preserving the purity of Aryan blood, he suggests, the Nazis actually operated on a modern premise of life that was characteristic of disciplinary and biopolitical society: the premise on which massacres and genocides are carried out as vital rather than as death events. Exterminations of entire populations are, from this perspective, performed for the progressive purpose of augmenting life (through the exaltation of a superior group) in an "indefinite extension of strength, vigor, health, and life" (*HS*, 1:125), which Foucault calls "a dynamic racism, a racism of expansion" (*HS*, 1:125). The seemingly ultimate act of negation—killing people—is thus subsumed under an eminently positive agenda, eugenics, with its implied intensification of micropowers over the social body, together with the promise of a better race and a better species to come. As Foucault comments in *"Society Must Be Defended,"* "The objective of the Nazi regime was . . . not really the destruction of other races."[26]

Interestingly, while dissecting the monstrosity of Nazism's modernity in *The History of Sexuality*, vol. 1, Foucault, in a memorably rare aside, compliments psychoanalysis on its comprehension of an older politics of life (and death) that is bound to law and prohibition (and thus, from that perspective, to the necessity of repression):

> It is to the political credit of psychoanalysis—or at least, of what was most coherent in it—that it regarded with suspicion (and this from its inception, that is, from the moment it broke away from the neuropsychiatry of degenerescence) the irrevocably proliferating aspects which might be contained in these power mechanisms aimed at controlling and administering the everyday life of sexuality: whence the Freudian endeavor (out of reaction no doubt to the great surge of racism that was contemporary with it) to ground sexuality in the law—the law of alliance, tabooed consanguinity, and the Sovereign-Father, in short, to surround desire with all the trappings of the old order of power. It was owing to this that psychoanalysis was—in the main, with a few exceptions—in theoretical and practical opposition to fascism. (*HS*, 1:150)

Foucault is probably thinking here of Freud's *Totem and Taboo* (1913), a work that speculates on the origins of human society by way of murder and sacrifice or that advances a theory of social formation as a phenomenon inseparable from transgressive originary violence. Although he goes on to call psychoanalysis's way of handling the sexual a "historical 'retro-version'" (*HS*, 1:150)—that is, obsolete—and although he criticizes the popularization of the repressive hypothesis as a type of belief (or of what, after his teacher Louis Althusser, may be called "ideology," a fictitious relation to lived reality that generates real subjection[27]), Foucault does justice to Freud by acknowledging the latter's grasp of the strategic historical place occupied by sexuality at the intersection of knowledge and power in modern Europe.[28]

To consider Foucault's relevance to the debates on race, it would therefore be necessary to see his major works—from *The History of Madness* and *The Order of Things* to *The Birth of the Clinic, Discipline and Punish, The History of Sexuality*, and the Collège de France lectures—as a continual series of critical commentaries on life's entry into history. This entry has to do not only with masses as individuated bodies but also with the methods and mechanisms by which masses are handled *in abstraction*—that is, systematically produced in the form of a calculable and manageable aggregate, *a social body* (or what Foucault in an interview calls "the great fantasy . . . of a social body constituted by the universality of wills"[29]). As he puts it in one of the lectures collected in *"Society Must Be Defended,"* a technology of power newly emerging in the second half of the eighteenth century applied "not to man-as-body but . . . to man-as-species" (*"Society,"* 242). This technology is addressed to a multiplicity of men "to the extent that they form . . . a global mass that is affected by overall processes characteristic of birth, death, production, illness, and so on" (*"Society,"* 242–43).[30] Foucault names this technology of power "a 'biopolitics' of the human race" (*"Society,"* 243). In using the word *race*, he clearly intends something akin to *group, class, type,* or *speciation*. As in his efforts to historicize how madness becomes legible through institutional compartmentalization and segregation in Western society, or how different fields of knowledge come into existence through gradual rearrangements of established boundaries and their fault lines, what fascinates him is how the will to know seems invariably, in the modern period, to devolve into computational moves (of dividing and multiplying) that in turn become enterprises of enclosure, partitioning, specification, and infinitization. It is in this process of random groups of human persons (or human traits) being amassed as aggregates of incorporeal affinities and, in that manner, correlated for purposes of statist management, that race, in tandem with sex, materializes as a relation of force.

Foucault's understanding of race may be glimpsed in a number of clarifying statements he makes in the Collège de France lectures gathered under the title *"Society Must Be Defended."* He writes that "the war that is going on beneath order and peace, the war that undermines our society and divides it in a binary mode is, basically, a race war" (59–60). "The social body is basically articulated around two races," he adds. "It is this idea that this clash between two races runs through society from top to bottom which we see being formulated as early as the seventeenth century" (60). He goes on to distinguish between a biological transcription of race war (in the form of evolutionism, such as that manifested in European policies of colonization) and a social transcription of race war (in the form of a class struggle) (60). He indicates his own attempt to trace this "biologico-social racism," with the important reminder that "the other race" is not from elsewhere but a race *"that is permanently, ceaselessly infiltrating the social body, or which is, rather, constantly being re-created in and by the social fabric"* (61, emphasis added). Finally, Foucault holds that the function of racism is twofold: "to fragment, to create caesuras within the biological continuum addressed by biopower," and *"to allow the establishment of a positive relation* of this type:... 'The very fact that you let more die will allow you to live more'" (255, emphasis added).[31]

In sum, Foucault's ongoing intellectual project has to do with the historical expansion of life, what he calls the "I—as species rather than as individual" (*"Society,"* 255), in the form of *an ideality*, a transcendent generality in whose name empirical practices flourish and proliferate. The endless endeavors to know life, involving ever more complicated mechanisms of measurement, surveying/surveillance, analysis, forecast, and projection, are part and parcel of the modern state's I-as-species mission. Seeing race primarily in these terms—that is, as part and parcel of a regime of growth,[32] dedicated to the normalization of the living and to the sanctification of humans, who are abstractly imagined as an integrated whole—raises a fundamental question: "How can a power such as this kill, if it is true that its basic function is to improve life, to prolong its duration, to improve its chances, to avoid accidents, and to compensate for failings?... Given that this power's objective is essentially to make live, how can it let die? How can the power of death, the function of death, be exercised in a political system centered upon biopower?" (*"Society,"* 254).

This is the juncture at which he introduces the remarks, given as the last epigraph at the beginning of this chapter, about racism as the state's way of introducing a break in the domain of life. Rather than understanding racism by way of tensions and antagonisms derived from positive markers such as skin color and geographical location, Foucault characteristically describes it as a relation of power (together with the historical discourses that revolve around such a relation). More specifically, racism is a means to an end rather than an end in itself; it is a technique of power that may be adopted whenever and wherever populations need to be brought under control in the state's biopolitical warfare. This is why, in a rather controversial gesture for the mid-1970s, he suggests that even socialism is marked by racism insofar as the socialist state can rationalize the murder of its enemies for purposes of advancing the class struggle (*"Society,"* 261, 262). In an astute discussion of the massive data-ification of the contemporary global environment, Patricia Ticineto Clough, writing along the grain of Foucault's arguments, proposes the term *population racism* to underscore the actuarialism that, as she argues, goes well beyond the state:

> With population racism, the calculations and measures of population in a variety of contexts—territory, class, ethnicity, gender, race—all are

put in terms of an analysis of biological activity. Of course, this is a biology (and now neuroscience) that is infused with technicity or technicality—the technicity of measuring, for starters. In turning all contexts of populations into a biotechnicity of calculation, quantification, and measure, population racism makes way for the health or lack thereof of populations to be part of a global market, beyond national boundedness, beyond the boundaries of the body as organism.[33]

Whereas our current understanding of racism tends to see it more or less psychically, as a form of prejudice and hatred or as mutual contempt, with all the subjective and subjectivizing connotations these words conjure, in Foucault's work racism is not simply a malicious frame of mind or, for that matter, a form of pathology. It is instead a systemic and *regulatory capacity*—a wedge that can be driven productively between groups in order to instigate a warlike struggle between those who can live (who can perpetuate and justify their lifestyles) and those who must die. As a technique of power, racism is eminently enabling—"the indispensable precondition that *allows* someone to be killed, that *allows* others to be killed. Once the State functions in the biopower mode, racism alone can justify the murderous function of the State" (*"Society,"* 256, emphases added), and the idea that "society must be defended" against the other (sub)races is thus "the internal racism of permanent purification," one of the basic dimensions of social normalization under state racism (*"Society,"* 61–62). For these reasons, it would be insufficient simply to ask who is being racialized. Far more critical for Foucault is the question of what institutional purposes such acts of racialization—negative *or* positive—serve to *norm*. (See the introduction in part I for a discussion of norming in Foucault's thinking.) Conversely, as an abstract category unsubstantiated by scientific definition yet thoroughly steeped in the historical power effects of racism, race cannot simply be claimed in the form of an identity politics in resistance to power. Under some circumstances, indeed, embracing the idea of race would be tantamount to being racist.[34]

The Afterlives of Pastoral Power; or, How "[Global] Society Must Be Defended"

Involving historically specific configurations yet pertaining to universals (the accident of birth and the inevitability of death), this "permanent class struggle" that is race (with its twin, biological-social makeup) can also be traced in Foucault's discussions of the processes of mental and physical subordination, in particular those associated with the legacy of the Christian pastorate.

Foucault offers a bold outline of the form of government he calls "pastoral power" in the essay "*'Omnes et Singulatim*': Toward a Critique of Political Reason."[35] Identifying various aspects of the conception of such power in pre-Christian antiquity and stressing the important changes introduced by the arrival of Christianity, he suggests that the religious-moral paradigm of leadership in the form of a shepherd king (or shepherd god) is key to the evolving practices of the political state "in the entirety of Western history" ("*Omnes*," 187). Charged with safeguarding the flock from danger and with binding it into a community, the shepherd figure embodies "the relations between political power at work within the state as a legal framework of unity, and a power we can call 'pastoral,' whose role is to constantly ensure, sustain, and improve the lives of each and everyone" ("*Omnes*," 187–88). As Johanna Oksala writes, pastoral power's "essential mechanisms are continuous care and the compulsory extraction of knowledge rather than violent coercion and the delimitation of rights."[36]

In Foucault's readings, this "salvation-oriented operation"[37] of governance between the shepherd and each member of the flock—the individual sheep—makes up Christianity's unique contribution to historically existing models of *obedience*. "In Christianity," he writes, "the tie with the shepherd is an individual one. It is personal submission to him.... Obedience is a virtue. This means that it is not, as for the Greeks, a provisional means to an end but, rather, an end in itself. It is a permanent state; the sheep must permanently submit to their pastors" ("*Omnes*," 189). This constantly renewed and indefinitely renewable bind between the leader and the individual on the basis of guidance produces a special kind of soul or conscience: "The sheep didn't let itself be led only to come through any rough passage victoriously, it let itself be led every second. *Being guided was a state* and you were fatally lost if you tried to escape it" ("*'Omnes,'*" 190, emphasis added). As for self-examination, a practice shared by the ancient Greeks, the Christian aim is "not to close self-awareness in upon itself but, rather, to enable it to open up entirely to its director—to unveil to him the depths of the soul" ("*'Omnes,'*" 190). Through "the organization of a link between total obedience, knowledge of oneself, and confession to someone else," Christianity's ultimate objective is "to get individuals to work at their own 'mortification' in this world"—that is to say, a kind of relation of oneself to oneself that involves "a renunciation of this world and of oneself, a kind of everyday death—a death that is supposed to provide life in another world" ("*'Omnes,'*" 190).[38]

In the rest of this remarkable essay, through a discussion of various seventeen- and eighteenth-century European authors such as Louis Turquet de Mayerne, N. De Lamare, Huhenthal, J. P. Willebrand, and in particular Johann Heinrich Gottlob von Justi, Foucault sketches an intellectual history in which *the police* emerges as the culminating instance of what he calls the reason of state—that is, as an apparatus with a palpably identified object. "Proceeding through the eighteenth century, and especially in Germany, we see that *what is defined as the object of the police is population*, that is, a group of beings living in a given area" ("*'Omnes,'*" 200, emphasis added).[39] This new object of the police, he states elsewhere, marked "a historical change in the relations between power and individuals ... not only according to their juridical status but as men, as working, trading, living beings."[40]

Taking the cue from Foucault's various remarks about a "gigantic thirst" for the state "that could not be tamed," a "desire for the State," and "a will to the State," Joseph Vogl offers a carefully considered account of the historical developments in Germany since the late seventeenth century.[41] According to Vogl, this modern and at the time new perspective on the state saw the police's function in terms of an optimization of social potential by way of positive intervention in a population's living conditions, conditions that were saturated with concrete variations, contingencies, and accidents. As he explains,

> The application of the term "police" tends to be unlimited and now takes on the task of positive intervention within the political government.... [T]he term "police" is concerned with the living conditions of the people (*Volk*), the forms of societal cohabitation, and the areas of the body politic. The police views these areas from the perspective of social relations and interaction, and renders—in a slightly paradoxical fashion—the development of the individual and common welfare into a general strengthening of the state. In this manner, the police encompasses the "realization" of how a given condition of the community can be preserved and improved....
>
> The police is ... simultaneously *a means of recognition, an instrument of governing, and a program of intervention*.... [T]he police fantasies of the eighteenth century ... gain their theoretical and systematic meaning precisely because they orient their patterns of intervention toward concrete factors and the "Nature of Things," and because they initially interrogate *the regulation of contingent incidents*. Be it in the branches of medicine, vocations, trade, personal property, public morality, internal security, or the politics of the population—a new perspective now conceives of the state as an institution of providence, prevention, and insurance vis-à-vis possible (mis)chance and accident.[42]

As the state kept an eye, so to speak, on how a complex mass of people went about their daily business and invented new means of securing the well-being and comfort of all, it became intimately and often unnoticeably present in all aspects of social relations and interactions. In this manner, to follow Foucault's suggestion, a modern political framework of governing can be seen as genealogically affined to a pastoral principle and technology, transposing the Judeo-Christian idea of the good shepherd caring for his flock into a utopian form of political rationalism, led and guarded by a good police force.

As in Foucault's thinking on sexuality and race, his decidedly Nietzschean reflections on Christianity should be contextualized within his sustained critique of Western political rationality. Two important features stand out in these admittedly intense reflections. On the one hand is the tremendous moral impact Christianity has exerted over the individual and over what may be called *the individuation of the soul* by way of pastoral techniques such as the ritual of confession. (A more extended discussion of confession is given in chapter 5.) On the other hand, the armed influence of the police is wielded as the supreme *objectification of the reason of state*. These two intimately linked anchorage points of Foucault's dissection of Western political rationality make his work freshly germane to the study of race and racism in the twenty-first century.

Unlike the postcolonial inflection of his notion of discourse, the relevant alignment Foucault proposes here is less a matter of suturing cultural forms to geopolitical or economic-political aggressions (as in Said's *Orientalism*) than a matter of tracing cultural practices to lingering religious dominance. Rather than featuring the couples such as master/slave, colonizer/colonized, and their variants, Foucault's analysis of political rationality foregrounds another type of twosome: shepherd/sheep; priest/confessant; police/citizen (alongside doctor/patient in *The Birth of the Clinic* and prison guard/inmate in *Discipline and Punish*). Absent here is the Manichaean logic of treating the two parties involved as absolute moral opposites. Instead, the couples—and their coupling—are epistemically and historically enmeshed through entrenched mechanisms of inculcating obedience and subordination to a higher, ineffable authority, mechanisms that have been passed down through Bible-based religion and its secular avatars. By spotlighting the police as the exemplary icon of government, and by placing this icon in a modern global situation still by and large dominated by residual Christian techniques of power—think of the widespread celebration of Christmas and Easter as public holidays, the common use of the Bible for swearing in officials of state, the prison protocol of having a Christian chaplain present at state executions, and the acceptability of wearing the cross as an item of jewelry—Foucault prepares the grounds for our early twenty-first-century confrontation with the phenomenon of *police racism*: racism as a type of combat gear the police routinely puts on in the service of law and order. I am referring to the random police murders of black people, including unarmed women and youth, that occur repeatedly in contemporary U.S. cities, murders that seem, in the context of the present discussion, quite logical mutations of Western political rationality as Foucault dissects it, with police officers being an extreme incarnation—and an absurd theatricalizaion—of the shepherd king.[43]

Furthermore, if the police is the core of the reason of state, the nations that take it upon themselves to safeguard the entire globe will perhaps need to be redefined as *transnationalism's* versions of the Christian pastorate, with its firm mandate to protect the flock that is the world population. As Klaus Mladek clarifies,

> The police as we know it today develops with the *Polizeistaat* of the eighteenth-century into one of the supreme concepts of bourgeois society; the new liberal sanctification of law and security, the rise of the state and the emancipation of the liberal subject are ensnarled in the institutions of police. The original thrust of the police function has remained intact up to today. New modes of police intervention and concepts of administrative order increasingly move across borders towards a planetary order, where a dense transnational framework of institutions and agencies forms what could be called *a global police force*.[44]

The guardianship exercised by this global police force—led in late capitalism by nations such as the United States, France, Britain, Germany, Australia, and Japan—together with the salvational bind it seeks to establish between itself and the ordinary citizen around the world, suggests that a new kind of race war is solidifying as a cross-cultural or, as Mladek calls it, planetary strategy and reality.

Since September 11, 2001, those associated with Islam have increasingly come to occupy the place of the subrace (those others who have to die in order for us to live, according to Foucault's formulation of racism). One instance of this new racism deployed by the global police force from within the new global order is the stigma of delinquency—a presumed propensity toward "terrorist" acts—now borne by Muslims (or, in a stereotyping fashion, by those with Muslim-sounding names or Muslim-seeming appearances). This new race war rests much less on a division of cultures in the form of mutual suspicion or contempt than on a *multinational consensus to govern*—that is, to legitimize and monopolize the terms or rationales of governing—the world by ostracizing specific groups of people. Although arrest, incarceration, torture, coerced confession, denial of legal representation, and execution are involved as governing techniques, this consensus is typically promulgated in the pastoral rhetoric of peace and order, tolerance, benevolent leadership, respect for diversity, and the well-being of the entire flock[45]—the rhetoric of how, to use Foucault's phrase, our "society must be defended" against the infidels, those who are not like us.

It is to these struggles in the current transnational setting that Foucault's work makes its singularly trenchant contributions today. Instead of discourses reifying "black," "brown," "yellow," and "white" in kneejerk or opportunistic fashions, his writings provoke us to ask: What if racialization is aligned instead with our democratic state institutions, our genteel social practices, and our well-intentioned conscience productions, all of which continue to be galvanized by Christian techniques of power? What if race becomes linked to controversies over embodied (including sartorial) religious conduct in an avowedly secular society? Finally, what if struggles against racism were to be waged alongside a rigorous historical analysis of vestiges of the Christian hermeneutics of the self[46]—including the self that, in our neoliberal present, is constantly led to embrace race as well as sexuality as a way of discovering, disclosing, and inventing itself?[47]

4
"Fragments at Once Random and Necessary"
The *Énoncé* Revisited, Alongside Acousmatic Listening

Outing the Inner Voice: Some Consequences

In his early works such as *Voice and Phenomenon* and *Of Grammatology* (both published in 1967), Jacques Derrida, as is well known, undertakes a critique of a foundational feature of Western philosophy having to do with the voice. The point of Derrida's critique is not so much the ascendency of the voice over writing as the tendency, which he shows through a meticulous analysis of the writings of Edmund Husserl, to attribute to the voice qualities of an inalienable inner meaning that seems immediately present to itself (as in the phenomenon of hearing oneself speak). According to Derrida, the voice has been the privileged carrier by default of that ineffable something that is referred to variously as the spirit, the soul, the mind, and the like. The fact that this ineffable something is assumed to be there, as though diaphanously, without mediation, is what he calls the Western metaphysics of presence, which is built on an idealization and universalization of the voice as a transcendent operation of pure auto-affection.

The appeal of such auto-affection to Husserl is its apparent self-sufficiency. Husserl is drawn to the familiar phenomenon whereby in hearing oneself speak one seems to be moving in a spontaneous, continuous, and unified circuit, with the ear and the mouth forming a single, closed loop. For him, it is when one hears one's own voice in silence—that is to say, in a solitary mental state, without going through the detour of the tongue and the mouth, the kind of externally mediated communication that he calls "indication"—that the inner voice is at its purest.[1] The essence of this "voice that keeps silent" is the result of what Husserl calls a "phenomenological reduction." Derrida's strategic move to open this inner-voice loop is worth repeating: "Hearing-oneself-speak is not the interiority of an inside closed in upon itself. It is the irreducible openness in the inside, the eye and the world in speech. *The phenomenological reduction is a scene.*"[2]

Jean-Luc Nancy, echoing Derrida but putting the emphasis on the act of sounding, describes this scene of hearing oneself speak in this manner: "To sound is to vibrate in itself or by itself: it is not only, for the sonorous body . . . to emit a sound, but it is also to stretch out, to carry itself and be resolved into vibrations that both return it to itself and place it outside itself."[3] As Mladen Dolar comments, "The Derridean turn has thus . . . turned the voice into a preeminent object of philosophical inquiry, demonstrating its complicity with the principal metaphysical preoccupations."[4] Derrida's point, it should be stressed, is not exactly to leverage writing against voice; rather, it is to argue that the voice, which (as a result of the phonocentric bias) seems readily self-same and self-present, is actually the effect of a prior—and ongoing—temporal series of inscription, an arche-writing that leaves traces (imprints of differentiation). Despite its lure of immediacy, the voice, even when it is heard in the solitary mental state, is not originary but already an artifact, a variant in a chain of emissions involving duration and spacing. Insofar as Derrida's utopian project of grammatology is meant to be a science of signs supposedly to be "founded" between signs' retention and escape, appearance and disappearance, the voice belongs in grammatology as much as does writing.

If we were to approach philosophy as an ethnographic exercise, Husserl's investment in the inner voice could be analogized to a type of nativism. Does not the attempt to salvage a virginal voice, as yet untouched and by implication untouchable by outside or foreign influences, remind us of certain anthropological endeavors to seek out and preserve primitive cultures? (Think of Derrida's well-known critique of Claude Lévi-Strauss's reading of the Nambikwara in *Tristes Tropiques* [1955].) Is not the inner voice like that putatively authentic native, whose contamination through contact with the outside world worries those who want to keep her in her pristine, indigenous condition? This longing for the origin in the form of the voice that keeps silent, far from the madding crowd, is what Derrida has taught us to deconstruct.

Derrida's focus on his project of grammatology also means that he has to sidestep or at least seem oblivious to some rather obvious issues. In his reflections on sonic experiences in everyday life, Michel Chion makes the perceptive observation that despite having correctly pried open Husserl's foreclosed "self-hearing" loop in *Voice and Phenomenon*, Derrida nonetheless fails to address the oddity of the situation in which external perceptions and internal perception of oneself, even while being bound to one another in the form of a "self-hearing," may not necessarily *merge as an imagined unit*. Chion is able to see this because he places the stress on hearing as well as on the emission of sound; accordingly, he is able to show that hearing "oneself" does not have to mean hearing oneself as looped through the voice. Whereas for Derrida "self-hearing" remains a matter of hearing oneself *speak* (and with it of the ideological baggage of all the philosophical and literary effects of the voice), for Chion, not working primarily or exclusively in the medium of human language, self-hearing can quite matter-of-factly involve other sonic circuits, such as those among hearing and various *embodied* functions and activities. When one knocks on the table with one's fist, makes noise stomping on the ground with one's feet, bounces a ball against the wall, or claps with one's hands, self-hearing materializes in circuits in which the voice as such does not need to figure, let alone become privileged.[5] As we shall see, this attachment to human language, speech, and voice—an attachment that tends in turn to prioritize sound over listening, information emission over information reception—constitutes a sticky and unresolved problem in theory even after the inner voice has, as it were, been irreversibly outed.

Although Derrida's incisive reading of Husserl is not informed by sound-reproduction technology, it was probably not a coincidence that the problematic of the inner voice, the essence of the phenomenological reduction, emerged at a time when the voice as such had become eminently reproducible with the invention of machines such as the phonograph. As Amy Lawrence reminds us, "Nearly all of Edison's proposed uses for sound recording are linked to the reproduction of the voice—in elocution, pronunciation, preservation of family histories . . . dictation, lectures, and recording phone calls. . . . Thus, almost before the phonograph had been invented, its special mission as preserver of the voice was set out for it. The ideology of the apparatus to a great extent pre-existed the invention of the apparatus."[6] Brian Kane also amplifies this important correlation between voice and reproductive technology in *Sound Unseen: Acousmatic Sound in Theory and Practice*, in which he suggestively prefaces a discussion of Husserl by a discussion of the arrival of the phonographic voice.[7] A landmark study of Western philosophy's responses to sound and voice *after* Edison invented the phonograph (that is, in the age of sound's and voice's mechanical recordability and iterability), Kane's book demonstrates in remarkable historical detail how a phenomenological approach to sound—such as Pierre Schaeffer's, an approach that began with an interest in ordinary objects of sound but culminated in the ideality of a sound object that is not reducible to ordinary objects—is fundamentally indebted to the philosophy of Husserl.[8]

Supplementing Derrida's reading of Husserl with Kane's analysis, we could argue that the inner voice, which Derrida places at the core of Western metaphysics, is *a post- appearing in the guise of a pre-*: a virginal self-presence that is recovered, so to speak, precisely when the voice has become—because of the irreversible happening of sound recording—ceaselessly repeatable, copyable, and dispersible. Douglas Kahn, adhering to Derrida's deconstructive logic, summarizes this epochal transition succinctly: "No longer was the ability to hear oneself speak restricted to a fleeting moment. It became locked in a materiality that could both stand still and mute and also time travel by taking one's voice far afield from one's own presence. . . . The voice no longer occupied its own space and time. *It was removed from the body where, following Derrida, it entered the realm of writing*[,] . . . *where one loses control of the voice because it no longer disappears.*"[9]

The Curtain Separates

The contemporary conceptualization of "acousmaticity"—of listening unaccompanied by the sight of sound's source—has become popularized largely through the sound and audiovisual work of Pierre Schaeffer and Michel Chion.[10] However, acousmaticity should also be conjoined to the aforementioned post-structuralist theoretical scene, in which the phenomenological effort to reessentialize (or *renativize*) the voice encounters its politicized resistance in the form of deconstruction. The consequences of this scene are far-reaching. Although Husserl's voice nativism or voice primitivism, if it may be so called, has been debunked (by Derrida and his followers) for its idealist presuppositions, the signature move of phenomenological reduction remains profoundly influential. Involving a *bracketing off* of the given (in Husserl's case, nature or some other factual existence), this move has implications on a number of intellectual, aesthetic, and mediatic fronts in ways that go considerably beyond the more esoteric circles of phenomenology and deconstruction.[11] In Schaeffer's and his followers' theorization of the so-called acousmatic situation, for instance—I think here of Chion, Dolar, Nancy,[12] Slavoj Žižek, and others, including myself, in their reflections on sound and voice—we are confronted with just how salient and powerful phenomenological reduction can be as a method or what might be called, after the media historian Bernhard Siegert, a *cultural technique*. How so?

As is typical of modern uses of antiquity (Freud's use of the legend of Oedipus being a foremost example), what is interesting in the Schaefferians' adaptation of the legend of the Pythagorean sect and its pedagogical practice—whereupon the pupils were separated from their master by a hanging curtain, so that they learned by hearing the master's voice but not seeing his face—is a certain dramatization.[13] What exactly is being staged? In what is commonly understood as sound's boundlessness—its all-encompassing ambience, its ability to envelope the listener as though in a continuum—Schaefferians install or, more properly speaking, underscore the crucial mechanism of a material divide (a break or caesura). In their rendition of the Pythagorean sect's practice, even as the interplay between presence (sound/voice) and absence (face/body) remains key, what is epistemically decisive is rather the part played by the curtain. This simple prop enables the master's voice, generalizable first as voice and then more broadly as sound, to spring forth in isolation as an object. As Kane suggests, this phantasmatic object's emergence in the acousmatic situation is akin to the inner voice's emergence (as a self-same presence) in the phenomenological situation; the Schaefferian acousmatique and the Husserlian *epoché* are two moments sutured together.[14] As the source of sound is obscured because withheld, the listeners are compelled to notice the sonic object's immanent logic, a logic that is not reducible to or accountable through external factors.

A bit more needs to be said about this legendary curtain. Before the emergence of the object, the curtain *separates*. If it serves as a means of concealment, it does so by way of *a cut through space*, a cut that institutes at once a boundary and a new beginning, conjuring at once a barrier and a novel coming-through. If in the realm of phenomenology the curtain functions as (a symbol of) the interruption—the bracketing—of a given (or assumed) way of thinking, in the realm of contemporary sound and music the curtain is rather the site where technology, together with its ideological effects, is to be located.[15] We may go so far as to say that the curtain is the very *hinge* where the Husserlian bracket meets not only Derridean deconstruction, as we learned during the heyday of post-structuralist theory, but also the recording machine. As

Schaeffer notes, "In ancient times, the apparatus was a curtain; today, it is the radio and the methods of reproduction, with the whole set of electro-acoustic transformations that place us, modern listeners to an invisible voice, under similar circumstances."[16] And whereas the Husserlian bracket does its work by closing things down, sound recording does its work in the opposite direction, by opening things up. Between the phenomenological reduction that represses (among other things the historical arrival of sound recording) and the phonographic supplementation that liberates (for instance, by freeing sound from previous traditions of abstract, note-based music), the conceptual grounds have radically shifted. A whole new way of thinking has come into play, resonating game-changing effects.

The curtain, in other words, is nothing short of a stand-in for a process of structuration, a geometric way of tracking thought wherein things acquire a kind of autonomy, a new recognizability, after they have been bracketed off—removed from traditional settings or severed from presumed origins. Between the nativist conservation of a metaphysics of (voice's) self-presence and the deconstructive-reproductive multiplication of such self-presence into infinite (sonic) traces, we hear echoes of other modernist philosophical gestures: Martin Heidegger's line across words, Derrida's coinage of the term *sous rature* (that is, the move of putting "under erasure"), and in an arguably affined but otherwise divergent operation Michel Foucault's depiction of the modern confinement–production of madness by way of spatial partitioning.[17] When lined up alongside these other instances, acousmaticity comes across less as a mechanism of obstruction than as an inaugurating event, one that involves a threshold artifact, a means of bringing things into focus. As Kane suggests, "By defamiliarizing everyday practices of listening, the acousmatic reduction makes these modes perspicuous . . . [or] brings these modes of listening into audibility."[18]

Beyond sound and music, we are reminded of other aesthetic experiments—the Russian Formalists' techniques of defamiliarizing poetry and narrative, early filmmakers' deployments of montage, Bertolt Brecht's epic theater and its alienation effects, Marcel Duchamp's *tout-faits* or readymades derived from *objets trouvés*, and so forth—that similarly depend on techniques of *bracketing-off cum estrangement* to make customary phenomena leap forward in a new frame. Does not the Schaefferians' adaptation of antiquity, too, belong in this larger history of modernism and its conceptual-aesthetic attempts at reflexivity and renewal? The "given" bracketed off could be anything: nature, convention, habit, or any jaded way of perceiving and doing things. The characteristic modernist move is that of letting a given something—be it phenomenological, imagistic, theatrical, sculptural, sonic, or vocal—become freshly noticeable through a deliberate, artful suspension, so much so that the beholder, whose perception is roughened (that is, challenged) in this process, is forced to come to terms with a different and often disturbing order of things.[19]

Foucault's *Énoncé*: The Thing Said, the Utterance Found

In hindsight, would it not be appropriate to align Foucault's work with this larger history of modernism and its techniques of bracketing-off cum estrangement, typically aimed at the experimental release of new objects for thought? I think in particular of what Foucault in *The Archaeology of Knowledge* describes as the phenomenon of the *énoncé*.[20]

As in many cases of post-structuralist conceptual interventions, the *énoncé*, usually translated as "things said" or "the statement," is derived from the medium of human language and signification. As a scholarly attempt to excavate the elided, forgotten, and buried but nonetheless continually present heterogeneities that govern the crisscrossing trajectories of modern knowledge formation, *The Archaeology of Knowledge* makes use of a structuralist analytic frame, only to exceed, inevitably perhaps, the boundaries of such a frame. To the incalculable excess of significations that serves as both the substance and the form of his discussion, Foucault assigns various names, such as *discourse, archaeology,* and *archive*—all of which suggest an open-ended field in which to situate the *énoncé* and its potentialities across periods of time. In an interview, Foucault defines his use of the term *archaeology* obliquely as a "play on words to designate something that would be the description of the *archive*," a word he further explains this way: "By the archives, I mean first the mass of things spoken in a culture, presented, valorized, re-used, repeated, and transformed. In brief, this whole verbal mass that has been fashioned by men, invested in their techniques and in their institutions and woven into their existence and their history."[21]

Foucault's epistemic and historiographic concerns pertain, in other words, to how "the mass of things spoken in a culture, presented, valorized, re-used, repeated, and transformed" constitutes the moving grounds on which claims to truth and history become rationalized and normalized. As cumulative, collective experience, knowledge is elusive not necessarily because it is inherently transient or opaque, but rather because it is traversed repeatedly and incessantly by countless *bodies* (implicitly equated in this case with voices, breaths, or *énoncés*) over centuries or millennia. Knowledge is a "verbal mass" because it is a temporal composite with physical remnants whose precise origins are no longer ascertainable. Hence, Foucault's conception of such collective experience in the passive voice as what *has been* spoken or, as he puts it in an interview on his study of the avant-garde author Raymond Roussel, what is simply "found."[22] As James Faubion comments, "Roussel's preoccupation with the prefabrication of language, with the 'ready-made' and artifactual quality of words and phrases and sentences, informs Foucault's conceptualization of discourses as scatterings of 'enunciations,' of words and phrases and sentences already spoken, of the linguistic but quite material deposits of thought itself."[23] When asked in the interview whether he feels challenged by the problem of how to define such "found language," Foucault responds forthrightly by reiterating his interest in the historical condition of things having been uttered, of elements of discourse having inhabited our world and remaining a part of it:

> Well, it is the interest I have in modes of discourse, that is to say, not so much in the linguistic structure which makes such a series of utterances

possible, but rather the fact that *we live in a world in which things have been said*. These spoken words in reality are not, as people tend to think, a wind that passes without leaving a trace, but in fact, diverse as are the traces, they do remain. *We live in a world completely marked by, all laced with, discourse, that is to say, utterances which have been spoken, of things said, of affirmations, interrogations, of discourses which have already occurred.* To that extent, the historical world in which we live cannot be dissociated from all the elements of discourse which have inhabited this world and continue to live in it as the economic process, the demographic, etcetera, etcetera.[24]

With this emphasis on discourse as something prefabricated—literally as a kind of *objet trouvé*, or found object (in the manner of Duchamp's *tout-fait* or readymade)—Foucault dispenses both with the instrumentalist notion of language as a communicative tool and with the idealist notion of language as an inner voice or soulful trait. Unlike Derrida, however, he does not go on to philosophize an arche-writing or become preoccupied with the effects of *différance* (the perpetual temporal deferment characteristic of lingual signification). Instead, he asks if discourse cannot be thought of as an assemblage of lived discontinuities, a network comprising what may be termed the *déjà énoncé*—the resonances, memories, associations, and affects (voluntary and involuntary) that, having been uttered and heard many times, cling to or hover around the most simple individual speech acts with a certain aura. As Foucault writes, "Of course, discourses are composed of signs; but what they do is more than use these signs to designate things. It is this *more* that renders them irreducible to the language (langue) and to speech. It is this 'more' that we must reveal and describe."[25]

Precisely because of Foucault's interest in this "more," this excess and heterogeneous mass of things said, his endeavor to explain the *énoncé* does not exactly result in clear or stable formulations. His reflections on the subject remain hypothetical and speculative in tone, as if he is unable, even after writing an entire book, to pin down the exact definition or expanse of the project he is proposing:

If the statement really is the elementary unit of discourse, what does it consist of? What are its distinctive features? What boundaries must one accord to it?

... [T]here is a statement whenever a number of signs are juxtaposed—or even, perhaps—when there is a single sign. The threshold of the statement is the threshold of the existence of signs.

... [The statement] plays the role of a residual element, of a mere fact, of irrelevant raw material. . . .

We must not seek in the statement a unit that is either long or short, strongly and weakly structured, but one that is *caught up*, like the others, in a logical, grammatical, locutory nexus.

[The statement] *is not in itself a unit, but a function that cuts across a domain of structures and possible unities*, and which reveals them, with concrete contents, in time and space.²⁶

Foucault's own hesitancy notwithstanding, the *énoncé* has received very helpful elucidating remarks from his contemporaries. Gilles Deleuze, for instance, writes: "The core of the notion [of the *énoncé*] is the constitution of a substantive in which *'multiple' ceases to be a predicate opposed to the One*." Succinctly pinpointing the "inherent variation" and "intrinsic variable" embedded in the "primitive function" of the *énoncé*, Deleuze sheds light on the *énoncé* as "a multiplicity that passes through all levels" and as *"an anonymous function which leaves a trace of subject only in the third person, as a derived function."*²⁷

Taking the cue from Deleuze, let me go a little further with the *énoncé* in more literary terms. Might it not be proposed that the *énoncé* is a kind of quotation with the quotation marks removed because the speaking subject behind it has, over the course of time, dissipated into the anonymity of collectivity? In the vocabulary of literary analysis, does not the *énoncé* bring to mind the free indirect style, in which an utterance or a thought, though to all appearances reported as coming from someone or somewhere specific, cannot be attributed with certainty to a single, nameable subject (such as a narrator, speaker, or character) because the conventional boundary between speaking subjects has become blurry in the process of enunciation, fuzzed as it is by the rivaling presences of more than one voice? This state of an incessant *murmur*—of things having been repeatedly said and heard with no clear-cut beginnings and ends—is for Foucault a most salient feature of historical knowledge. Such knowledge is laden with the material deposits of acts of saying, but the acts have transpired—have become passive or objectlike in their reverberations over time—and are no longer unambiguously attachable to any individuated agent or subject. (I return to this question of the free indirect style toward the end of this chapter.)

If history is hitherto assumed to be a continuous, measurable sum of all things said and done, the notion of the *énoncé* suggests rather that history needs to be reconceptualized in the form of an untotalizable field of disjointed discourse events. History avails itself much less in the form of solid connections than through mutations, ruptures, and breaks and much less in the form of stable sovereign subjects than through contingent eruptions of scattered, forgotten, or unformalized data fragments. As Foucault elaborates it in his well-known essay on authorship,

> All discourses . . . would then develop in the anonymity of a murmur. We would no longer hear the questions . . . Who really spoke? Is it really he and not someone else? With what authenticity or originality? . . . Instead, there would be other questions, like these: What are the modes of existence of this discourse? Where has it been used, how can it circulate, and who can appropriate it for himself? What are the places in it where there is room for possible subjects? Who can assume these various subject functions? And behind all of these questions, we would hardly hear anything but the stirring of an indifference: What difference does it make who is speaking?[28]

To put it differently, the *énoncé*'s appearance at a particular moment in time—its condition of being found, so to speak—is often an index to a vast subterranean, even if as-yet invisible and inaudible, agglomerate of discourse relations. His known reservations about psychoanalysis notwithstanding, Foucault goes so far as to name these massive discourse relations an "unconscious":

> But these invisible relations would in no way constitute a kind of secret discourse animating the manifest discourses from within; it is not therefore an interpretation that could make them come to light but, rather, the analysis of their coexistence, of their succession, of their mutual dependence, of their reciprocal determination, of their independent or correlative transformation. All together (though they can never be analyzed exhaustively), they form what might be called, by a kind of play on words—for consciousness is never present in such a description—*the "unconscious," not of the speaking subject, but of the thing said.*[29]

In this ambitious undertaking to capture the murmur of the *énoncé*, to know something in history is to get at the myriad layers and strata of what has been said *and* to get at the "more" that has been generating around this ever-receding, ever-mutating verbal mass. If human language is no longer viewed in the sense of a linear, logical progression but rather as actual discourses found in bits and pieces, human signification would amount to a new type of act—an archiving in process, so to speak, involving shifting series of transitions among different levels of deposits, excavations, adaptations, repurposings, and projections. At once individuated and impersonal, human signification would mean coming into contact with the temporally cumulative yet often vague and seldom entirely verifiable experiences left behind by others.[30]

In Bits and Pieces: From Acousmatic Sound to the Fragment as Knowledge Object

Returning to the more specialized terrains of voice and sound, we can now make the following propositions. By naming the acousmatic situation, the Schaefferians have, in tandem with other modernist endeavors, established a special kind of knowledge object, which is defined essentially as a (cut) fragment, for which the whole (a coherent, organic unity) is, for one reason or another, irrecoverable and unavailable. This kind of knowledge object is, in retrospect, interestingly resonant with Foucault's linguistically derived notion of the *énoncé*. Maurice Blanchot, for instance, describes the *énoncé* in terms of "fragments at once random and necessary" and compares Foucault's concept to serial music:

> The sparseness of the statement is a function of the fact that it can be nothing other than positive, without a cogito to which it might refer, without a unique author to authenticate it, free from every context that might help to situate it in an organized set.... The enigmatic statement is already multiple in itself, or, more precisely, it is a non-unitary multiplicity: it is serial because the series is its way of grouping, having repeatability as its essential property ... even as it constitutes, along with other series, a tangle or reversal of singularities that at times, when stationary, form a tableau, and, at others, by dint of their successive relations of simultaneity, are inscribed as fragments at once random and necessary, seemingly comparable to the perverse efforts (as Thomas Mann put it) of serial music.[31]

Theodor Adorno, for his part, associates the fragment with death. "The fragment is the intrusion of death into the work," he writes. "While destroying it [the work], it [the fragment] removes the stain of semblance."[32] If Adorno's assertion holds validity, the question remains why what he calls death—presumably the state of disintegration that absolves the fragment of the culpability ("the stain") of mimesis, the culpability of having an identity or being like something—seems to intrude so readily in modernity's processes of producing knowledge. Again, Michel Chion, working in the realm of sound, provides an unwitting rejoinder to Adorno when he invokes the acousmatic voice resulting from technology. According to Chion, there is an intimate link between acousmaticity as such and death because in both cases voices have been cut off from bodies: "Ever since the telephone and gramophone made it possible to isolate voices from bodies, the voice naturally has reminded us of the voice of the dead. And more than our generation, those who witnessed the birth of these technologies were aware of their funerary quality. In the cinema, the voice of the acousmêtre is frequently the voice of one who is dead."[33]

Is not Chion speaking here to a certain kind of historicity, borne aptly though by no means exclusively by acousmatic sound, whose operations simply help underscore the emergence of the fragment *as* knowledge object and of knowledge itself as an assemblage of fragments? For Adorno, this historicity manifests as a collective imprint of things having been torn out of their integrated contexts—things having had their "stain of semblance" removed, as he puts it, and (re)appearing in isolated and funerary form. For Foucault, this historicity manifests in the sparse version of the enigmatic *énoncé*, a kind of knowledge object that is "without a cogito to which it might refer," as Blanchot writes, and "without a unique author to authenticate it." These qualities of deadness and authorlessness are emblematic of such fragments' participation in modernity. The sociocultural complexity of this state of affairs, whereby the world acquires the status of knowledge—that is, becomes knowable—primarily through the condition of being disjointed, disembodied, dead, or originless, cannot be overstated.[34]

What do such fragmented knowledge objects imply for those on the receiving end? Again, the sonic context presents some convenient answers once we realize that the more special notion of acousmatic sound can serve quite reasonably as a stand-in for a general ambience of *information dispersion*.

From the sound receiver's perspective, the fragmentation of objects-for-knowledge is evident in the considerable list of sound- and music-receiving apparatuses (and the experiences they enable) developed since recording became possible.[35] From the phonograph, the gramophone with its loudspeaker, the radio, and the turntable playing vinyl records at different speeds to the portable transistor radio, the cassette-tape recorder, the Walkman, the Discman, and digital electronic devices such as iPods, smartphones, tablets, and laptops, sounds—and let us assume that they are sounds we choose to receive and listen to—have been coming to us in bits and pieces. From being captured in the grooves of an old-fashioned LP to being downloadable from companies such as Apple Music, sound increasingly tends to reach us without our seeing where it originates; and what we can see, the mechanical or electronic equipment, is typically not the cause or the source of the sound. Even when one seems to know the source, as it were, the source is never one thing: Is it the composer, the performer (with her vocal cords, instruments, recording studio, and sound-editing procedures), the station or channel playing a piece of music, or the device with which one streams, downloads, plays, and listens to the sound being transmitted? This ever-widening chasm between the seemingly straightforward event of listening (that is, of sound reception for those who are not hearing impaired) and the proliferating multitude of causes and sources, a multitude that renders the question "Where are these sounds coming from?" by and large moot, is one reason acousmaticity—the physical separation of sound source and sound effect—has become such an indispensable concept. Further still, it is possible to argue that acousmaticity need no longer be confined to the sonic as such but can also be applied to the postmodern condition of information dispersion, of which acousmatic sound—much like Foucault's *énoncé*—is perhaps simply one outstanding example.

Such information dispersion includes all the acousmatic bits and pieces that come at us not by our choosing—music in public places such as elevators, restaurants, malls, gyms, supermarkets, and airports; tunes and advertisements we have to listen to while being put on hold when phoning businesses and institutions—but that nonetheless punctuate and permeate our global urbanized existences. There are also the global positioning systems that help us navigate. Even when they sound like humans (with different national and gendered accents), the simulated voices giving us directions on the road, like their counterparts talking to us from electronic screens big and small, are among the most advanced configurations of fragmented knowledge objects, of sounds as bytes. In these intimate yet inhuman daily encounters, the basic formulation of acousmaticity—as (sonic or emitted) data whose cause or origin is not (visibly) present or accessible—remains on the mark. In fact, the *nonconvergence* of information source and information reception has become such a definitive feature of contemporary social interactions that it is difficult to imagine everyday life in a different format. By simply separating, the curtain has, to wit, thoroughly restructured and redefined human perceptual experiences and the collective imaginaries arising therefrom.[36]

Although nonacousmatic sound arguably still exists—and it is easy enough to give examples from nature such as birds chirping, dogs barking, trees falling, and so forth *within one's view*—it is important to ponder the fact that contemporary listening, rather than a pristine activity, function, or capacity, has long been acclimatized to acousmaticity (of which the infinite mass of sound fragments released with the virtually nonstop inventions of "smart" devices is only one conspicuous example). If we accept that such listening is now often trained, indeed generated, by acousmatic situations of various kinds, a more daunting set of questions ensues. How are we to conceptualize listening and, for that matter, information reception after we have grasped the pervasive extent of acousmaticity in our time? Should we think of listening as singular and particular (and still tied to human perceptual attributes) or as plural and anonymous (a drifting series of attention spans, ever adaptable to the vast information webs around us)? As independent of or as coevolving with technology? As humanly reflexive or as robotically automated or both?

Human "Listening" in the Age of Information Dispersion

What does it mean to hear or listen to something? A random list of commonsensical examples may include a doctor listening to a patient's heartbeat through a stethoscope; an entomologist listening to cicadas' chirping; a linguist catching the tones of a tonal language; a musician discerning the different parts and instruments of a musical composition; a mechanic figuring out a car's trouble by the sound of its engine; and so forth. These mundane instances foreground what may be called a sensory-cognitive paradox even for trained specialists and skilled technicians: *Is listening an activity, or is it a form of passivity?* The fact that *to listen* is, in the English language at least, both a transitive and an intransitive verb suggests that the line between the two states may not always be so clear and that "to listen" straddles action and reaction. To borrow from Jean-Luc Nancy's comparison between sight and sound: "In terms of the gaze, the subject is referred back to itself as object. In terms of listening, it is, in a way, to itself that the subject refers or refers back."[37] The acousmatic situation, in which the source of sound is hidden, further compounds the intrigue: Is listening in such a situation a matter of doing something, or is it not, more precisely speaking, a sensorially truncated mode of receiving something—a matter of something *happening to* the listener in discontinuous form? Should listening be aligned with what we call *consciousness*—in which case all the old-fashioned humanistic values of understanding and interpretation based on subjectivity as agency would need to remain valid—or should it be aligned with a mechanistic or electronic *sensor*, for which sounds, whether in the form of refined classical music, recorded human voices, or raw street noise, are signals, pieces of data to be algorithmically decoded, measured, preserved, and remixed?[38] How can we talk about listening as what takes place between or aside from these usual poles of categorization?

One approach has been to return listening to a kind of embodied materialism. A relatively early example of such an approach is found in Roland Barthes's well-known essay "The Grain of the Voice," in which the language of the body becomes the singular aspect of a vocal deliverance. Barthes writes: "The 'grain' is . . . the materiality of the body speaking its mother tongue; perhaps the letter, almost certainly *signifiance*"; such *signifiance*, he goes on, "cannot better be defined, indeed, than by the very friction between the music and something else, which something else is the particular language (and nowise the message)." Finally, Barthes asserts: "The 'grain' is *the body in the voice* as it sings, the hand as it writes, the limb as it performs."[39]

In a more full-fledged version of such embodied materialism, the divisions among sounds, listening, instruments, and their capacities for sonority and resounding tend to dissolve altogether, giving way instead to an alignment of mutually *touching* matrices of resonance. An exquisite instance of this type of theorization is found in Nancy's *Listening*, a work that makes the case for sound as a sensation distinct from and other to the kind of sense (that is, meaning) based in the logos and, with it, in logic and language. On the inextricable codependence between emission and reception, Nancy is insistent: the resonance or "sonance" of sound, he writes, is an expression we should hear "as much from the side of sound itself, or of its emission, as from the side of its reception or its listening: it is precisely from one to the other that it 'sounds.'" Accordingly, the subject of listening (or the subject who listens) is, he argues, neither a phenomenological nor a philosophical subject and perhaps not a subject at all, except as "the place of resonance, of its infinite tension and rebound."[40] The most unforgettable lexicon from Nancy's discussion is *timbre*. He defines *timbre* as the resonance of a stretched skin and the expansion of this resonance in the hollow of a drum, which he in turn associates with a pregnant woman's belly, that cavity where a new life forms that first listens on the inside and then arrives at the outside with a cry. For Nancy, timbre—and by implication *subjectless listening*—is "above all the unity of a diversity that its unity does not reabsorb."[41]

Notwithstanding the subtlety and sophistication of Nancy's analysis, a disquieting question looms: Is not his materialist approach to sound another form of nativism, primitivism, and origination myth, this time localized in the (female) body rather than, as in the case of Husserl, idealized through the mind?

And what if, contra Nancy, the subject is not so quickly dissolved? How otherwise might listening be conceptualized? Grammar—indeed, human language—offers some provocative, if unexpected, assistance here. First is the illumination made by the proverbial active and passive voices, which break up actions into source and target (e.g., "I tell" as opposed to "I am told"). Interestingly, in the case of listening, "active" and "passive" seem readily reversible or become fuzzy: "I tell" is more or less equivalent to "I am heard," while "I am told" is another way of saying "I hear." Second, perhaps more perplexingly, *what is the pronoun that best describes the listener in relation to what she hears?* Does the listener function in the capacity of an "I" with respect to the sound coming at her? Does not the listener also function as a "you," an addressee? Can the listener be conceived as an "it" or a "them"?

In linguistics, pronouns belong to a class of nouns known as "shifters" because of the ambiguous character of their significations.[42] Although pronouns are seldom invoked in the study of sound, the question about pronouns seems appropriate—indeed logical, even if irresolvable—by virtue of the fact that a certain relationship with another is explicit or implicit in the activity or experience of listening. Does the pronouns' ambiguity in this case imply that the *places* that listening might *mark*—or shall we say touch? pass through? remember? differentiate?—as it proceeds are unfixable, interchangeable, or nonexistent? Does not such shiftiness or fluidity of place become ever more acute when listening is mediated by various apparatuses of recording, transmission, and simulation? Think of karaoke, the popular form of entertainment in which, in order to sing along, one is supposed to lip-sync with a song by following the lyrics displayed on a screen. Is the listener in this case an active "I" (the one singing and performing by lip-syncing), a "you" (the one addressed and sung to by the song), or an "it" or "them" (*anyone* participating and mimicking in tandem with the sounds "coming from" the machine, the performance on the screen, the composer of the music, the author of the lyrics, and so forth)?

The question raised by pronouns in acousmatic listening—that is, listening in a surround of sounds and voices whose sources or causes are unseen, unavailable, or altogether irrelevant—is perhaps paradigmatic of a conceptual, aesthetic, and mediatic ecology considerably more expansive than that covered by the specialized terrains of sound and music studies. Accompanying the endless (re)producibility of acousmaticity in the contemporary world—among *musique concrète* practices, avant-garde experiments, high-tech inventions and their spin-offs, and all the commercial exploitations of sound as fragments—is also, as we notice, the evisceration of a viably unified and authoritative site of command, or of what some might call a transcendental subject position. The knowledge object produced in this situation is, to echo once again Blanchot's comments on Foucault's *énoncé*, "without a cogito to which it might refer, without a unique author to authenticate it." How might such evisceration of the transcendental subject position be articulated in conjunction with processes of listening and, by implication, with information reception?

Some Pertinent Hints from Literary Studies

Across disciplinary boundaries, scholars of literature have been grappling with a parallel set of questions for quite some time. In the realm of modern fiction, for instance, the ambiguity or instability of the narrative voice—encapsulated in the classic narratological question "Who is speaking?"—has long been deemed a key feature of modern literary form. As the type of narrator traditionally presumed to be omniscient gives way to the so-called unreliable narrator, issues of origination, authorship, authority, and trust are played out with existential and sociopolitical ramifications. To what extent could such literary scholarship—based on the medium of human language and signification—be shared or perhaps adapted for a comparative study of the acousmatic voice in the realm of sound theory? To what extent might literary studies be regarded, if somewhat belatedly or anachronistically, as partaking of the transdisciplinary discourse about acousmatic listening and reception?

To give a prominent example: in his reading of Fyodor Dostoyevsky's novels and stories, the literary critic Mikhail Bakhtin defines the enunciated word as the locus of an intersubjective struggle. According to Bakhtin, Dostoyevsky's texts exemplify a noteworthy quality: even when only one voice is apparently speaking, a multitude of voices can be *heard*; different people's opinions and attitudes have been internalized, are anticipated and responded to in advance, and/or are controverted at the moment of utterance.[43] The copresence of clashing voices in the Underground Man, Raskolnikov, Prince Mishkin, the brothers Karamazov, and numerous other narrators and characters, a copresence that is usually implicit—detectable in the mute yet also garrulous chasms between perception and expression, between hearing and speaking, between direct speech and reported speech—leads Bakhtin to describe the word in Dostoyevsky as "double-voiced" or "polyphonic." Bakhtin's intervention serves to amplify the voice's inherent heterogeneity, its anxious "sideward glance" at and quarrel with others in the midst of enunciation.[44] Insofar as the double-voiced or polyphonic utterance is, rather than a space of unison and harmony, an echo chamber, an opening for a struggle for dominance, the voice (as enunciation) in Bakhtin's reading is partial, interferential, and internally split. Double-voicedness or polyphonicity signifies not neoliberal inclusion or peaceful coexistence (as is sometimes assumed) but rather a politics of antagonism, insubordination, and dissent, in which the constant is an animated existential crisis and combat.

Just as Jacques Lacan describes the voice as "the alterity of what is said,"[45] so does Bakhtin's work highlight the voice's permeable and far-from-tranquil borders. Double-voicedness or polyphonicity, as made evident in Dostoyevsky's fiction, suggests that a word may be emitted in one way but is usually heard and received in plural and oftentimes conflictual or incommensurate ways. Indeed, a word's (or language's) emission and reception never entirely coincide because different speakers and listeners, whose interactions are traversed by different lived temporalities, are involved. The appearance of a word in the form of a singular vocal emission is always underwritten (and underspoken) by other voices; even when silent, these other voices are audible and can exert a powerful impact. Such fundamentally non-synchronized and nonsynchronizable workings of the voice make up the neurotic and silently deafening dynamics of a novelistic universe such as Dostoyevsky's.

What remains germane from Bakhtin's discussion is the pressing concern of the voice as nonunified because *unclosable*: as a social phenomenon, the voice is inflected with otherness, with the pressures of temporal or vocal exteriority. Going a step further, I'd venture that although Bakhtin focuses our attention on the voice (as an object of study), *what he has contributed is a de facto theory of acousmatic listening in a scenario of intensified information dispersion*. The reason is simple: for the voice to be apprehended as double or polyphonic, it has to be heard as such—it has to be heard as coming from ambiguous or uncertain causes or sources. Rather than of the double-voiced emission, as Bakhtin so carefully delineates it, it would be more accurate to speak of the double- or multiple-listening "ear"—that is, a listening that carries in its mode of receptivity a capacity for discerning contending wills, desires, intentions, and implications—a capacity, in short, for handling divergences *aurally*. Could not exactly the same point be made about the *énoncé*—namely, that the stress needs to be placed equally on how it is being heard and received rather than simply, pace Foucault, on its status as what is said?

In the field of fiction, such a theory of listening cum reception—even though listening is seldom given the spotlight—is embedded in the narrative convention known as the free indirect style. The "free indirect" intermixing of different voices in storytelling—for instance, by taking the syntax and verbal tenses from one and the tones, attitudes, and pronouns from another to form a particular utterance—marks a crucial literary-historical transition, as was evident in the writings of eighteenth- and nineteenth-century western European novelists such as Johann Wolfgang von Goethe, Jane Austen, and Gustave Flaubert. It is easy to see how the basic feature of reporting another's speech or thought, so fundamental to narration, carries with it the potential for dispute, negotiation, compromise, and subordination. How to convey another's speech act or thought process in such a way as to transmit not only its linguistic content but also its tone and affect, its emotional and stylistic attributes? Rather than producing an exact overlap with what is being reported (even if this were possible), the persona doing such reporting—often a narrator, a character, or the author—enters a delicate situation in which, to keep some distance from what is reported, she may need to assume an ironic, sarcastic, or analytical stance. In brief, she may need to introduce the artifact of a space—a curtain, a fold line, an editing cut—in order to demarcate her position from that of the reported speech or thought. Such competition with another (or another's) speech act or thought process, competition that can have the effect of throwing that speech act's or thought process's stylistic characteristics (or what might be called its immanent logic) into sharp relief, amplifies nothing other than the stark copresence of multiple, discordant, or quarrelsome voices (and, we should add, *listenings and receptions*).[46] For some, such vocal and tonal (and, we should add, *aural and receptive*) intermixing announces a progressively democratizing society, one that has become tolerant of disagreements and conflicting viewpoints. For more skeptical observers, this apparent intermixing of information—speeches, attitudes, opinions, and thoughts—signals rather Western modernity's increasingly genteel ways of exerting authority and power. The transformed, though usually implicit and unspoken, rules, codes, etiquette, and politics of socialization mean that voices (and, we should add, *listenings and receptions*) now materialize in the interstices between the lines. Sponsoring the latter view—that in the context of modern Europe the free indirect style amounts to a new, gentle mechanism of social control—the literary historian Franco Moretti suggests that it should be considered a kind of stylistic Panopticon.[47]

Nevertheless, as in the case of Bakhtin's study of the voice in Dostoyevsky, the name *free indirect style* may be part of the problem here. Insofar as such naming focuses on the externalizable instance of emission (such as voice, speech, or style) as its object of study, listening and reception tend always to be given short shrift (as my parenthetical insertions in the previous paragraph indicate). The labels *double-voiced word* and *free indirect style*—and I would add Foucault's *énoncé* to the list—are, in this regard, as misleading as they are instructive precisely because they surreptitiously cover up the very factors without which the voice could not have been double or polyphonic: listening, reception, and attention. For acousmatic sound (as a ubiquitous form of information dispersion) to work productively among and across the disciplines, therefore, it cannot simply be a matter of amassing comparable concerns in established fields such as philosophy, literature, music, film, and sound studies. More critically, it will need to be a matter of coming to grips with the persistently underacknowledged yet indisputable and ineluctable part played by listening, reception, and attention—together with all the epistemic issues that arise with specific situations of information dispersion—in the making of fragmented knowledge objects.

5
From the Confessing Animal to the Smartself

Rather than assuming a generally acknowledged repression, . . . we must begin with these positive mechanisms, insofar as they produce knowledge, multiply discourse, induce pleasure, and generate power; we must investigate the conditions of their emergence and operation, and try to discover how the related facts of interdiction or concealment are distributed with respect to them.
—Michel Foucault, *The History of Sexuality*, vol. 1

A political ordering of life, not through an enslavement of others, but through an affirmation of self.
—Michel Foucault, *The History of Sexuality*, vol. 1

Most readers will agree that one of the unforgettable themes to emerge from Michel Foucault's study of sexuality in the West is his unreserved criticism of the ritual of confession. In hindsight, we seem far from having fully grasped why Foucault was so passionate about this topic, not least because Foucault did not exhaust or complete the task he set before us. To see this, we need to begin by posing a simple question: What exactly was the object to which Foucault was directing his fierce eloquence when he made his scathing remarks on confessional discourse?

For decades, since the publication of volume 1 of *The History of Sexuality*, the obvious answer seems to lie with sexuality—after all, these scathing remarks appear throughout the study. To be sure, this sexuality is not the *ars erotica* that Foucault, in a broad comparative stroke, names as the categorically different way of handling sexual matters exhibited by certain parts of the world (China, Japan, India, Rome, and the Arabo-Muslim societies) but rather the *scientia sexualis* that he asserts has evolved from the early Christian church all the way to the modern, disciplinary, and biopolitical society in the West. "In the erotic art," he writes, "truth is drawn from pleasure itself, understood as a practice and accumulated as experience; pleasure is not considered in relation to an absolute law of the permitted and the forbidden, nor by reference to a criterion of utility, but first and foremost in relation to itself; it is experienced as pleasure, evaluated in terms of its intensity, its specific quality, its duration, its reverberations in the body and the soul."[1] Foucault's obviously idealizing and schematic description of *ars erotica* should be read less for its historical accuracy than for its rhetorical effectuality; his generalization of *ars erotica*'s definitive *difference* is perhaps simply a way of sharpening the contours of the object of his critique, *scientia sexualis*. Rather than being derived from an intense relation to oneself, as is characteristic of *ars erotica*—together with the self-sufficiency and mastery that come with seasoned practice and accumulated experience—Western *scientia sexualis* is, according to Foucault, organized around a set of external validating procedures (iterative tests, proofs, regulations, protocols, and their like) in which one is obligated to individualize oneself as an ever insufficient and unworthy entity always in need of correction, improvement, verification, and oversight.

The Internal Ruse of Confession

For Foucault, the act of confession constitutes the core of such external validating procedures. Some reminders of his riveting depictions:

> Since the Middle Ages at least, Western societies have established the confession as one of the main rituals we rely on for the production of truth.... The evolution of the word *avowal* and of the legal function it designated is itself emblematic of this development: from being a guarantee of the status, identity, and value granted to one person by another, it came to signify someone's acknowledgement of his own actions and thoughts. For a long time, the individual was vouched for by the reference of others and the demonstration of his ties to the commonweal (family, allegiance, protection); then he was authenticated by the discourse of truth he was able or obliged to pronounce concerning himself....
>
> One has to be completely taken in by this *internal ruse of confession* ... in order to believe that all these voices which have spoken so long in our civilization—repeating the formidable injunction to tell what one is and what one does, what one recollects and what one has forgotten, what one is thinking and what one thinks he is not thinking—are speaking to us of freedom. (*HS*, 1:58, Foucault's emphasis, 60, emphasis added)

By "internal ruse," Foucault is referring to a process of *inversion* of the power dynamics embedded in the widespread uses of confession. Whereas, or so his argument goes, confession is a form of coercion, it is often regarded as a source of freedom; whereas it is an effect of a power that constrains us, we tend to attribute to it a capacity to liberate us from power. This inverted logic compels the belief that "the expression alone, independently of its external consequences, produces intrinsic modifications in the person who articulates it: it exonerates, redeems, and purifies him; it unburdens him of his wrongs, liberates him, and promises him salvation" (*HS*, 1:62). Moreover, by virtue of the power structure immanent to it as a discourse, confession "cannot come from above, as in the *ars erotica*, through the sovereign will of a master, but rather from below, as an obligatory act of speech"; "the agency of domination does not reside in the one who speaks ... but in the one who listens and says nothing.... And this discourse of truth finally takes effect, not in the one who receives it, but in the one from whom it is wrested" (*HS*, 1:62).

Although Foucault's analysis of confession is inextricable from sexuality, sex is merely, to cite his words, "a privileged theme of confession" (*HS*, 1:61). His object of critique is not sex per se but something else. In tandem with his elaboration of sexual practices as spread throughout Western history ("from the Christian penance to the present day" [*HS*, 1:61]) is a stress on a mode of relation to oneself that takes the specific form of a discursive surrender, a forced revelation of secrets to another, typically someone who is placed in the position of authority. *If sexuality is a theme*, Foucault shows, *confession is the form*: what he is really targeting is the impersonal apparatus of governance instantiated through religion, science, medicine, law, education, and other bourgeois institutions and relying on rationalist procedures of objectification and regularization as the means of authenticating lived experience. Although originally entrenched in the practices of the early Christian church, this apparatus of *truth extortion* was disseminated across European society over the centuries: "With the rise of Protestantism, the Counter Reformation, eighteenth-century pedagogy, and nineteenth-century medicine, it gradually lost its ritualistic and exclusive localization; it spread; it has been employed in a whole series of relationships: children and parents, students and educators, patients and psychiatrists, delinquents and experts. ... For the first time ... , a society has taken upon itself to solicit and hear the imparting of individual pleasures" (*HS*, 1:63).

A society for which truth functions by being ferreted out through procedures of active solicitation also faces a theoretical and methodological conundrum: As this society evolves into the Enlightenment norms of scientific regularity, how is the older, juridicoreligious model of confession to be brought up to date? This is the leading question to which Foucault provides his well-known analyses not only in *The History of Sexuality* but also in *Discipline and Punish*,[2] in which he theorizes the prison cell not only as a detention platform but also as a surveillance laboratory where a criminal can be subjected to regular scrutiny, reform, and rehabilitation. In the modern penitentiary system, that is, the prisoner's physical body is pre-recruited as part of an updated confessional apparatus that Foucault describes, after Jeremy Bentham, as Panopticism. In alignment with a consciousness of being watched at all times by an authority figure who remains invisible and nonlocatable, this incarcerated and disciplined docile body becomes the key instrument in a cost-effective economy of collective soul making, the production of genteel subjects.

An Unfinished Analytic?

Foucault's dissection of confessional discourse offers powerful insights into the project he consistently invokes as the will to knowledge. As he suggests, precisely because of how truth has been functioning in Western society from religious to secular times—as what needs to be lured, pried, and ferreted out; as what needs to be discovered not only because it is a secret but also because it is unknown to the individual himself—a host of responses have been developing alongside truth's production network and the many relationships this network has spawned. These responses historically include "the long discussions concerning the possibility of constituting a science of the subject, the validity of introspection, lived experience as evidence, or the presence of consciousness to itself" (*HS*, 1:64). It would not be an exaggeration to say that in the twenty-first century we remain caught in the throes of such responses. Before we proceed to some intriguing examples of such truth production—examples that fall outside Foucault's purview—a couple of crucial points need to be made.

First, despite its wide-ranging ramifications, Foucault's analysis remains centered on the few prominent institutions that consolidate the ascendancy of the Western *bourgeois* domain: the Christian church in collaboration with reigning monarchies and the gradual waning of that collaboration; the declining monarchical establishment and the increasingly autonomous political state; the rising disciplinary society with its proliferation of truth-production mechanisms through professionalized grids of intelligibility. It is to the evolving rationalizations of governmentality as distributed among various state and civil organs of the secularizing bourgeois social order—the police, law, medicine, education, family, the penitentiary, and psychiatry—that Foucault dedicates his inimitable critical energies. Even though he refrains from dwelling on the subjective experiences of life in such a society—instead, he considers individual subjects to be vehicles through which the effects of power are channeled, in what Giorgio Agamben calls subjectification (see Agamben's remarks quoted a few lines later)—and even though he disabuses his readers of the idea that there can be pure resistance (asserting that there is no resistance without power), the epic sweep of his indictment of disciplinary society has undoubtedly set certain trends for subsequent scholarly thinking on these topics. Following Foucault's arguments, it seems logical, for instance, to surmise that subjective experiences in disciplinary society are grounded in coercion and violation—indeed, to imagine the condition of being coerced or being violated as constitutive of normative subject formation. If Foucault himself has not made such claims, his work has nonetheless made it eminently possible, if not necessary, to make them. Reading along the grain of Foucault's arguments, Agamben, for instance, remarks that "every apparatus implies a process of subjectification, without which it cannot function as an apparatus of governance, but is rather reduced to a mere exercise of violence.... Apparatus... is first of all a machine that produces subjectification, and only as such is it also a machine for governance."[3] Subjectification, in other words, is a largely negative phenomenon; a subject's capacity to be herself is strictly the outcome of the coercive apparatus.

Foucault's reticence or ambivalence about what may be loosely called subjective renditions of lived experience thus leaves something unfinished—and open—in the examination of the bourgeois social order that he has so forcefully initiated. This unfinished something is the status of the subject as a recipient of and respondent to those institutional controls that are, according to Foucault, designed to capture and trap her. Is this subject an obedient and submissive one? What if the subject is disobedient and recalcitrant? Beyond these typical descriptions of essential ontological qualities (obedience, submissiveness, disobedience, recalcitrance), what *fields* of capacitation, potentiality, flexibility, resilience, intractability, and indifference lie between incarceration and surveillance, on the one hand, and the unstable loci of subjective existence and practice, on the other? Is *de*subjectification—the negation of the negative phenomenon of subject formation as tied to the coercive apparatus—necessarily a catastrophe, as some philosophers suggest? I return to these interesting questions in the final section of this chapter.

Second, closely related to issues of subjectification and desubjectification is another prominent feature: Foucault's relative inattention to a major connection in contemporary society—what, following Max Horkheimer and Theodor Adorno, may be broadly referred to as the "culture industry."[4] The issue with Foucault's inattention to this topic is not necessarily that he should have, like his Frankfurt School contemporaries, proceeded to repudiate mass-cultural representations or, more specifically, the aggressive postwar Americanization of the globe into a global marketplace. It is rather that Foucault's dissection of confessional discourse, for all its incisiveness, has curiously stopped short of an exploration of confession's prolific, mediatized afterlife in the age of biopolitics. The story of confession as Foucault tells it has adhered to a particular institutional trajectory: beginning with the early Christian church, confession migrates in various mutations through the European Middle Ages to arrive at the period of the Enlightenment, now geared toward progressive scientific process; from that point on, confession is brought up to date as a key mechanism of secular society's will to knowledge, its most important deployments being the monitoring and regularization of sex through modern institutions such as the nuclear family, schools, prisons, hospitals, clinics, and in particular the practice of psychiatry. However, as Foucault himself repeatedly suggests, the target of bureaucratic management in the ongoing transition from disciplinary to biopolitical society is that of *population*, a mathematically calculated and statistically correlated form of totality that, we might say, amounts to a new transcendental index.[5] How does confessional discourse figure in this biopolitical context, in relation to innumerable abstract groupings of people organized as "us" and "them" in everyday culture around the world? What are some of confessional discourse's more popular and mass scenarios, East and West?

By the mid- to late twentieth century, in the increasingly polarized global environment of the cold war, confession seems to recur in ever more innovative and politicized appearances. Between Communist regimes' rituals of political purgation and capitalist nations' routines of civic consciousness raising, confessional discourse has been propelled into brand-new careers in the mass media—and often since the 1960s as full-fledged media events. These new careers cannot be overstated, not least because they extend the implications of Foucault's classic narrative in fascinating, ubiquitous directions. As I go on to argue, the types of subjects (or desubjects) that emerge from these new confessional directions also seem quite different from the ones he has so memorably portrayed.

Confession's Newer Careers, with External Enemies

It is well known that in Communist regimes the interrogation of those suspected of being class enemies has often involved the forced confession of their misdeeds, their supposed crimes against the people. The last imperial ruler of China, the Manchu aristocrat Aisin-Gioro Pu Yi, was subjected to such a process of interrogation and correction when he was an inmate at the Fushun Detention Center in the early 1950s after he had been repatriated to the People's Republic of China as a prisoner of war by the Soviets. As the film *The Last Emperor* (Bernardo Bertolucci, 1987) demonstrates, Pu Yi was subjected to long hours of harsh questioning by party cadres and required to admit his crimes in writing; in effect, he was obliged to denounce his former, privileged life as a sovereign (in particular in the puppet state Manchukuo under the Japanese) as a betrayal of the Chinese people.[6]

At the other end of the demographic spectrum, the late 1940s through the 1950s was the early period of the founding of the People's Republic of China, during which peasants in rural areas were actively mobilized in support of the new political state. One method of such mobilization was for peasants to deliver reports on themselves, their livelihoods, and their family heritages during communal gatherings so that they could be appraised collectively and given a proper classification of their class status. Designed by the Chinese Communist Party as a way to reorganize society from the bottom up so that those who occupied the lowest rungs of the social ladder would have an opportunity to start over, 翻身 *fanshen*, as the peasants' revolutionary movement came to be named, was supposedly a process of mass spiritual and empirical rebirth. As William Hinton, whose English-language observations of a northern Chinese village, Long Bow, during 1948 remain a rare and unique historical record, writes:

> Every revolution creates new words. The Chinese Revolution created a whole new vocabulary. A most important word in this vocabulary was fanshen. Literally, it means "to turn the body," or "to turn over." To China's hundreds of millions of landless and land-poor peasants it meant to stand up, to throw off the landlord yoke, to gain land, stock, implements, and houses. But it meant much more than this. It meant to throw off superstition and study science, to abolish "word blindness" and learn to read, to cease considering women as chattels and establish equality between the sexes, to do away with appointed village magistrates and replace them with elected councils. It meant to enter a new world.[7]

Just as Pu Yi was admonished for his imperial lineage, so were the peasants of Long Bow inspired to report on their lives in such ways as to bring about, as far as possible, a downgrading of their class status. In the new political climate, the lower one's class status and the more impoverished one's family, the higher would be one's social worth. "Every family wanted to be classed as far down the scale as possible.... Only those classed as poor peasants could expect to gain," Hinton explains.[8] In a similar vein, after undergoing the proper reforms, Pu Yi, the former emperor, was released and allowed to live out the rest of his life as an ordinary citizen—a gardener—until his death in 1967.

Although these events of self-reflection and self-reportage in an East Asian country during the cold war seem a considerable remove from the ones analyzed by Foucault, the family resemblance they share is unmistakable: a procedure, officiated by authoritative representatives, during which an individual *avows* things about himself through a process of revelation; what is revealed is then subject to the judgment of those who are listening and watching. In the case of Christianity, the confession is by definition a confession of one's sins, for which one must seek absolution; if there is blame, that blame is directed at oneself as a sinner who needs guidance. In the case of (Chinese) communism, things are less straightforward because of the introduction of an important additional device: the class enemy.[9] With class comes a boundary between virtue and evil and thus a self-righteous reasoning for war. Although the villagers in Long Bow as studied by Hinton were still in the early stages of this class-mobilization effort (when the preoccupation was still with classifying where people belonged on the social ladder), by the mid-1960s class warfare, based on the identification of class enemies (those branded as spiritually polluted, such as landlords, feudalists, intellectuals, and the running dogs of Euro-American capitalist imperialism or of Soviet revisionism) became a common social practice. During the frenzy of the Chinese Cultural Revolution (1966–1976), the assault on such enemies and the parading of them in dunce caps, accompanied by forced confessions and other staged public humiliations, was a routine. The Red Guards, militant regiments of adolescents unleashed by Mao Zedong around the country to further his thought in pursuit of perpetual revolution, were among class warfare's most vigorous agents of moral rectitude.[10]

The introduction of class enmity in the secular, totalitarian state's utilization of confession as a population-management technique brought fundamental changes to confessional discourse. Class displaces the vertical, hierarchical relationship with God and his delegate, the priest, onto the horizontal, rhizomic relationships among different social groups. If a former emperor must confess, it is not because he has sinned against God but because he has committed crimes against the people. In a system where there is no transcendent deity to guarantee one's atonement and redemption—that is, no metaphysical or otherworldly being to obfuscate the man-made nature of truth extortion—confession becomes in effect *an art of war* (鬥爭 *douzheng*, "struggle" or "combat") aimed at wiping out adversaries. As the Chinese peasants observed by Hinton quickly learned, *one can top from the bottom, seizing the moral high ground by occupying the downtrodden position.* Whereas Foucault's emphasis is consistently on the coerciveness of self-revelation in the name of freedom from sin (as mediated by religious authorities), the workings of the totalitarian state bring to the fore instead a triangulation of players (the reporting self, the state authorities, and the class enemy), with a spotlight on the outward-turning rather than inward-turning moves of the reporting self. Whatever negative energy or violence is directed at the self in the Christian tradition—Foucault cites practices such as self-flagellation or mortification of the flesh—is now aimed at another. Moreover, whereas in Foucault's narrative the confessing self is deemed unworthy, an obstacle and a limit to be overcome, in totalitarian confession the obstacle is not (in) myself but elsewhere, and its removal will vindicate me (and my class), elevating "us" to a stronger and more esteemed position. (As mentioned in chapter 3, Foucault associates such hunting of class enemies in socialist regimes with racism also.)

Would it be at all far-fetched to suggest that some of these totalitarian confessional dynamics have long found their way into late capitalist society?[11] The crucial demarcation between the self and an enemy, made strictly along class lines in totalitarian confession, seems eminently adaptable for other identity-based accounts of the self, including though not limited to neoliberal autobiographical narratives of gender and race. An addiction to drugs and alcohol, for instance, can now be scripted as a form of testimonial, delivered in public, to the struggle between the self and an enemy "substance" that the self is said to have "abused" or, in fact, been abused by; with the help of others, this confessing self has hopes of becoming "clean" and redeemed. The major shift from Foucault's confessional model lies, to wit, in *the value ascribed to the self.* Whereas for Foucault truth production is a rationalization process, an introspective gaze forcibly imposed on the self, in more contemporary confessional discourse that rationalization process has become increasingly voluntary. If giving an account of oneself (to the authorities) in Foucault's narrative is synonymous with self-devaluation and self-destruction, in late capitalist society giving an account of oneself (in public) promises rather a way *out of* self-devaluation and self-destruction. If the confessing self in Foucault's narrative is regarded as the source of trouble and the limit to be transcended metaphysically, the source of trouble is now consistently externalized, deflected onto a culprit. In brief, *confession has turned into a means of outsourcing blame.*

What this shift advances is a concept of the self that is, first and foremost, *a discursive capacity: a verbal ability to allege that something injurious has happened to me (or us).* Salvation in this case is imagined to be an outcome of worldly rather than otherworldly intervention. Instead of being acknowledged confidentially in a cloistered space to a trusted professional auditor (such as a priest, a nun, a medical doctor, a counselor, a psychotherapist, or a psychiatrist), even the most shameful secrets are now confessable in public, to be heard by strangers. Instead of to the divine light, traditionally the revered source of absolution, the confessing self must be ready to expose herself as a *complainant*, a bearer of grievance against something or someone else, to the profane light of the mass media.

In this newer confessional order, as the complainant's discursivity in relation to her injury is understood as a passage to freedom, a number of characteristics are worth highlighting. Oriented around misery suffered in the past, the confessing self has morphed steadily into a present *show*, an ostentatious exposition in the basic understanding of a stage, a screen, and other forms of artistic display. Even more germanely, the confessing self is increasingly constituted through a practice of *making visible*—hence, perhaps, the indispensable feature of having something to divulge, which is to say, having some secret content ready for disclosure. Such secret content is precisely what sex is in Foucault's argument, but it is *the form of confessional discourse*—the performativity of "myself" through speech—that lends itself to creative iterations and renditions so that the exercises of making oneself visible become, as we will see in some famous cases, a show business.

The Self as Enterprise, the Self as Entrepreneur

For the self to function as a business venture, it must at the same time become an entrepreneur—that is, an enthusiastic manager and promoter of the said enterprise. In *The Birth of Biopolitics*, Foucault suggests that a fundamental difference introduced by neoliberalism is that *homo economicus* is no longer the partner of exchange that he is in the classical conception. Rather, *homo economicus* is now "an entrepreneur, an entrepreneur of himself"—"being for himself his own capital, being for himself his own producer, being for himself the source of [his] earnings." Going still further, Foucault writes: "The man of consumption, insofar as he consumes, is a producer. What does he produce? Well, quite simply, he produces his own satisfaction. And we should think of consumption as an enterprise activity by which the individual, precisely on the basis of the capital he has at his disposal, will produce something that will be his own satisfaction."[12]

Nowhere is this entrepreneurial turn of selfhood—what may be abbreviated as "my self, my show"—better illustrated than in contemporary mass-media culture. Many readers will recall, for instance, the sensational episode of Princess Diana's formal interview with the BBC in 1995 as part of a strategy to publicize her marriage troubles.[13] As the estranged wife of Charles, the duke of Windsor and successor to the British throne, Diana had long been the beloved fodder for the paparazzi's gossip-mongering machinery. What was unprecedented, however— and much to the disgrace of the British royal family—was her proactive gesture of 訴苦 *suku*, or "voicing bitterness," a kind of speech act that lowly peasants in Communist China were once encouraged actively to practice. This voluntary solicitation of—indeed, surrender to—global media's snare by an aristocratic white woman is a good reminder that the confessing self's entrepreneurial turn is not necessarily about money, fame, or strictly material benefits. What could someone of Diana's wealth, popularity, and iconic status still want by further feeding the media frenzy that she already commanded?

At one level, of course, this instance of a media spectacle demonstrates yet again tabloid news' victory over journalism proper as a social technology based on voyeuristic gazing. As Byung-Chul Han writes, "The Latin verb *spectare*, from which spectacle derives, is voyeuristic gazing that lacks deferential consideration—that is, respect (*respectare*). Distance is what makes *respectare* different from *spectare*. A society without respect, without the pathos of distance, paves the way for the society of scandal."[14] With its specialization in scandals—especially sex scandals but also any unseemly detail having to do with the private lives of the rich and famous—tabloid news routinely deploys spectacle as a tactic of war in the age of information overload, and the success of such a tactic is such that even highly reputable news establishments such as the BBC must follow its lead. What scandal generates is audience attention, which, though not necessarily deferential, is an increasingly scarce commodity.[15] Princess Diana was obviously not in need of money or fame, but wasn't her complaint precisely about the *lack* of attention (or love) from her husband? In a way reminiscent of the workings of the repressive hypothesis, this coupling of a purported oppression (the rejection of poor Diana) and the garrulous presentation of it as *grievance cum satisfaction* is perhaps the key to entrepreneurial selfhood. Thanks to an official channel for verbalization—the

From the Confessing Animal to the Smartself

Q-and-A process of an interview—enhanced by the glare and stare of global media, the unspeakable secret (in this case a princess's domestic distress) now spoke volumes. There were clear villains in the story: the unfaithful, clownish husband, the wicked witch with whom he had been having an affair, and the cold, uptight, and unsympathetic in-laws. Although airing such dirty laundry in public amounted to a form of self-laceration, it was also a means of self-elevation. Indeed, as we say when a company puts its stock on the market, *going public* was a measured way to create value, in this case by converting a deficit (victimhood caused by the lack of husbandly attention) into a surplus (victory won with an abundance of worldly attention).

Foucault's famous discussion of Panopticism in *Discipline and Punish* as what undergirds the gentle coerciveness of soul making in disciplinary society has often been faulted for being too stark and depressing.[16] This impression stems largely from how the Panoptic effect, as he describes it, is associated with an injunction of transparency, which, once internalized by the individual inmate, produces the paranoid feeling of being watched at all times and thus the compulsion to conform to what is perceived as the norm. What the burgeoning enterprise of the confessing self suggests, however, is that Foucault is, if anything, perspicacious rather than pessimistic. For not only is Panopticism consensually implemented in neoliberal times—think of all the advanced surveillance equipment people feel they, like everyone else, have to own and all the multitasking portable screens on which they, like everyone else, are transfixed[17]—but it also collaborates efficiently with the low-tech, widespread discursive capacity for alleging injury. If such allegation typically furnishes a story—in Diana's case, a tale of domestic horror, replete with villains and victims, among whom she is the leading victim—Panopticism typically furnishes the bureaucratic and technological support: the BBC's research, scripting, and production teams; the cameras and other technical essentials; the postproduction editing, circulation, and marketing efforts; and so forth. It is to the efficacy of such collaboration between "voicing bitterness" and a Panopticist infrastructure complex that entrepreneurs of selfhood increasingly turn to generate attention for their enterprises of "autoillumination."[18]

Still, among the many possibilities, why does the voicing of one's misery (rather than of one's sins, as in classical confession) seem so instrumental to this mediatized confessional discourse as to have attained the status of a global currency? One response could be that sights of cruelty have, under some historical circumstances, not only made for popular spectator sports but also formed part of a seasoned political strategy of governance (think of the gladiators' contests in ancient Roman times).[19] But how are we to legitimize the enjoyment of cruelty and its violation of humane boundaries amid the hegemonic neoliberalist affects of gentility and tolerance and in such ways as to incite broad dissemination (bringing in viewers, repeat customers, advertisers, and thus profits)? Instead of confronting the audience with the cruel—that is, messy and gaudy—scenes of domestic disputes (as caused by the husband's frequent absence because of adultery or by the wife's anorexic, bulimic, or suicidal episodes), the lone and lonesome figure of the unhappy wife subjecting herself to the harsh light of the camera and telling of her misfortunes in a subdued voice with an upper-class British accent *compresses* the lurid melodrama of such cruelty in an evocative, because tastefully elegant, format. Such techniques of evocation, amalgamating discursive *and* Panopticist capabilities, are crucial to the augmentation of the self, much less as a subject than as an ongoing project.[20] In hindsight, Project Diana was nothing short of a forerunner of aggressive crowdsourcing—here, crowdsourcing as a means to assetize self-esteem.

Evocative aesthetics aside, the voicing of one's bitterness in public also exemplifies what Nikolas Rose has described as a therapeutic relation to ourselves that characterizes contemporary Western and westernized society. Rose elaborates the term *therapeutic* as follows: "Problematizing oneself according to the values of normality and pathology, diagnosing one's pleasures and misfortunes in psy terms, seeking to rectify or improve one's quotidian existence through intervening upon an 'inner world' we have enfolded as both so fundamental to our existence as humans and yet so close to the surface of our experience of the everyday. It is this therapeutic relation to ourselves, and the authoritative components of this relation that have multiplied in our present."[21]

In a number of thought-provoking studies that resonate with Rose's (though with a different kind of emphasis), Eva Illouz, too, has offered a methodical analysis of the foundational role played by therapy as a sociocultural frame in the twentieth century and beyond. In particular, Illouz highlights the myriad dimensions of the influential conjunction between therapeutic discourse as such and feminist politics.[22] She explains the conjunction in a succinct formulation: "Because of its emancipatory structure, the therapeutic discourse offered a powerful narrative of growth and liberation that resonated with the feminist political claim for liberation. Thus the conjunction of feminism and psychology actually contributed to convert the private self into a public construct and even . . . into a public performance."[23]

For Illouz, as for Rose, the therapeutic outlook has become "one of the centers of that amorphous and vague entity known as Western civilization"[24] not least because therapy, as a realm of expert knowledge, has effectively spilled into virtually every sector of modern and contemporary society. To see this, we need only heed how frequently the concepts of "caring" and "healing" are promulgated in our economic organizations, corporate management and public relations, military establishments, international conflicts, intimate and social relationships, mass media, journalism, prison rehabilitation, child rearing, and adult as well as youth education. It is thus necessary, Illouz argues, to think of *therapy as nothing less than a predominant form of rationalization*, understood specifically as "the process of expansion of formal systems of knowledge, which in turn lead to an 'intellectualization' of everyday life: that is, to the fact that everyday life is increasingly shaped by knowledge systems and by the systematization of beliefs about the world."[25] Be this as it may, why the frequent voicing of bitterness? Why does selfhood's entrepreneurial turn seem so inextricably entwined with the public revelation of one's private woes? As Illouz expounds on this, what she calls "an extraordinary paradox," her thoughts steer us back toward Foucault:

Therapeutic culture—the primary vocation of which is to heal—must generate a narrative structure in which suffering and victimhood actually define the self. Indeed, the therapeutic narrative functions only by conceiving of life events as the markers of failed or thwarted opportunities for self-development. Thus *the narrative of self-help is fundamentally sustained by a narrative of suffering*. This is because suffering is the central "knot" of the narrative, what initiates and motivates it, helps it unfold, and makes it "work." Therapeutic storytelling is thus inherently circular: to tell a story is to tell a story about a "diseased self." As Michel Foucault laconically remarked in his *History of Sexuality*, *the care of the self, cast in metaphors of health, paradoxically encouraged a view of a "sick" self in need of correction and transformation.*[26]

Accordingly, by making the publicization of psychic suffering central to the account of oneself, the therapeutic narrative has fundamentally transformed and redefined autobiographical—and, we should add, confessional—discourse. Nowadays, even when one is rich and famous, psychic suffering is believed to be able to persist, calling for an act of will and volition to overcome it and thereby to regain one's authentic self. Illouz's paradigmatic case of such a project of self-authentication is Oprah Winfrey.[27] If Diana's grievance belongs in the genre of aristocratic domestic melodrama, Oprah's narrations of her life experiences as a black woman from a lower-class background traverse the genres of the weepie, noir, and the Western, as well as the self-help manual on everything from sexual abuse, weight gain, dietary disorder, destructive love relationships, and the quest for spiritual rejuvenation. The *Oprah Winfrey Talk Show*, which ran for twenty-five years from 1986 to 2011 and commanded a level of popularity and influence unprecedented in television history, offered regular instances of glamorized public self-exposure. As Illouz reminds us, Oprah's "vast cultural and economic enterprise has depended on her capacity to perform her inner self, that is, on her capacity to convince her audience of the authenticity of her suffering and self-overcoming."[28] As is well known, the *Oprah Winfrey Show* spawned numerous greatly successful subsidiary branches of business, including a book club, a magazine, a radio show, a cable network, and multiple acts of national and international philanthropy. In the late 2010s, Oprah was rumored to have expressed interest in running for the U.S. presidency. As Tim Wu writes, even though Oprah relied on a Christian view of human existence (that is, of life as filled with struggle and torment), there was a major difference between her preaching and more traditional religions. Whereas the latter typically warn of the dangers of materialism, Oprah's "prescriptions for personal growth always included consumption as a means of self-actualization and self-reward." Commercial transactions were unabashedly at the core of Oprah's model of emotional capitalism, in which, as Wu explains, "spiritual growth and consumption were theologically linked, not in tension."[29]

As Illouz elaborates it, the therapeutic persuasion functions as an enlarged cultural trading zone—that is, a zone in which groups with diverse interests and methods of thinking are engaged in the exchange of knowledge and symbols, even when they may not agree on the meaning of whatever they are exchanging.[30] Some of the most recognizable and enthusiastically traded ideas include the following: a person is a free agent who does things only by conscious choice and contractual agreement; growth is an inherent component of the human condition; to have meaning in life, one must seek self-fulfillment; wanting such self-fulfillment is a sign of health; anything that stands in the way, such as one's psychic suffering, needs to be exposed because exposure is the path to healing and liberation. Especially salient, Illouz writes, is a split model of responsibility regarding oneself:

> In making this suffering a public form of speech, in which one must expose to others the injuries inflicted on the self by others, one becomes ipso facto a public victim.... In becoming public, this speech not only allows the subject to obtain symbolic reparation (in the form of recognition) but also compels him or her to change and to improve his or her condition. It thereby inaugurates a new model of selfhood and responsibility: *it makes one responsible for one's future but not for one's past.* It

promotes a self that is passive—in that it is defined by wounds inflicted by others—but is commanded to become highly active, in that it is summoned to change. *It is highly responsible for self-transformation, yet it is not held morally accountable for its deficiencies. This split model of responsibility marks . . . a new cultural model of selfhood.*[31]

Illouz's comments on the politics of temporalities involved here may be paraphrased and amplified with neoliberalist stresses on *choice*, *consent*, and *ownership*. That is to say, what may be experienced as existential *limits* (such as psychic suffering caused by injuries dealt to one by others, by biological constraints, or by repressive hypotheses of various kinds) are, through rituals of public self-exposure and performative verbalization, magically transformed into identity, lifestyle, and agency—that is, *options*.[32] Whereas limits are unfortunate obstacles in the past, options are what one can exercise shrewdly henceforth. Confessional narration of one's victimhood is thus simultaneously a voluntarist pledge to the future, a way of laying claim to one's potentiality as a new deal.

Another Kind of Mirror Stage; or, Selfhood as Heterotopia

The examples of Diana and Oprah bring to the fore an additional and vital consideration of confessional discourse. As a mass-cultural phenomenon, confession has become not only a public airing of hurt and pain but also a *technosocial* event evolving in step with the mutating gadgetry of contemporary mass media. Be it in the form of scandal or therapy writ large, salacious self-exhibitionism, or benevolent life counseling of others, the spectacles of confession enjoyed by tens of millions of viewers these days are typically accessed on various types of electronic screens—television sets, personal computers, laptops, cell phones, tablets, and smartwatches. The very *setting* of confession, in other words, has undergone a significant shift from the dark, shadowy enclosure of the confession booth in the Christian church and the Panoptically visible, atomized inmate cell in the penitentiary (the two major loci of the coercive yielding of the self in Foucault's discussions). This epochal remodeling of confession's operational premises, so to speak, makes it necessary to modify and reboot the critical language we use regarding this historically changing practice.

When talking about the newer phenomena of mass mediatization, some critics tend (often with good reason) to harbor a generally dismissive attitude, judging the unprecedented proliferation of capture devices and of the habits—indeed, lifestyles—they engender with a stern sense of moral disdain. In his discussion of the connection between the apparatus and subjectification, as mentioned earlier, Giorgio Agamben, for instance, expresses such disdain by using the word *desubjectification* (which he associates with the current phase of capitalism), citing as his examples those who let themselves be captured by contemporary media such as the cell phone and television: "He who lets himself be captured by the 'cellular telephone' apparatus—whatever the intensity of the desire that has driven him—cannot acquire a new subjectivity, but only a number through which he can, eventually, be controlled. The spectator who spends his evenings in front of the television set only gets, in exchange for his desubjectification, the frustrated mask of the couch potato, or his inclusion in the calculation of viewership ratings."[33] In a similar vein, in his book *In the Swarm: Digital Prospects* Byung-Chul Han describes how "the mounting narcissification of perception" accompanies digital communication, how the smartphone "totalizes the imaginary" and "undermines our ability to encounter and work with negativity," and how digital technology "has proven to be a narcissistic ego machine."[34] Other critics echo Agamben and Han when they indict the seemingly endless consumerist capabilities brought about by the internet, together with the endless varieties of self-branding and self-promotion that have become ready to hand. (Think of everything from hookups with casual sex partners to selections of reproductive programs, from searches for one's genealogy through DNA testing to the profit-generating, side-hustling trends on social media.)

Although these critics are not mistaken about the disturbing social impact of many of these recent technosocial happenings, which may be summarized as self-affirmation run amok, I believe that their often unwitting reliance on the older (phenomenological) associations of the *bourgeois* subject—one who has a considerable attention span and a capacity for emotional depth and who is capable of being gripped by or of losing herself in an aesthetic experience—is no longer adequate to the tasks before us.[35] As we have seen with the various instances of confessional discourse's newer careers, our critical language may well have become anachronic when applied to human behaviors in the digital age. If media spectacles such as Diana and Oprah are any indication, the entrepreneurialization of the self as project requires a mode of analysis that would suspend rather than simply recycle the more familiar—and reassuring—paradigm of the self as an interiority, an internal space cultivated with sensitive reflection and reflexivity. How do we come to terms with a kind of self that, instead of being rife and torn with inner antagonisms (as in the case of the confessing Christian sinner or psychotherapy patient), is habituated to ephemeral images, voices, sounds, emails, and text messages coming at it incessantly from "ambient screens" big and small?[36]

I turn here to a less frequently discussed section of Foucault's famous essay on heterotopia, "Different Spaces."[37] Readers will recall that he offers there a brief account of the changing relations of what he calls *emplacement*—that is, the nexus of functions and values associated with particular arrangements of social spaces—in Western religious and secular cultures. A number of points are worth underscoring for the present discussion.

As Foucault proceeds to flesh out his notion of heterotopia (which he mentions in conjunction with utopia[38]), he clarifies that he intends to speak not so much of "internal space" as "of the space outside [*du dehors*]."[39] Interestingly, among the numerous examples he introduces of this space outside is the mirror, the reflective object that, after a certain discussion by Jacques Lacan, seems ineluctably evocative of selfhood and subjectivity as an unresolved drama of self-identification, mediatized spatially through the lure of an integrated image. Whereas Lacan writes that the mirror stage seems to be "the threshold of the visible world,"[40] Foucault, for his part, describes the mirror as a "mixed, intermediate experience" that is at once utopic and heterotopic. Utopic, because the mirror is a "placeless place," "an unreal space that opens up virtually behind the surface." But the mirror is also heterotopic because, he writes, it "has a sort of *return effect* on the place that I occupy."[41] This is how Foucault elaborates on this "return effect":

> [The mirror] is also a heterotopia in that *the mirror really exists*, in that it has a sort of return effect on the place that I occupy. Due to the mirror, I discover myself absent at the place where I am, since I see myself over there. From that gaze which settles on me, as it were, I come back to myself and I begin once more to direct my eyes toward myself and to reconstitute myself there where I am. The mirror functions as a heterotopia in the sense that it makes this place I occupy at the moment I look at myself in the glass both utterly real, connected with the entire space surrounding it, and utterly unreal—since, to be perceived, it is obliged to go by way of that virtual point which is over there.[42]

The most remarkable thing about Foucault's passage, I contend, is its divergence from Lacan's influential model, in which the subject's (mis)recognition of itself (as a unified entity) is based, psychoanalytically speaking, in narcissism. The mirror reflection in Lacan is a mere externalization of a psychic stage—that is, a means of objectifying what (Lacan proposes) is the *inner* event of a narcissistic binding, a oneness. For Foucault, in contrast, the intrigue of the mirror does not reside in the subject's being an interiority (opaque, invisible, inaccessible, yet determinant). In his description, the mirror is neither an implement nor a metaphor for *méconnaissance*, the metaphysical process of *suturing* that psychically organizes an infant's as yet uncoordinated reflexes and motor incapacity into a coherent self-image.

Rather than being a facilitator of make-believe and self-deception, the mirror according to Foucault "really exists" and stands as a geometric divide—one might say a kind of cut—between a space that is physically immanent and present, over here, and another space that is a nowhere, a nonplace, over there. For Foucault, in other words, the intrigue of the mirror is that it enables an experience of *two* places rather than an experience of an imaginary *one* place (the unified self or self-image, however much of a misrecognition that might be). Seeing oneself in the mirror means, quite literally, seeing oneself in another place that is beyond one's physical grasp and access, even while that very sight returns one to this place that one occupies here and now. The self as such is part and parcel of this "return effect" from the space outside; selfhood is, in this sense of *a shuttling back and forth* as specified by Foucault, heterotopic.

This notion of the mirror as an emplacement between utopia and heterotopia seems to me a more appropriate description of the contemporary confessional self's relationship to the media spectacle on the digital screen. Because of that back-and-forth movement between the two places and the return effect from the space outside, as Foucault writes, "I discover myself absent at the place where I am, since I see myself over there." In the case of the media spectacle, this "over there" is now filled not so much by an imaginary integrated self-image as by an (invisible) infrastructure complex embedded in mathematical abstractions: viewer hits, frequencies, and rankings; statistical calculations such as polls and surveys; and other fancy data permutations and manipulations.[43] Even though the entrepreneur of the self may be physically localized in one space, this self must now regularly project ahead and "find" itself through the mirror that is the electronic screen, precisely because the place occupied by the self, to be perceived at all, "is obliged to go by way of that virtual point which is over there." When the self's confessional performativity is transmitted anonymously to tens of millions, what is "seen" or "reflected"—and returned to the self—is not necessarily a coherent self-image or a psychically binding process (the excessiveness of which would turn into what Han terms "the mounting narcissification of perception"). Instead, what is seen, reflected, and returned to the self is more precisely a computational augmentation and optimization of the self as well as an infinite displacement and serialization of that self through interactivity or interpassivity.[44]

The appeal of the digitized-media world is that it is additive. As Han writes, it is a world devoid of negativity: "The way of the digital is addition."[45] Structurally speaking, there is always more and still more to come because the algorithms, becoming ever more sophisticated, are busily generating more possibilities *from the choices you just made*. This mechanically and electronically additive generativity founds an endless and endlessly capacitated sense of growth, expandability, and upgradability. Rather than a finitude, the self of this digital age is, as we witness with Oprah, a CEO in charge of a corporation that is, to all appearances, unlimited. This is the self that Foucault presciently describes as an "abilities-machine."[46]

In sum, precisely because of the overwhelming interference of machinic intelligence, whether we like it or not, it behooves us to configure a somewhat different set of terms to talk about the contemporary confessional self. Rather than being pulled together by an act of misrecognition that empowers it to imagine itself as a unified me, the self in the era of Panopticist, mediatized spectacles should be rethought as being constituted by the impersonal gazes coming from outside, nowadays often in the form of digital screens. Like Foucault's mirror, this outside suggests an irreducible emplacement between two different spaces. In this *heterotopicality*—a link that is at the same time a variation, a return that is a return from nowhere, a series of transferences and reciprocities whose exact originating point is lost—the self will henceforth have to find its definitions and bearings.

Let us also not forget that the ubiquitous shiny surfaces' reflections, driven by algorithmic formulations, are (much like Denis Diderot's indiscreet jewels) loquacious and solicitous. Rather than following the formulation of the classical confessional self, these digital screens are incessantly, garrulously talking back to the self about the self's own secrets: what the self supposedly wants, needs, or likes; what the self's tendencies and preferences are; how the self's past decisions translate into possible present and future choices; what customers from what regions of the world have accessed the self's interests and productions; and so forth. In addition, these talkative screens gossip: they actively report to the self what other people have picked—be it a book by Foucault or a type of shampoo, a pair of shoes or a brand of toilet paper—thus performing the function of socializing the self and its private choices in a purportedly sharing economy and placing the self in a competitive because comparative electronic grid of commodified intelligibility.

If the digital screen is a mirror, it is because a return effect comes back therefrom, rendering the self a *prosthetic force field*. Instead of striving (as in the older, psychoanalytic paradigm of *méconnaissance*) to be an integrated unit (replete with the misery of feeling alienated), this self is euphorically innovative, determinedly mobile, and at all times energetically multitasking. In the human form of a products inventory that works off endless add-ons—exercise programs, dietary regimens, spiritual-training exercises, travel and vacation imperatives, investment portfolios, remodeling initiatives, polyamorous partnerships, plastic surgical enhancements, and, in some cases, gender-reassignment procedures as well as ever-proliferating self-actualization apps—the self, as it races to transcend itself by keeping up with all the machinic devices that are supposedly only "assistants," is coming increasingly to resemble the devices themselves. It is in this evolving ethos of *homo prostheticus*—to borrow a perceptive coinage from Peter Sloterdijk[47]—and in a progressivist global environment decked with smartphones, smartcars, smarthouses, smartcities, smartweapons, and their like that we should mark the coming of age of what, for lack of a better term, must be dubbed the *smartself*.

CODA
Intimations from a Series of Faces Drawn in Sand

Although it takes days or even weeks to finish a single [Tibetan] sand painting, each piece of artwork is destroyed as a final symbolic act. Once a mandala is completed, the monks must then dismantle it by following a specific process in which parts of the sand painting are ruined in a particular order. Once the sand has been brushed together, it is then mixed with water—often dispersed into the ocean—to fully symbolize the impermanence of life and a non-attachment to material objects.[1]

❖ ❖ ❖

One thing in any case is certain: man is neither the oldest nor the most constant problem that has been posed for human knowledge. Taking a relatively short chronological sample within a restricted geographical area—European culture since the sixteenth century—one can be certain that ... man is an invention of recent date. And one perhaps nearing its end.

If those arrangements were to disappear as they appeared, if some event of which we can at the moment do no more than sense the possibility—without knowing either what its form will be or what it promises—were to cause them to crumble, as the ground of Classical

Coda

thought did, at the end of the eighteenth century, then one can certainly wager that man would be erased, like a face drawn in sand by the edge of the sea.²

❖ ❖ ❖

Sand paintings, as created by Native American Navajo Indians, were not made to be an "art object," but rather were made as part of an elaborate healing ritual or ceremony. The artist, or in the Navajo context, the medicine man, would use naturally colored grains of sand, and pour them by hand to create these elaborate "paintings." After the medicine man completed the sand painting, the person who needed the healing was asked to sit on top of the sand painting.... The belief was that the sand painting provided a portal so that the healing spirits could come through the painting and heal the patient.

After removing the illness from the person, the healing spirits returned to the sand painting, and therefore the illness was believed to have been transferred over to—or was now contained within—the sand painting itself. So once the healing ceremony was over, the painting was destroyed in order to destroy the illness as well.³

Acknowledgments

Like many publications, this monograph comprises a series of intensive studies that began in different contexts. Although the final shape of the book is quite a remove from those original contexts, I would like to acknowledge them to mark the occasions behind the book's making. A much shorter, preliminary version of chapter 1 was published in the anthology *New Directions in Philosophy and Literature*, ed. David Rudrum, Ridvan Askin, and Frida Beckman (Edinburgh University Press, 2019). Chapter 2 was written first as a lecture for the conference "Impatient Concepts" at Brown University in 2013 in honor of Professor Réda Bensmaïa; a version of the lecture was published in "Pleasure and Suspicion," ed. Rachel E. Greenspan and John Paul Stadler, a special issue of *Polygraph* 26 (December 2017). A brief preliminary version of chapter 3 appeared in *After Foucault: Culture, Theory, and Criticism in the 21st Century*, ed. Lisa Downing (Cambridge University Press, 2018). A preliminary version of chapter 4 first appeared under a different title in *Sound Objects*, ed. James A. Steintrager and Rey Chow (Duke University Press, 2019). All these previous versions have been substantially rewritten and expanded for inclusion in this book.

Writing this book was my way of staying intellectually alive during the years I served as a department chair (2014–2017, 2018–2020). I

Acknowledgments

am grateful to my beloved students at Brown and Duke who studied Foucault with me over the past decade and a half and whose curiosity and enthusiasm have helped sustain my own interest in his work. Sophie Smith and Xuenan Cao provided splendid assistance during different stages of my research. I owe a special debt to Austin Sarfan, my teaching assistant and coinstructor in two recent undergraduate seminars on Foucault at Duke, who sharpened my understanding of Foucault's scholarship at multiple turns. Thanks are also due to the many audiences in western Europe, East Asia, and North America who listened to my presentations of portions of various chapters over the years. To the dear friends who continue to inspire me with their sheer love for humanistic learning, please pardon me for putting you in the impersonal form of a list, which does not begin to do justice to the singular gifts I have received from each of you: Zahid Chaudhary, Chris Cullens, Ken Haynes, Ani Maitra, Livia Monnet, Pedram Navab, Pooja Rangan, and James Steintrager. About Austin Meredith, my companion and co-conspirator, words simply fall short.

This book would not have happened without the endorsement of Columbia University Press. Jennifer Crewe, Columbia's associate provost and press director, chaperoned the book's preparation in the midst of her extremely hectic schedule; I cannot thank her enough for the decades of professional recognition and encouragement she has so kindly bestowed on me. The book's publication benefitted from the energetic and effective efforts of the press's first-rate production teams (my thanks in particular to Sheniqua Larkin, Michael Haskell, Annie Barva, and Lisa Hamm). Several anonymous reviewers and press board members provided deeply responsive and constructive comments, both on the book proposal and on the final manuscript. I remain humbled by the privilege of these colleagues' generous feedback, which helped make this a stronger and better work.

Finally, I would like to acknowledge Duke's Trinity College of Arts and Sciences for providing the ample research support that facilitated the completion of this project.

Notes

Introduction: Rearticulating "Outside"

1. David Gelles, "Giving Away Billions as Fast as They Can," *New York Times*, October 27, 2017, Business sec.
2. Nicole Aschoff, *New Prophets of Capital* (New York: Verso, 2015), 108.
3. Gelles, "Giving Away Billions as Fast as They Can."
4. In "Giving Away Billions as Fast as They Can," Gelles quotes this phrase from David Callahan, the founder of the website Inside Philanthropy and the author of *The Givers: Wealth, Power, and Philanthropy in a New Gilded Age* (New York: Knopf, 2017), who distinguishes the "problem-solving mentality" from the "stewardship mentality."
5. According to David Gelles in "The Moral Voice of Corporate America," *New York Times*, August 19, 2017, Business section:

    Diversity—of opinions, ideologies and religions—is what makes taking a stand on moral issues so treacherous for C.E.O.s. Yet paradoxically, it is also diversity—of races, genders and worldviews, among customers and the work force—that makes many of the executives, when forced to take a stand, come down on the side of inclusion, tolerance and acceptance.

    Business leaders looking to the future are accepting that it is unwise to isolate swaths of the population by coming off as racist, sexist or intolerant. Instead, for the sake of the bottom line, it is imperative that they appeal to the widest possible audience.

6. Bruno Latour, "Why Has Critique Run Out of Steam? From Matters of Fact to Matters of Concern," *Critical Inquiry* 30 (Winter 2004): 225–48; subsequent citations to this essay are given parenthetically in the text.
7. For an incisive discussion of Latour's writings on religion and of his role as a (Catholic) missionary to the moderns, see Barbara Herrnstein Smith, "Anthropotheology: Latour Speaking Religiously," *New Literary History* 47, nos. 2–3 (Spring–Summer 2016): 331–51.
8. Latour's main target on the count of fetishes is what he perceives to be the fear of objects among some social scientists. See, for instance, his interesting discussion in "On Interobjectivity," *Mind, Culture, and Activity* 3, no. 4 (1996): 228–45.
9. Benjamin Ginsberg, *The Fall of the Faculty: The Rise of the All-Administrative University and Why It Matters* (New York: Oxford University Press, 2011), xi.
10. See Chris Lorenz, "If You're so Smart, Why Are You Under Surveillance? Universities, Neoliberalism, and New Public Management," *Critical Inquiry* 38, no. 3 (Spring 2012): 599–629. Lorenz's account, drawing on numerous informative discussions on the topic of European and North American universities under neoliberalism, offers an analysis of the rationales, culture, rhetoric, and practices of what he calls New Public Management, which he likens to totalitarianism. Lorenz takes the concept of bullshit from Harry G. Frankfurt, *On Bullshit* (Princeton, NJ: Princeton University Press, 2005). For definitions of the bullshit nature of New Public Management discourse, see pages 625–29 of Lorenz's article: "The bullshitter," he writes, "is only interested in effects and does not necessarily believe in what he states himself" (627).
11. Bill Readings, *The University in Ruins* (Cambridge, MA: Harvard University Press, 1996), 6.
12. Readings, *The University in Ruins*, 3. See in particular the introduction and the chapter "The Idea of Excellence" (1–20, 21–43) for elaborations of how the new bureaucratic criterion of excellence has steadily replaced the older criteria of the German idealist model—national culture, citizenry, *Bildung*, aesthetic cultivation, judgment, critique, rules of thought, and so forth—as the rationale for university education.
13. Lorenz, "If You're so Smart, Why Are You Under Surveillance?," 607.
14. Michel Foucault, *The History of Sexuality*, vol. 1: *An Introduction*, trans. Robert Hurley (New York: Vintage, 1980), 28; subsequent citations to this volume (abbreviated *HS*) are given parenthetically in the text. For

Christopher Newfield, the internal discourse of the institution is not accountability but innovation; see his essay "'Innovation' Discourse and the Neoliberal University: Top Ten Reasons to Abolish Disruptive Innovation," in *Mutant Neoliberalism: Market Rule and Political Rupture*, ed. William Callison and Zachary Manfredi (New York: Fordham University Press, 2019), 144–68. According to Newfield, "Michel Foucault developed the notion of biopower in large part through his studies of the history of sexuality.... For its nonstudents at least, innovation is the university's sexuality" (145), and "innovation is a discourse that lashes the university firmly to the economy and its imperatives of pecuniary gains (revenues, salaries, assets)" (144).

15. See Bruno Latour, *Reassembling the Social: An Introduction to Actor-Network-Theory* (Oxford: Oxford University Press, 2005).
16. The special issue entitled "Recomposing the Humanities with Bruno Latour," *New Literary History* 47, nos. 2–3 (Spring–Summer 2016), is clearly an organized response to Latour's counsel.
17. See Rey Chow, *The Age of the World Target: Self-Referentiality in War, Theory, and Comparative Work* (Durham, NC: Duke University Press, 2006), 1–23.
18. For a defense of Kant's importance for the contemporary American academic debates about critique, see Judith Butler, "Critique, Dissent, Disciplinarity," *Critical Inquiry* 35, no. 4 (Summer 2009): 773–95.
19. Paul Ricoeur, *Freud and Philosophy: An Essay on Interpretation*, trans. Denis Savage (New Haven, CT: Yale University Press, 1970), 27, 32.
20. See, for instance, Ian Hunter, "Scenes from the History of Poststructuralism: Davos, Freiburg, Baltimore, Leipzig," *New Literary History* 41, no. 3 (Summer 2010): 491–516; Herrnstein Smith, "Anthropotheology."
21. These sample descriptions of critique are taken from Rita Felski, *The Limits of Critique* (Chicago: University of Chicago Press, 2015), 2, 4, 6, 15, 18, 186. For related interest, see also the essays in Elizabeth S. Anker and Rita Felski, eds., *Critique and Postcritique* (Durham, NC: Duke University Press, 2017).
22. Felski, *The Limits of Critique*, 129.
23. Felski, *The Limits of Critique*, 9.
24. Elizabeth Weed, "Gender and the Lure of the Postcritical," *differences* 27, no. 2 (2016): 158. Although Weed mentions Eve Kosofsky Sedgwick's work in passing, her main object of criticism is Stephen Best and Sharon Marcus's essay "Surface Reading: An Introduction," in "The Way We Read Now," special issue of *Representations* 108, no. 1 (2009): 1–21.

25. Eve Kosofsky Sedgwick, "Paranoid Reading and Reparative Reading, or, You're so Paranoid, You Probably Think This Essay Is About You" (1997), in *Touching Feeling: Affect, Pedagogy, Performativity* (Durham, NC: Duke University Press, 2003), 123–51; subsequent citations to this version of the essay are given parenthetically in the text. This essay was first published as the introduction to the anthology *Novel Gazing: Queer Readings in Fiction*, ed. Eve Kosofsky Sedgwick (Durham, NC: Duke University Press, 1997).
26. Ashley Barnwell, "Entanglements of Evidence in the Turn Against Critique," *Cultural Studies* 30, no. 6 (2015): 907, Barnwell's emphasis.
27. For a very short list of instructive titles published over the past two decades alone, see Ranajit Guha, *History at the Limit of World-History* (New York: Columbia University Press, 2003); Chandra Talpade Mohanty, *Feminism Without Borders: Decolonizing Theory, Practicing Solidarity* (Durham, NC: Duke University Press, 2003); Dipesh Chakrabarty, *Provincializing Europe: Postcolonial Thought and Historical Difference* (Princeton, NJ: Princeton University Press, 2007); Maurice Godelier, *The Metamorphoses of Kinship*, trans. Nora Scott (London: Verso, 2012); Pheng Cheah, *What Is a World? On Postcolonial Literature as World Literature* (Durham, NC: Duke University Press, 2016); Aamir R. Mufti, *Forget English! Orientalisms and World Literatures* (Cambridge, MA: Harvard University Press, 2016).
28. See, for instance, Gayatri Chakravorty Spivak, *Outside in the Teaching Machine* (New York: Routledge, 1993); Hortense Spillers, *Black, White, and in Color: Essays on American Literature and Culture* (Chicago: University of Chicago Press, 2003); Audre Lorde, *Sister Outsider: Essays and Speeches* (N.p.: Crossing Press, 2007); Alexander Weheliye, *Habeas Viscus: Racializing Assemblages, Biopolitics, and Black Feminist Theories of the Human* (Durham, NC: Duke University Press, 2014); Lisa Lowe, *The Intimacies of the Four Continents* (Durham, NC: Duke University Press, 2015).
29. For well-known arguments about the intimate relations between area studies and U.S. State Department prerogatives, see Edward W. Said, *Orientalism* (New York: Vintage, 1979); and Masao Miyoshi and Harry Harootunian, eds., *Learning Places: The Afterlives of Area Studies* (Durham, NC: Duke University Press, 2002). For a different type of argument (that is, different from Said's and his allies' argument) about the institutionalization of area studies, see Zachary Lockman, *Field Notes:*

The Making of Middle East Studies in the United States (Stanford, CA: Stanford University Press, 2016).

30. For an engaging examination of identity studies, see Robyn Wiegman, *Object Lessons* (Durham, NC: Duke University Press, 2012).

31. The term *intersectional* is usually attributed to Kimberlé Williams Crenshaw, "Demarginalizing the Intersection of Race and Sex: A Black Feminist Critique of Antidiscrimination Doctrine, Feminist Theory, and Antiracist Politics," in *Critical Race Feminism: A Reader (Critical America)*, ed. Adrien Katherine Wing (New York: New York University Press, 2003), 23–33. Crenshaw calls for a new way of understanding oppression, which she argues can be experienced along more than one axis at once.

32. See Michel Foucault, *The Order of Things: An Archeology of the Human Sciences*, trans. Alan Sheridan (London: Tavistock, 1970), xv–xxiiv.

33. See my discussion in Rey Chow, "A Discipline of Tolerance," in *The Companion to Comparative Literature*, ed. Ali Behdad and Dominic Thomas (New York: Wiley-Blackwell, 2011), 15–27.

34. For an informed discussion of the historical origins and ramifications of the hegemonic rhetoric of diversity and inclusion among career administrators on U.S. campuses, see Anthony Kronman, *The Assault on American Excellence* (New York: Free Press, 2019), 119–62.

35. For a key text in the eighteenth-century classical tradition, see Friedrich Schiller, *On the Aesthetic Education of Man* (1795), trans. and with an introduction by Reginald Snell (New York: Dover, 2004). For brief histories of such classical humanistic inquiry in Germany, England, and the United States, see Readings, *The University in Ruins*, chapters 3–7 and throughout. For critical reflections on the continuing relevance of classical humanistic pedagogical concerns such as the vital significance of language and literature, see Gayatri Chakravorty Spivak, *An Aesthetic Education in the Era of Globalization* (Cambridge, MA: Harvard University Press, 2013).

36. The term *self-culpabilization* is taken from Slavoj Žižek, "The Varieties of Surplus," *Problemi International* 1, no. 1 (2017): 12. Žižek is mocking a prevalent logic of "political correctness" in the European Union, though his words may also be applied to dominant trends in North American neoliberal contexts: "The positive form of the White Man's Burden (responsibility for civilizing the colonized barbarians) is ... merely replaced by its negative form (the burden of white man's guilt): if

we can no longer be the benevolent masters of the Third World, we can at least be the privileged source of evil, patronizingly depriving them of their responsibility for their fate (if a Third World country engages in terrible crimes, it is never their full responsibility, but always an after-effect of colonization: they merely imitate what the colonial masters were doing, etc.). This privilege is the *Mehrlust* earned by self-culpabilization" (13).

37. For related interest, see Elizabeth V. Spelman, *Repair: The Impulse to Restore in a Fragile World* (Boston: Beacon Press, 2002), in which the author coins the term *homo reparans*; and David Eng, "Reparations and the Human," *Columbia Journal of Gender and the Law* 21, no. 2 (2011): 561–83.

38. See Jacques Derrida, "'... That Dangerous Supplement...,'" in *Of Grammatology*, trans. Gayatri Chakravorty Spivak (1977; reprint, Baltimore: Johns Hopkins University Press, 1998), 141–64.

39. Austin Sarfan, "Foucault and the Limits of Power," appendix in "On Foucault's Use of Nietzsche: 1975–1976," B.A. thesis, Department of Philosophy, University of Chicago, 2016, 34.

40. Michel Foucault, *Maurice Blanchot: The Thought from Outside*, trans. Brian Massumi, in Michel Foucault and Maurice Blanchot, *Foucault/Blanchot* (New York: Zone Books, 1990), 54, 28.

41. See Maurice Blanchot, *The Infinite Conversation*, trans. and with a foreword by Susan Hanson (Minneapolis: University of Minnesota Press, 1993), 196–201, for a succinct discussion of such limits—as borne by a culture's obscure gestures of rejection and exclusion—in Foucault's study of the confinement of madness.

42. Michel Foucault, "First Preface to *Histoire de la folie à l'âge classique* (1961)," trans. Alberto Toscano, *Pli* 13 (2002): 2.

43. Michel Foucault, "Nietzsche, Genealogy, History," in *Language, Counter-Memory, Practice: Selected Essays and Interviews by Michel Foucault*, trans. Donald F. Bouchard and Sherry Simon, ed. and with an introduction by Donald F. Bouchard (Ithaca, NY: Cornell University Press, 1977), 154. For related interest, see Georges Didi-Huberman, "Knowing When to Cut," in *Foucault Against Himself*, ed. François Caillat, trans. David Homel, foreword by Paul Rabinow (Vancouver: Arsenal Pulp Press, 2015), 77–109.

44. Michel Foucault, "What Is Critique?," in *The Essential Foucault: Selections from Essential Works of Foucault, 1954–1984*, ed. Paul Rabinow and Nikolas Rose (New York: New Press, 2003), 265.

45. See Michel Foucault, "Of Other Spaces: Utopias and Heterotopias," trans. Jay Miskowiec, *diacritics* 16, no. 1 (Spring 1986): 22–27. A second translation of the same essay is Michel Foucault, "Different Spaces," in *Essential Works of Foucault, 1954–1984*, vol. 2: *Aesthetics, Method, and Epistemology*, ed. James D. Faubion, trans. Robert Hurley (New York: New Press, 1998), 175–85. At the end of this essay, Foucault writes that the ship is the heterotopia par excellence. Along the way, he alludes to the mirror as both a utopia and a heterotopia. These references to utopia, heterotopia, and the mirror are also found in the preface and part 1, chapter 1, of *The Order of Things*, xviii, 7–16. For a discussion of Foucault's thought-provoking reading of the mirror, see chapter 5.

46. Although this is not the place to discuss in detail the topic of debt as a neoliberal form of governance, I would like to note the inspiring work of Maurizio Lazzarato in *The Making of the Indebted Man: An Essay on the Neoliberal Condition*, trans. Joshua David Jordan (Los Angeles: Semiotext(e), 2012), and *Governing by Debt*, trans. Joshua David Jordan (South Pasadena, CA: Semiotext(e), 2015).

47. A good instance of such laudably intensive critical attention can be found in the symposium "In the Humanities Classroom: A Set of Case Studies," *Common Knowledge* 23, no. 1 (January 2017): 57–103. In her afterword, Caroline Walker Bynum, the organizer of the symposium, invites readers to submit other examples of humanities classroom experience to the journal or to discuss possible contributions with her (103). Nonetheless, it is difficult not to notice the rather restrictive scope of the subject matter selected for the inaugural set of case studies, which offer few clues about the issues facing humanities scholarship and pedagogy that I have been trying to describe.

48. Alenka Zupančič makes the important suggestion that Foucault is actually using the notion of "repression" not in the strict Freudian sense of *Verdrängung* but in a looser, Freudo-Marxist sense of *oppression*, meaning the exercise of a more or less violent authority. This conflation of repression and oppression, she writes, works particularly well in the English language. See her article "Biopolitics, Sexuality, and the Unconscious," *Paragraph* 39, no. 1 (2016): 49–64, esp. 51 and 62 n. 4.

49. Michel Foucault, *Discipline and Punish: The Birth of the Prison*, trans. Alan Sheridan (New York: Vintage, 1979), 182–83, Foucault's emphasis. For Foucault's remarks on normalization as related to the penitentiary system in modern France, see the concluding chapter to *Discipline and Punish*, 293–308. For his concise statements on normalization as a

mode of productive rather than repressive power, see the lecture on January 15, 1975, in *Abnormal: Lectures at the Collège de France 1974–1975*, ed. Valerio Marchetti and Antonella Salomoni, trans. Graham Burchell (New York: Picador, 2003), 31–54. This lecture marks Foucault's transition from *Discipline and Punish* to *The History of Sexuality*.

50. Pierre Macherey, "Towards a Natural History of Norms," in *Michel Foucault, Philosopher*, essays translated from the French and German by Timothy J. Armstrong (New York: Routledge, 1992), 176–91. (These essays were based on an international conference that took place in Paris, January 9–11, 1988.) For related interest, see also Pierre Macherey, *Hegel or Spinoza*, trans. Susan M. Ruddick (Minneapolis: University of Minnesota Press, 2011).

51. Macherey, "Towards a Natural History of Norms," 186–87, 187, 187–88, emphasis added in all three quotations. Macherey's discussion should be read in tandem with Foucault's memorable remarks on the principle that explains history. From the basic materials of bodies, accidents, and passions, Foucault writes, "something fragile and superficial will be built on top . . . : a growing rationality. The rationality of calculations, strategies, and ruses; the rationality of technical procedures that are used to perpetuate the victory, to silence, or so it would seem, the war, and to preserve or invert the relationship of force. This is, then, a rationality which, as we move upward and as it develops, will basically be more and more abstract, more and more bound up with fragility and illusions, and also more closely bound up with the cunning and wickedness of those who have won a temporary victory. And given that the relationship of domination works to their advantage, it is certainly not in their interest to call any of this into question" (*"Society Must Be Defended": Lectures at the Collège de France, 1975–76*, ed. Mauro Bertani and Alessandro Fontana, trans. David Macey [New York: Picador, 2003], 54–55).

52. See Foucault's remarks in *History of Sexuality*, 1:6.

53. See note 48 for Zupančič's suggestion that for Foucault *repression* means "oppression."

54. Foucault puts it this way: "The statement of oppression and the form of the sermon refer back to one another; they are mutually reinforcing" (*History of Sexuality*, 1:8).

55. Wendy Brown's book *States of Injury: Power and Freedom in Late Modernity* (Princeton, NJ: Princeton University Press, 1995) remains an exemplary text in its articulation of the genealogies of this situation.

56. See the chapter "The Realpolitik of Race and Gender" in Ginsberg, *The Fall of the Faculty*, 97–130. Ginsberg's point is that "issues that to many professors represent moral imperatives have been transformed into powerful instruments of administrative aggrandizement" (97).
57. See Readings, *The University in Ruins*, 32 and throughout, and Lorenz, "If You're so Smart, Why Are You Under Surveillance?"
58. Ferdinand de Saussure, *Course in General Linguistics*, ed. Charles Bally and Albert Sechehaye in collaboration with Albert Reidlinger, trans. Wade Baskin, with an introduction by Jonathan Cullter (Glasgow: Fontana/Collins, 1974), 120, Saussure's emphasis.
59. Explaining the same point a little differently, Maurice Blanchot writes that Foucault "could sense in structuralism a residual whiff of transcendentalism: for what might be the status of those *formal* laws alleged to govern every science, while at the same time remaining alien to the vicissitudes of history on which, nevertheless, their appearance and disappearance depended?" (*Michel Foucault as I Imagine Him*, trans. Jeffrey Mehlman, in Foucault and Blanchot, *Foucault/Blanchot*, 71, Blanchot's emphasis).
60. Foucault, *"Society Must Be Defended,"* 254.
61. Paul Veyne, "The Final Foucault and His Ethics," trans. Catherine Porter and Arnold I. Davidson, in *Foucault and His Interlocutors,* ed. and with an introduction by Arnold I. Davidson (Chicago: University of Chicago Press, 1997), 229, emphasis added.
62. See Foucault's remarks on the principle that explains history, as mentioned in note 51.
63. Mark Cousins and Athar Hussain, *Michel Foucault* (New York: St. Martin's Press, 1984), 75.

1. Literary Study's Biopolitics

1. Michel Foucault, *The History of Sexuality*, vol. 1: *An Introduction*, trans. Alan Sheridan (New York: Pantheon, 1978); *"Society Must Be Defended": Lectures at the Collège de France 1975–1976*, ed. Mauro Bertani and Alessandro Fontana, trans. David Macey (New York: Picador, 2003); *The Birth of Biopolitics: Lectures at the Collège de France 1978–1979*, trans. Graham Burchell (New York: Palgrave MacMillan, 2008).
2. Michel Foucault, *The Order of Things: An Archaeology of the Human Sciences*, trans. Alan Sheridan (London: Tavistock, 1970).

1. Literary Study's Biopolitics

3. T. S. Eliot, "The Love Song of J. Alfred Prufrock," in *T. S. Eliot, Collected Poems, 1909–1962* (London: Faber and Faber, 1970), 13–17.
4. Eliot, "The Love Song of J. Alfred Prufrock," 16.
5. Michel Foucault, "A Preface to Transgression," in *Language, Counter-Memory, Practice: Selected Essays and Interviews*, ed. and trans. Donald F. Bouchard (Ithaca, NY: Cornell University Press, 1977), 51.
6. Jean-François Lyotard, *The Postmodern Condition: A Report on Knowledge*, trans. Geoff Bennington and Brian Massumi (Minneapolis: University of Minnesota Press, 1984).
7. Martin Heidegger, *Poetry, Language, Thought*, trans. Albert Hofstadter (New York: Harper Colophon, 1971), 198, 208, 210.
8. Archibald MacLeish, "Ars Poetica," *Poetry* 28, no. 3 (1926): 126–27.
9. For a concise study of the legacy of New Humanism in twentieth-century U.S. literary culture, a legacy that contributed to the large profile of New Criticism in U.S. high schools and colleges from the 1940s to the 1970s and to the rise of creative writing as a discipline during the cold war era, see Eric Bennett, *Workshops of the Empire: Stegner, Engle, and American Creative Writing During the Cold War* (Iowa City: University of Iowa Press, 2015), in particular the introduction and chapters 1–3.
10. See in particular the chapter "Speaking" in Foucault, *The Order of Things*, 78–123.
11. For an argument, interestingly drawing on Foucault's *The Order of Things*, of how the rise of a new philology in late eighteenth- and nineteenth-century Europe—as evident in the work of William "Sanskrit" Jones—needs to be made part of a historical understanding of comparative literature and world literature, see Siraj Ahmed, "Notes from Babel: A Colonial History of Comparative Literature," *Critical Inquiry* 39 (Winter 2013): 296–326. Referring to Foucault's remarks on page 240 of *The Order of Things*, Ahmed suggests that, for Foucault, Jones was as critical to the new configuration between language and knowledge as Adam Smith was to the new configuration of political economy. Like Smith's, Jones's work contains a philosophic duality "involving two different concepts of language: on one hand, language as a veridical discourse, the transparent medium of knowledge; on the other, language as a historical system, an opaque object of knowledge." "Because the new philology transformed the very terms by which we understand language's relationship to knowledge, its consequences have been, according to Foucault, the most far-reaching of any of the modern

sciences and at the same time the most unperceived. It replaced Babel's confusion with a critical method that claimed to know humanity across space and time" (310, 305). A modified version of Ahmed's article appears as the introduction to his book *Archaeology of Babel: The Colonial Foundation of the Humanities* (Stanford, CA: Stanford University Press, 2018), 18–49.

12. Foucault, *The Order of Things*, 300.
13. As is well known, Foucault shifted his interest away from literature after 1970, when he began a course of research in power, knowledge, institutions, and subjects. For a deeply informed discussion of this major shift in his work, see Timothy O'Leary, "Foucault's Turn from Literature," *Continental Philosophy Review* 41 (2008): 89–110. For an argument of the continued importance of literary thinking throughout Foucault's work, as evidenced in the recurrence of the concept of *partage* in his writings, see the chapter "Foucault's Transgression" in Robert Harvey, *Sharing Common Ground: A Space for Ethics* (London: Bloomsbury Academic, 2017), 191–241. For an earlier book-length study of related interest, see Simon During, *Foucault and Literature: Towards a Genealogy of Writing* (New York: Routledge, 1992).
14. Michel Foucault, "The Functions of Literature," in *Politics, Philosophy, Culture: Interviews and Other Writings 1977–1984*, ed. and with an introduction by Lawrence D. Kritzman (New York: Routledge, 1988), 308.
15. Foucault, *The Order of Things*, 296, 297, emphases added. Although Foucault did not name them, his discussion calls to mind the venerable pedigree of philosophers in the analytic tradition—Friedrich Ludwig Gottlob Frege, Bertrand Russell, Ludwig Wittgenstein, Rudolf Carnap, and A. J. Ayer, among others—who were preoccupied with or haunted by the idea of a perfectly neutral language.
16. Lorraine Daston and Peter Galison, *Objectivity* (New York: Zone, 2007), 374.
17. See the chapter "The Thing" in Heidegger, *Poetry, Language, Thought*, 165–86.
18. Roland Barthes, "The Rhetoric of the Image," excerpt from *Image, Music, Text*, ed. and trans. Stephen Heath (New York: Hill and Wang, 1977), in *Visual Culture: The Reader,* ed. Jessica Evans and Stuart Hall (London: Sage, 1999), 39.
19. Eliot, "The Love Song of J. Alfred Prufrock," 13, 14.
20. Barthes, "The Rhetoric of the Image," 36–37.

21. Mladen Dolar, "The Burrow of Sound," *differences* 22, nos. 2–3 (Summer–Fall 2011): 123, emphasis added.
22. This is why, as Barthes points out in his analysis of ideology (mythology), the language of modern mathematics, which is supposed to resist interpretation, tends under some circumstances to become easy prey to ideology. Against such resistance, for instance, ideology can turn a formula such as $E = mc^2$ into a mythical signifier for "mathematicity" itself. See Roland Barthes, *Mythologies*, trans. Annette Lavers (London: Paladin, 1973), 132–33.
23. Franco Moretti, *Graphs, Maps, Trees: Abstract Models for Literary History* (New York: Verso, 2005), 24, Moretti's emphasis.
24. See Moretti's discussion of how a change of the object can be brought about by quantification, whereas in comparative literary study of the novel the status of the object has remained unchanged, in Ursula Heise, "Comparative Literature and Computational Criticism: A Conversation with Franco Moretti," in *Futures of Comparative Literature*, ed. Ursula Heise (New York: Routledge, 2017), 273–84, with Moretti's mention of the novel's unchanged status on 276. See also Franco Moretti, "'Operationalizing' or, the Function of Measurement in Literary Theory," in *Canon/Archive: Studies in Quantitative Formalism from the Stanford Literary Lab*, ed. Franco Moretti (New York: n+1 Foundation, 2017), 97–114, where Moretti defines "operationalizing" as building a bridge between concepts and measurements (98).
25. See Franco Moretti, "Conjectures on World Literature," in *Distant Reading* (London: Verso, 2013), 43–62.
26. "The rise of the New Critics is a story told again and again in the annals of literary scholarship, but seldom with the financial bottom line underscored.... The New Criticism gained a high profile largely by way of funding from the philanthropic arm of Standard Oil. It was part of an extra-institutionally supported internationalist vision for global culture under the terms of a liberal democratic capitalist American order" (Bennett, *Workshops of the Empire*, 60–61). According to Eric Bennett, a happy exception to this neglect of finances in the story about New Criticism is Lawrence H. Schwartz, *Creating Faulkner's Reputation: The Politics of Modern Literary Criticism* (Knoxville: University of Tennessee Press, 1988) (*Workshops of the Empire*, 189 n. 17).
27. "At bottom, it's a theological exercise—[a] very solemn treatment of very few texts taken very seriously" (Moretti, "Conjectures on World Literature," 48).

1. Literary Study's Biopolitics

28. Moretti, *Graphs, Maps, Trees*, 26, 1 (Moretti's emphasis), 4. For some more recent examples, see the chapters in *Canon/Archive*, ed. Moretti, whose titles offer glimpses into the quantification-based research involved: for example, "Preface: Literature, Measured," "Quantitative Formalism," "Style at the Scale of the Sentence."
29. Moretti, *Graphs, Maps, Trees*, 24.
30. Elaborating on what literary maps do, Moretti writes: "You *reduce* the text to a few elements, and *abstract* them from the narrative flow, and construct a new, *artificial* object like the maps that I have been discussing.... Not that the map is itself an explanation, of course: but at least, it offers a model of the narrative universe which rearranges its components in a non-trivial way, and may bring some hidden patterns to the surface" (*Graphs, Maps, Trees*, 53, Moretti's emphases).
31. Moretti, *Graphs, Maps, Trees*, 29.
32. Franco Moretti, "Literature, Measured," in *Canon/Archive*, ed. Moretti, xi, Moretti's emphasis. He is describing the collective work of the Stanford Literary Lab. The next new thing, he goes on to say, is the captions.
33. Dennis Tenen, "Visual-Quantitative Approaches to the Intellectual History of the Field: A Close Reading," in *Futures of Comparative Literature*, ed. Heise, 262.
34. Heise, "Comparative Literature and Computational Criticism," 273, 276.
35. See David Damrosch, *What Is World Literature?* (Princeton, NJ: Princeton University Press, 2003); Pascale Casanova, *The World Republic of Letters*, trans. M. B. Debevoise (Cambridge, MA: Harvard University Press, 2007); Eric Hayot, *On Literary Worlds* (New York: Oxford University Press, 2012); Emily Apter, *Against World Literature: On the Politics of Untranslability* (New York: Verso, 2013); Siraj Ahmed, "Notes from Babel" and *Archaeology of Babel*; Warwick Research Collective (WReC), *Combined and Uneven Development: Towards a New Theory of World-Literature* (Liverpool: Liverpool University Press, 2015); Pheng Cheah, *What Is a World? On Postcolonial Literature as World Literature* (Durham, NC: Duke University Press, 2016); Simon Gikandi, "Introduction: Another Way in the World," in "Literature in the World," special topic in *PMLA* 131, no. 5 (October 2016): 1193–206; Aamir Mufti, *Forget English! Orientalisms and World Literatures* (Cambridge, MA: Harvard University Press, 2016).
36. Moretti, "'Operationalizing' or, the Function of Measurement in Literary Theory," 113.

1. Literary Study's Biopolitics

37. In one such anthology to which I am a contributor, David Der-wei Wang, ed., *A New Literary History of Modern China* (Cambridge, MA: Harvard University Press, 2017), authors were required to begin their essays uniformly with a specified date and an important incident so as to be consistent with the format of the publisher's volumes on other national literary histories.
38. Richard Grusin, "The Dark Side of Digital Humanities: Dispatches from Two Recent MLA Conventions," *differences* 25, no. 1 (2014): 83.
39. Bill Readings, *The University in Ruins* (Cambridge, MA: Harvard University Press, 1996), 87. Readings's chapter offers a concise account of how the decline of literary study is a historical outcome of the increasingly weakened ties between citizenry and national literary culture.

2. "There Is a 'There Is' of Light"; or, Foucault's (In)visibilities

1. Michel Foucault, *The Birth of Biopolitics: Lectures at the Collège de France, 1978–79*, ed. Michel Senellart, trans. Graham Burchell (New York: Palgrave MacMillan, 2008), 279–80, emphases added.
2. Many people have tried to fill this gap, of course. Foucault names Marx as a representative of those who rushed in to fill it with a realist criticism of capitalism, a realist criticism Foucault believes should be discontinued because it misses the point of exactly how labor is abstracted in economic discourse. See the lecture dated March 14, 1979, in *The Birth of Biopolitics*, esp. 221 and following.
3. Foucault, *The Birth of Biopolitics*, 283.
4. Foucault, *The Birth of Biopolitics*, 282.
5. See Gilles Deleuze, *Foucault*, trans. Seán Hand, with a foreword by Paul A. Bové (Minneapolis: University of Minnesota Press, 1988); John Rajchman, "Foucault's Art of Seeing," *October* 44 (Spring 1988): 88–117; Gary Shapiro, *The Archaeologies of Vision: Foucault and Nietzsche on Seeing and Saying* (Chicago: University of Chicago Press, 2003); Joseph J. Tanke, *Foucault's Philosophy of Art: A Genealogy of Modernity* (New York: Continuum, 2009); Catherine M. Soussloff, *Foucault on Painting* (Minneapolis: University of Minnesota Press, 2017).
6. Michel Foucault, *The Birth of the Clinic: An Archaeology of Medical Perception*, trans. A. M. Sheridan Smith (New York: Vintage, 1975), xiii.
7. For an in-depth discussion of the recurrence of the concept of *partage* in Foucault's writings, see the chapter "Foucault's Transgression" in Robert

Harvey, *Sharing Common Ground: A Space for Ethics* (London: Bloomsbury Academic, 2017), 191–241.
8. Michel Foucault, *Discipline and Punish: The Birth of the Prison*, trans.
Alan Sheridan (New York: Pantheon, 1977), 200.
9. For a discussion—through the work of Michel Foucault, Maurice
Merleau-Ponty, and Michel Henry—of the anomalies of spatiality,
meaning, and visibility that painting problematizes, see David Nowell
Smith, "Surfaces: Painterly Illusion, Metaphysical Depth," *Paragraph*
35, no. 3 (2012): 389–406.
10. For the detractors, Merleau-Ponty's ontology is ultimately another version of the untenable idealism they identify with the Cartesian cogito,
the Husserlian consciousness, and the Sartrean subject. For an illuminating discussion of these philosophical tensions, see James Schmidt,
Maurice Merleau-Ponty: Between Phenomenology and Structuralism
(New York: St. Martin's, 1985).
11. Gérard Raulet, "Structuralism and Post-structuralism: An Interview
with Michel Foucault," *Telos*, no. 55 (1983): 199, quoted in Schmidt,
Maurice Merleau-Ponty, 165.
12. Giorgio Agamben, *Homo Sacer: Sovereign Power and Bare Life*, trans.
Daniel Heller-Roazen (Stanford, CA: Stanford University Press, 1998).
13. For an interesting example of work in media studies that articulates
such bareness to the image, see Hito Steyerl, *The Wretched of the Screen*
(Berlin: Sternberg Press, 2013), in particular the chapter "In Defense of
the Poor Image," 31–45.
14. For a fascinating study of the figure of the void in postwar U.S. cinematic culture, see Matt Tierney, *What Lies Between: Void Aesthetics and
Postwar Post-politics* (London: Rowman and Littlefield International,
2014).
15. Michel Serres, "The Geometry of the Incommunicable: Madness," in
Foucault and His Interlocutors, ed. and with an introduction by
Arnold I. Davidson (Chicago: University of Chicago Press, 1997), 39.
16. For the record, Foucault does, in a dialogue, echo Hélène Cixous in
using the phrase "art of poverty" to describe the literary and filmic work
of Marguerite Duras. However, when elaborating, he rephrases Cixous's
idea this way: "It's this art of poverty, or what might be called memory
without remembering . . . a memory that has been completely cleansed
of all remembering, which is nothing more than a kind of fog, perpetually referring to memory, a memory of memory, with each memory eras-
ing all remembering, and so on indefinitely" (Michel Foucault, Patrice

Maniglier, and Dork Zabunyan, *Foucault at the Movies*, trans. and ed. Clare O'Farrell [New York: Columbia University Press, 2018], 124–25).

17. I borrow the phrase "force of flight" from Foucault's essay "La force de fuir," *Derrière le miroir: Rebeyrolle*, no. 202 (March 1973): 1–8, quoted in Tanke, *Foucault's Philosophy of Art*, 86, 212.

18. See Otto Fenichel, "The Scoptophilic Instinct and Identification," in *The Collected Papers of Otto Fenichel*, ed. Hanna Fenichel and David Rapaport (London: Routledge and Kegan Paul, 1954), 373–97.

19. See Michel Foucault, *This Is Not a Pipe*, with illustrations by and letters from René Magritte, trans. and ed. James Harkness (Berkeley: University of California Press, 1983); and Michel Foucault, *Manet and the Object of Painting*, trans. Matthew Barr, with an introduction by Nicolas Bourriaud (London: Tate, 2009). The Manet volume consists of a lecture Foucault gave in Tunis in 1971 (transcribed from the only recording of a series of lectures on Manet that Foucault delivered in different countries between 1967 and 1971); see Matthew Barr, "Translator's Introduction," in Foucault, *Manet*, 23. The book on Manet that Foucault had planned to publish never materialized.

20. See Foucault, *Manet*, 27.

21. For a helpful discussion of Foucault's departure both from conventional art history and from philosophy, see Soussloff, "Introduction: What Painting Does," in *Foucault on Painting*, 13–24.

22. Foucault, *Manet*, 31, emphasis added. Soussloff proposes "object painting" to translate the terms *le tableau-objet* and *la peinture-objet* as used by Foucault. She writes: "For Foucault, the object painting signaled the meta-space between painting as *le tableau* and painting as *la peinture*, that is, the special place of *the* object, painting" (*Foucault on Painting*, 54, Soussloff's emphasis).

23. Deleuze, *Foucault*, 59, Deleuze's emphasis. For related interest, see my more extended discussion of Deleuze's reading of Foucault, including Foucault's notion of visibilities, in the chapter "Postcolonial Visibilities: Questions Inspired by Deleuze's Method," in Rey Chow, *Entanglements, or Transmedial Thinking About Capture* (Durham, NC: Duke University Press, 2012), 151–68.

24. Rajchman, "Foucault's Art of Seeing," 92.

25. Deleuze, *Foucault*, 58. Putting the stress on the act of seeing (in a manner somewhat different from Deleuze's), Rajchman argues that Foucault's attention to visibilities raises the possibility of an opening, a gap,

of nonparticipation: "'Seeing' in this sense is part of doing. We cannot see what to do because we are 'prisoners' of the self-evidence of one *way* of seeing what to do. We participate, we do our bit, in the practices which make that way of seeing self-evident to us—a participation or acceptance we can refuse" ("Foucault's Art of Seeing," 94, Rajchman's emphasis). In a comparable manner, Soussloff, while acknowledging Foucault's suggestion of downplaying a theory of the knowing subject (*Foucault on Painting*, 47), puts the stress on the potential transformation of the observing subject: "For Foucault, paintings and their history demonstrated how an observing subject could be transformed through art and what such a transformation might offer for a politics of the present" (4 and throughout).

26. For discussions in the English language of the full spectrum of Foucault's writings on painting and photography, I refer readers to Shapiro, *The Archaeologies of Vision*; Tanke, *Foucault's Philosophy of Art*; and Soussloff, *Foucault on Painting*. My own task is to offer a theoretical sketch, in connection with the other chapters of the present book, of the vital role played by (in)visibilities in Foucault's conceptual provocations in general.

27. For a concise recapitulation of Foucault's remarks on Manet as well as an extended discussion of the spectacle of invisibility (or the "temporary blindness") that characterizes Manet's contribution to the history of painting and to the nature of vision, see John Nale, "Divisions of Manet," *Philosophy Today* 51, no. 1 (Spring 2007): 17–25.

28. Foucault, *Manet*, 66.

29. Tanke, *Foucault's Philosophy of Art*, 44.

30. See John Berger, *Ways of Seeing* (New York: Penguin, 1972) (as based on the BBC series). In this influential book, which features paintings by Magritte on its front cover, Berger discusses (among other topics) the genre of the nude in European paintings, distinguishing between nudity and nakedness.

31. Deleuze, *Foucault*, 65. For related interest, see Georges Didi-Huberman, "Knowing When to Cut," in *Foucault Against Himself*, ed. François Caillat, trans. David Homel, with a foreword by Paul Rabinow (Vancouver: Arsenal Pulp Press, 2015), 77–109. See also the interviews and dialogues in Foucault, Maniglier, and Zabunyan, *Foucault at the Movies*.

32. For extended discussions of the viewer's gaze and questions of subjection and subjectivity in Foucault's work on art, see Kevin Hetherington,

"Foucault, the Museum, and the Diagram," *Sociological Review* 59, no. 3 (2011): 458–75; Catherine M. Soussloff, "Foucault on Painting," *History of the Human Sciences* 24, no. 4 (2011): 113–23; and Soussloff, *Foucault on Painting*.

33. In a comparable fashion, Foucault notices the many arrows in Paul Klee's paintings. As Shapiro writes, "Foucault points to the importance of the arrows that appear so frequently in Klee, making explicit not only the movement to be attributed to an element in a painting, like a boat moving down the river, but displaying the way in which painting generally directs the viewer's attention, encouraging the reading of a painting in a certain way" (*The Archaeologies of Vision*, 275).

34. Foucault similarly identifies or imagines such a fold line in a number of other paintings by Manet: see, for instance, his remarks on *The Masked Ball at the Opera* (1873), *The Execution of Maximilien* (1869), and *In the Greenhouse* (1879) in *Manet*, 35–38, 38–42, and 46–49.

35. Foucault, *Manet*, 62–63, emphasis added.

36. Foucault, *Manet*, 28.

37. Deleuze points out the significance of description in Foucault in this manner: Foucault, he writes, has a "passion for describing scenes, or, even more so, for offering descriptions that stand as scenes: descriptions of *Las Meninas*, Manet, Magritte, the admirable descriptions of the chain gang, the asylum, the prison and the little prison van, as though they were scenes and Foucault were a painter" (*Foucault*, 80). See also Soussloff's comments on Louis Marin's influence on Deleuze's thinking about description as a place where language and image intertwine (*Foucault on Painting*, 22).

38. Foucault, *This Is Not a Pipe*, 45. As James Harkness, the translator of *This Is Not a Pipe*, notes, "[The term] *décalcomanie* means transference, transferency, or decal; it is also a painterly technique (often mentioned by Breton) in which pigment is transferred from one side of a painted surface to another by folding over the canvas. Finally, *décalcomanie* refers to a species of madness bound up with the idea of shifting identities" (62 n. 3).

39. Foucault, *This Is Not a Pipe*, 44, 46.

40. Foucault, *This Is Not a Pipe*, 44–45.

41. See Soussloff, *Foucault on Painting*, 69–95, for a richly informative discussion of Foucault's handling of Magritte's series of different paintings featuring the pipe.

42. Foucault, *This Is Not a Pipe*, 23–24, emphasis added.

43. See *This Is Not a Pipe*, 26–31, for Foucault's inimitable explication.
44. Foucault, *This Is Not a Pipe*, 26.
45. Foucault, *This Is Not a Pipe*, 28. Hence, Foucault suggests, Magritte went on to make a second painting about pipes, turning the play unleashed by the first painting into a pedagogical exercise, tying together all the elements that have been torn asunder by art. But whatever stability in communication that pedagogy (as personified by the schoolteacher) might provide is quickly overthrown by the unstoppable series of negations issuing forth from Magritte's separation of words and images (*This Is Not a Pipe*, 29–31).
46. Tanke, *Foucault's Philosophy of Art*, 105–6.
47. Foucault, *This Is Not a Pipe*, 28.
48. Michel Foucault, *The Archaeology of Knowledge and the Discourse on Language*, trans. A. M. Sheridan Smith (New York: Random House, 1972), 48. As Soussloff comments, "Rules allow objects to be seen as such" (*Foucault on Painting*, 55).
49. Shapiro, *Archaeologies of Vision*, 308.
50. Foucault, *Manet*, 71, emphasis added.
51. Tanke, *Foucault's Philosophy of Art*, 82.
52. "In some of his most interesting pages Foucault singles out Bataille's obsessive image of the eye upturned in ecstasy, and the corresponding transformation of language that this condition makes possible" (Gerald L. Bruns, "Foucault's Modernism," in *The Cambridge Companion to Foucault*, 2nd ed., ed. Gary Gutting [Cambridge: Cambridge University Press, 2003], 367). See also Nicolas Bourriaud, "Michel Foucault: Manet and the Birth of the Viewer," in Foucault, *Manet*, 17–19, for a brief discussion of the impact of Bataille's writings on Foucault. And see Soussloff, *Foucault on Painting*, throughout for discussions of the influence of Bataille as well as of other major figures, including Merleau-Ponty, Paul Klee, Wassily Kandinsky, and Louis Marin, on Foucault's thinking on art and visibility.
53. David Nowell Smith argues that for Foucault the "invisible" in question in Manet's painting is a kind of "play of invisibility . . . an ellipsis taking place within the sphere of the visible" ("Surfaces," 393).
54. Michel Foucault, *"Society Must Be Defended": Lectures at the Collège de France 1975–1976*, ed. Mauro Bertani and Alessandro Fontana, trans. David Macey (New York: Picador 2003), 245.
55. "The interest Foucault sustained for [Manet] came first of all from the fact that Manet proved himself a founder of discursivity, that he instituted a

2. "There Is a 'There Is' of Light"; or, Foucault's (In)visibilities

'discursive field,' in the same way as the works of Darwin, Buffon, Marx or Freud.... Foucault did not approach Manet as though he were an individual whose life it was a matter of studying like a collection of anecdotes—to such an extent that he did not even mention his first name, Édouard.... [I]nstead, he seemed to describe an intensity, an electric field, an event named Manet which unfolds in pictorial language" (Bourriaud, "Michel Foucault," 12–13).

56. Tanke puts this somewhat differently, as an indifference toward the external world: "The real legacy of Manet's work is the annulment of the obligation to represent the external world. Painting's indifference to its capacity for external reference is a central aspect of modernity" (*Foucault's Philosophy of Art*, 86.)
57. Michel Foucault, "Governmentality," in *The Essential Foucault: Selections from Essential Works of Foucault, 1954–1984*, ed. Paul Rabinow and Nikolas Rose (New York: New Press, 2003), 240–41.
58. Shapiro, *Archaeologies of Vision*, 303, 310, emphasis added.

3. Thinking "Race" with Foucault

1. Edward Said, *Orientalism* (New York: Pantheon, 1978), 21, Said's emphasis. See also Edward Said, *Culture and Imperialism* (New York: Vintage, 1993).
2. Johannes Fabian, *Time and the Other: How Anthropology Makes Its Object* (New York: Columbia University Press, 1983).
3. This situation is in part what James Clifford refers to as the "predicament of culture." See James Clifford, *The Predicament of Culture: Twentieth-Century Ethnography, Literature, and Art* (Cambridge, MA: Harvard University Press, 1988).
4. Roxann Wheeler, *The Complexion of Race: Categories of Human Difference in Eighteenth-Century British Culture* (Philadelphia: University of Pennsylvania Press, 2000), 10, 45. For an ambitious account along the lines described by Wheeler, see Denise Ferreira da Silva, *Toward a Global Idea of Race* (Minneapolis: University of Minnesota Press, 2007), in which the author describes her project as an "analytics of raciality" based on an examination of "how the tools of nineteenth-century scientific projects of knowledge produced the notion of the racial" (xviii, xii–xiii).

5. Michel Foucault, *Discipline and Punish: The Birth of the Prison*, trans. Alan Sheridan (New York: Vintage, 1979), 253.
6. See Nikolas Rose, *The Politics of Life Itself: Biomedicine, Power, and Subjectivity in the Twenty-First Century* (Princeton, NJ: Princeton University Press, 2007), 162 (in the chapter "Race in the Age of Genomic Medicine").
7. For an erudite discussion, see Sylvia Wynter, "Unsettling the Coloniality of Being/Power/Truth/Freedom: Towards Human, After Man, and Its Overrepresentation—an Argument," *CR: The New Centennial Review* 3, no. 3 (2003): 257–337. Wynter begins her essay with a quote from *The Order of Things* about the geopolitical historicity of the notion of "man" since the sixteenth century.
8. Nikolas Rose argues that in the prevalent racial science that took shape in the eighteenth and nineteenth centuries, "whatever differences there were in its different versions, race was understood at a molar level. It was thought of as an inherited constitution that shaped the whole character and all capacities of each racialized individual. This constitution could be observed in visible characteristics, not merely skin color but physiognomy, body morphology, and the like. And as racial science encountered genetics, it was this molar notion of racial specificity and racial difference that was encoded in genes, seen as equally molar, determining these individual physical, mental, and moral characteristics and severely limiting the scope for modification by environment or experience. But the molecular gaze of contemporary genomics transforms this perception" (*The Politics of Life Itself*, 161).
9. For an examination of the historical usages of the term *racism* and analyses of the antiracism that is the spirit of our time, see Pierre-André Taguieff, *The Force of Prejudice: On Racism and Its Doubles*, trans. and ed. Hassan Melehy (Minneapolis: University of Minnesota Press, 2001). As George M. Fredrickson comments, "The French sociologist Pierre-André Taguieff has distinguished between two distinctive varieties or 'logics' of racism—'le racisme d'exploitation' and 'le racisme d'extermination.' . . . One might also call the two possibilities the racism of inclusion and the racism of exclusion" (*Racism: A Short History*, rev. ed., with a foreword by Albert M. Camarillo [Princeton, NJ: Princeton Classics, 2015], 9).
10. See Suzanne Marchand, *German Orientalism in the Age of Empire: Religion, Race, and Scholarship* (Cambridge: Cambridge University Press,

3. Thinking "Race" with Foucault

2009); and Urs App, *The Birth of Orientalism* (Philadelphia: University of Pennsylvania Press, 2010).

11. See Gayatri Chakravorty Spivak, "Can the Subaltern Speak?," in *Marxism and the Interpretation of Culture*, ed. Cary Nelson and Lawrence Grossberg (Urbana: University of Illinois Press, 1988), 271–313, and "Who Claims Alterity?," in *Remaking History*, ed. Barbara Kruger and Phil Marian (Seattle: Bay Press, 1989), 269–92.

12. According to Roxann Wheeler, our contemporary confusion over skin color was caused in part by the historical shift from a more elastic sensibility toward color based on humoral and climate differences to a more rigid attitude toward color based on anatomy (introduction to *The Complexion of Race*, esp. 27–48).

13. Michel Foucault, *The History of Sexuality*, vol. 1: *An Introduction*, trans. Robert Hurley (New York: Vintage, 1980), 8–9; subsequent references to this volume (abbreviated *HS*) are given parenthetically in the text.

14. See the depiction of this famous scene in Frantz Fanon, *Black Skin, White Masks*, trans. Charles Lam Markmann (New York: Grove, 1967), 109, 111, 112, 113.

15. For a full-fledged discussion, see Pooja Rangan and Rey Chow, "Race, Racism, and Postcoloniality," in *The Oxford Handbook of Postcolonial Studies*, ed. Graham Huggan (Oxford: Oxford University Press, 2013), 396–411.

16. Michel Foucault, "The Confession of the Flesh," in *Power/Knowledge: Selected Interviews and Other Writings, 1972–1977*, ed. Colin Gordon, trans. Colin Gordon, Leo Marshall, John Mepham, and Kate Soper (New York: Pantheon, 1977), 222. For a helpful discussion of Foucault and race, see Stuart Elden, "The War of Races and the Constitution of the State: Foucault's 'Il faut défendre la société' and the Politics of Calculation," *boundary 2* 29, no. 1 (2002): 125–51. See also the informed debates in the special issue "Foucault and Race" in *Foucault Studies* 12 (October 2011).

17. On society's monitoring of populations, see Michel Foucault, "Governmentality," in *The Essential Foucault: Selections from Essential Works of Foucault, 1954–1984*, ed. Paul Rabinow and Nikolas Rose (New York: New Press, 2003), 229–45; on the art of not being governed quite so much, see Michel Foucault, "What Is Critique?," in *The Essential Foucault*, 263–78.

18. Sigmund Freud, "Instincts and Their Vicissitudes (1915)," in *The Standard Edition of the Complete Psychological Works of Sigmund

Freud, vol. 14, trans. James Strachey et al. (London: Hogarth, 1957), 110–40.

19. Following Foucault's lead, Ann Laura Stoler in *Race and the Education of Desire: Foucault's* History of Sexuality *and the Colonial Order of Things* (Durham, NC: Duke University Press, 1995) examines this nexus in the context of the Dutch Indies, showing how the regulations and controls Foucault describes are in play in European states' and citizens' practices in the colonies overseas.

20. See chapter 1 for a discussion of Foucault's detailed accounts of the three modes of knowledge in the respective chapters in *The Order of Things: An Archaeology of the Human Sciences*, trans. Alan Sheridan (London: Tavistock, 1970).

21. Foucault, *The Order of Things*, 273, emphasis added; subsequent references to this volume (abbreviated *OT*) are given parenthetically in the text.

22. Davide Tarizzo, *Life: A Modern Invention*, trans. Mark William Epstein (Minneapolis: University of Minnesota Press, 2017).

23. For related interest, see also the informative discussions in Michel Foucault, "Cuvier's Situation in the History of Biology," trans. Lynne Huffer, *Foucault Studies* 22 (January 2017): 208–37.

24. Jeffrey T. Nealon, *Plant Theory: Biopower and Vegetable Life* (Stanford, CA: Stanford University Press, 2016), 5–6, Nealon's emphasis.

25. Foucault, "The Confession of the Flesh," 223.

26. Michel Foucault, *"Society Must Be Defended": Lectures at the Collège de France, 1975–1976*, ed. Mauro Bertani and Alessandro Fontana, trans. David Macey (New York: Picador 2003), 259; subsequent references to this volume (abbreviated *"Society"*) are given parenthetically in the text. See also the last part of Davide Tarizzo's book *Life*, where he explores the role played by Darwinian articulations of life—which bear metaphysical underpinnings even as they are regarded as scientific—in contemporary manifestations of racism (202–20).

27. For an incisive discussion of how Foucault handles Althusser's arguments about ideology, see Warren Montag, *Althusser and His Contemporaries: Philosophy's Perpetual War* (Durham, NC: Duke University Press, 2013), 141–70.

28. See Foucault's similar remarks in an earlier section in *The History of Sexuality*, volume 1: "It is very well to look back from our vantage point and remark upon the normalizing impulse in Freud; one can go on to denounce the role played for many years by the psychoanalytic institution;

but the fact remains that in the great family of technologies of sex, which goes so far back into the history of the Christian West, of all those institutions that set out in the nineteenth century to medicalize sex, it was the one that, up to the decade of the forties, rigorously opposed the political and institutional effects of the perversion-heredity-degenerescence system" (119).

29. Michel Foucault, "Body/Power," in *Power/Knowledge*, 55.
30. See Tarizzo's discussions of these points in *Life*, 59–63, 87–89.
31. In *Abnormal*, referring to psychiatry, Foucault uses the term *neoracism* to describe the abnormalizations created from within the social fabric (in this case by biomedical interventions) (*Abnormal: Lectures at the Collège de France 1974–1975*, ed. Valerio Marchetti and Antonella Salomoni, trans. Graham Burchell [New York: Picador 2003], 317).
32. See Foucault's interesting remarks on the variables of growth in natural history's handling of individuals and species and on how sexuality modified such variables in "Cuvier's Situation in the History of Biology," 234–35.
33. Patricia Ticineto Clough, "Rethinking Race, Calculation, Quantification, and Measure," in *The User Unconscious: On Affect, Media, and Measure* (Minneapolis: University of Minnesota Press, 2018), 125.
34. For discussions of the nuances and complications involved, see, for instance, Taguieff, *The Force of Prejudice*; Fredrickson, *Racism*; Paul Gilroy, *Against Race: Imagining Political Culture Beyond the Color Line* (Cambridge, MA: Harvard University Press, 2002); and Frieda Ekotto, *Race and Sex Across the French Atlantic: The Color of Black in Literary, Philosophical, and Theater Discourse* (Lanham, MD: Lexington Books, 2011).
35. Michel Foucault, "'*Omnes et Singulatim*': Toward a Critique of Political Reason," in *The Essential Foucault*, 180–201; subsequent references to this essay (abbreviated "'*Omnes*'") are given parenthetically in the text. Some of the arguments in this essay can also be found in "The Political Technology of Individuals," chapter 8 in *Technologies of the Self: A Seminar with Michel Foucault*, ed. Luther H. Martin, Huck Gutman, and Patrick H. Hutton (Amherst: University of Massachusetts Press, 1988), 145–62. See also Michel Foucault, "The Subject and Power," in *The Essential Foucault*, 126–44, for another detailed discussion of pastoral power.
36. Johanna Oksala, "From Biopower to Governmentality," in *A Companion to Foucault*, ed. Christopher Falzon, Timothy O'Leary, and Jana Sawicki (London: Blackwell, 2013), 328.

37. Michel Foucault, "What Is Critique?," in *The Essential Foucault*, 264.
38. For related interest, see also the chapter "Christianity and Confession" in Michel Foucault, *About the Beginning of the Hermeneutics of the Self: Lectures at Dartmouth College, 1980*, ed. Henri-Paul Fruchaud and Daniele Lorenzini, trans. Graham Burchell, with an introduction by Laura Cremonesi, Arnold I. Davidson, Orazio Irrera, Danieli Lorenzini, and Martina Tazzioli (Chicago: University of Chicago Press, 2016), 53–92.
39. For an informative discussion of studies of the police in relation to Foucault's work and beyond, see Klaus Mladek, "Introduction: Police Forces: A Cultural History of an Institution," in *Police Forces: A Cultural History of an Institution*, ed. Klaus Mladek (New York: Palgrave MacMillan, 2007), 1–9. For a more extended philosophical discussion of the topic, see also Klaus Mladek, "Exception Rules: Contemporary Political Theory and the Police," in *Police Forces*, ed. Mladek, 221–65.
40. Foucault, "The Political Technology of Individuals," 156.
41. Joseph Vogl, "State Desire: On the Epoch of the Police," in *Police Forces*, ed. Mladek, 57–58, 71 n. 39, citing Michel Foucault, "Méthodologie pour la connaissance du monde: Comment de débrarrasser du marxisme," in *Dits et écrits (1954–1988)*, 4 vols., ed. Daniel Defert and François Ewald (Paris: Gallimard, 1994), 3:617–18.
42. Vogl, "State Desire," 52–53, emphases added. Vogl goes on to describe how this new conception of police and population found its way into the aesthetics of bourgeois dramaturgy, as in Friedrich Schiller's work *Die Polizei*.
43. For a comprehensive study of the use of lethal force by police in the contemporary United States, see Franklin E. Zimring, *When Police Kill* (Cambridge, MA: Harvard University Press), 2017.
44. Mladek, "Introduction," 3, emphasis added.
45. "What makes Western racism so autonomous and conspicuous in world history has been that it developed in a context that presumed human equality of some kind [including Christianity and the European and American revolutions of the eighteenth and nineteenth centuries]" (Fredrickson, *Racism*, 11).
46. For some of Foucault's reiterated remarks about the Christian hermeneutics of the self, see, for instance, "Technologies of the Self," chapter 2 in *Technologies of the Self*, 16–49, and "The Political Technology of Individuals."
47. It is beyond the scope of this chapter and my ability to address the paradigm-shifting impact of molecularization on biopolitics in the

3. Thinking "Race" with Foucault

twenty-first century, but Nikolas Rose's consistently Foucauldian arguments in *The Politics of Life Itself* are well taken: "In our present configuration of knowledge, power, and subjectivity, what is at stake in [the] arguments about human genome variations among populations is not the resurgence of racism, the specter of stigmatization, a revived biological reductionism, or the legitimation of discrimination: it is the changing ways in which we are coming to understand individual and collective human identities in the age of genomic medicine and the implications of these for how we, individually and collectively, govern our differences" (185).

4. "Fragments at Once Random and Necessary": The *Énoncé* Revisited, Alongside Acousmatic Listening

1. For this chapter's purposes, the relevant texts by Husserl are *The Logical Investigations*, vol. 1, trans. Dermot Moran (New York: Routledge, 1970); *On the Phenomenology of the Consciousness of Internal Time (1893–1917)*, trans. John Barnett Brough (Dordrecht: Kluwer Academic, 1991); and *Ideas for a Pure Phenomenology and Phenomenological Philosophy: First Book*, trans. Kersten Englis (Dordrecht: Kluwer Academic, 1983).
2. Jacques Derrida, *Voice and Phenomenon: Introduction to the Problem of the Sign in Husserl's Phenomenology*, trans. Leonard Lawlor (Evanston, IL: Northwestern University Press, 2011), 74, emphasis added. The quote is taken from the chapter "The Voice That Keeps Silent," which is especially illuminating for my thinking in the present chapter and where Derrida often references his own introduction to Husserl's *The Origin of Geometry*. See also Leonard Lawlor, "Translator's Introduction: The Germinal Structure of Derrida's Thought," in Derrida, *Voice and Phenomenon*, xviii–xxiv, for a helpful discussion. For discussions of logocentrism and phonocentrism in other major authors, discussions that constitute Derrida's deconstruction of the premises of Western philosophy, see Jacques Derrida, *Of Grammatology*, trans. Gayatri Chakravorty Spivak, corrected ed. (Baltimore: Johns Hopkins University Press, 1997).
3. Jean-Luc Nancy, *Listening*, trans. Charlotte Mandell (New York: Fordham University Press, 2002), 8. Nancy goes on to elaborate the notion of presence in sound as "not the position of a being-present" but rather

4. "Fragments at Once Random and Necessary"

"a *coming* and a *passing*, an *extending* and a *penetrating*. Sound essentially comes and expands, or is deferred and transferred" (13, Nancy's emphases).

4. Mladen Dolar, *A Voice and Nothing More* (Cambridge, MA: MIT Press, 2006), 38.
5. See Michel Chion's interesting remarks in *Sound: An Acoulogical Treatise*, trans. James A. Steintrager (Durham, NC: Duke University Press, 2016), 94, under the section titled "The Audio-Phonatory Loop."
6. Amy Lawrence, *Echo and Narcissus: Women's Voices in Classical Hollywood Cinema* (Berkeley: University of California Press, 1991), 11–12. Lawrence offers an informative discussion of the close links between sound recording and the reproduction of voice (1–32).
7. Brian Kane, *Sound Unseen: Acousmatic Sound in Theory and Practice* (Oxford: Oxford University Press, 2014); see in particular the chapter "The Acousmatic Voice," 180–95.
8. See, for instance, the following works by Pierre Schaeffer: *In Search of a Concrete Music* (originally published in French in 1952), trans. Christine North and John Dack (Berkeley: University of California Press, 2012); *Traité des objets musicaux* (Paris: Éditions du Seuil, 1966); and *Treatise on Musical Objects: An Essay Across Disciplines*, trans. Christine North and John Dack (Oakland: University of California Press, 2017). See also John Dack, "Pierre Schaeffer and the (Recorded) Sound Source," in *Sound Objects*, ed. James A. Steintrager and Rey Chow (Durham, NC: Duke University Press, 2019), 33–52.
9. Douglas Kahn, *Noise, Water, Meat: A History of Sound in the Arts* (Cambridge, MA: MIT Press, 1999), 8, emphasis added.
10. See note 8 for representative works by Schaeffer. For references to the acousmatic in Chion's analysis of Hitchcock's *Psycho*, see Michel Chion, *The Voice in Cinema* (originally published in French in 1982), trans. Claudia Gorbman (New York: Columbia University Press, 1999), 140–51. Chion's analysis also appears in a modified translation under the title "An Impossible Embodiment," in *Everything You Always Wanted to Know About Lacan (but Were Afraid to Ask Hitchcock)*, ed. Slavoj Žižek (London: Verso, 1992), 195–207. This translation includes a long note on Schaeffer's retrieval in the 1950s of the ancient term *acousmatic*, supposedly the name given to a Pythagorean sect "whose adepts used to listen to their Master speaking from behind a hanging, so that, it was said, the sight of the sender would not distract them from the message" (206). For related interest, see Chion, *Sound*, and Michel Chion, "Reflections

4. "Fragments at Once Random and Necessary"

on the Sound Object and Reduced Listening," in *Sound Objects*, ed. Steintrager and Chow, 23–32.

11. For reasons of space, this point will need to be elaborated on a separate occasion.
12. See, for example, Nancy, *Listening*, 3.
13. For an account of the complex details about Pythagoras and his different groups of disciples, see the chapter "Myth and the Origin of the Pythagorean Veil" in Kane, *Sound Unseen*, 45–72.
14. "Just as the Husserlian theory of the object allows Schaeffer to define the sound object, the phenomenological *epoché* allows for a definition of *l'acousmatique*. The two moments are sutured together" (Kane, *Sound Unseen*, 22).
15. Schaeffer, *Traité des objets musicaux*, 93, quoted in Kane, *Sound Unseen*, 24.
16. Schaeffer, *Traité des objets musicaux*, 91, quoted in Kane, *Sound Unseen*, 24.
17. Because of Foucault's acute orientation toward the inherent relations between thinking and spacing, Michel Serres argues for reading his work on madness as geometrical; see Michel Serres, "The Geometry of the Incommunicable: Madness," in *Foucault and His Interlocutors*, ed. and with an introduction by Arnold I. Davidson (Chicago: University of Chicago Press, 1997), 36–56. For related interest, see also Georges Didi-Huberman, "Knowing When to Cut," in *Foucault Against Himself*, ed. François Caillat, trans. David Homel, with a foreword by Paul Rabinow (Vancouver: Arsenal Pulp Press, 2014), 77–109.
18. Kane, *Sound Unseen*, 30.
19. For a more extended discussion of these modernist conceptual-aesthetic attempts at interrupting the given, see the chapter "When Reflexivity Becomes Porn," in Rey Chow, *Entanglements, or Transmedial Thinking About Capture* (Durham, NC: Duke University Press, 2012), 13–30.
20. Michel Foucault, *The Archaeology of Knowledge and the Discourse on Language*, trans. A. M. Sheridan Smith (New York: Pantheon, 1972). It should be emphasized that my interest here is in rethinking the *énoncé* in relation to the theorization of acousmaticity. For an admirable and broader exploration of the ramifications of sound and hearing in Foucault's work in general, see Lauri Siisiäinen, *Foucault and the Politics of Hearing* (New York: Routledge, 2012).
21. Michel Foucault, *Foucault Live: Collected Interviews, 1961–1984*, ed. Sylvère Lotringer, trans. Lysa Hochroth and John Johnston (New York: Semiotext(e), 1989), 65–66, Foucault's emphasis.

4. "Fragments at Once Random and Necessary"

22. This interview was conducted by Charles Ruas only nine months before Foucault's death. See Michel Foucault, *Death in the Labyrinth: The World of Raymond Roussel*, trans. Charles Ruas (1986), with an introduction by James Faubion, postscript by John Ashbery (New York: Continuum, 2004), 171–88.
23. James Faubion, "General Introduction," in Foucault, *Death in the Labyrinth*, xiii.
24. Foucault, *Death in the Labyrinth*, 179, emphases added.
25. Foucault, *The Archaeology of Knowledge*, 49, Foucault's emphasis.
26. Foucault, *The Archaeology of Knowledge*, 80, 84, 84, 86 (emphasis added), 87 (emphasis added).
27. Gilles Deleuze, *Foucault*, trans. Seán Hand, foreword by Paul Bové (Minneapolis: University of Minnesota Press, 1988), 13–14, emphases added.
28. Michel Foucault, "What Is an Author?," trans. Josué V. Harari, in *The Essential Foucault: Selections from Essential Works of Foucault, 1954–1984*, ed. Paul Rabinow and Nikolas Rose (New York: New Press, 2003), 391.
29. Michel Foucault, "On the Archaeology of the Sciences: Response to the Epistemology Circle," in *The Essential Foucault*, 402, emphasis added.
30. I have elsewhere discussed this process in terms of *languaging*. For an extended account in which Foucault's *énoncé* is explored in conjunction with Walter Benjamin's *mémoire involontaire*, see Rey Chow, *Not Like a Native Speaker: On Languaging as a Postcolonial Experience* (New York: Columbia University Press, 2014), 47–57.
31. Maurice Blanchot, *Michel Foucault as I Imagine Him*, trans. Jeffrey Mehlman, in Michel Foucault and Maurice Blanchot, *Foucault/Blanchot*, trans. Jeffrey Mehlman and Brian Massumi (New York: Zone Books, 1990), 75.
32. Adorno's metaphor for works of art is cited at the beginning of Gretel Adorno and Rolf Tiedemann, "Editors' Afterword," in Theodor W. Adorno, *Aesthetic Theory*, ed. Gretel Adorno and Rolf Tiedemann, trans. Robert Hullot-Kentor (London: Athlone Press, 1997), 361. The editors go on to offer an account of the productive and negative associations Adorno attaches to fragmentariness in his various works (362).
33. Chion, *The Voice in Cinema*, 46. For a fairly recent fictional treatment of this link between sound-media technologies and the dead (in the expanding popular genre of New Age connectivity), see the episode "Be Right Back" in season 2 of the British television series *Black Mirror*

4. "Fragments at Once Random and Necessary"

(2011). Part science fiction and part sentimental drama, the episode features a woman who talks with her dead husband by way of chat-room software and cell phone and through biochemical maneuvers eventually brings him back as a "live" partner who is programmed to "replay" (or respond) to her verbally and physically but not emotionally.

34. To this extent, I tend to disagree with Kane's critique of Schaeffer—that Schaeffer is producing a phantasmagorical version of the Pythagorean story through a *metaphysics* (understood in a pejorative sense) of the sound object. Describing how Schaeffer, despite stressing the importance of phenomenological experience and using concrete materials for his sound objects early on (as in his search for a concrete music), became increasingly focused on ideal objects in his mature works, Kane argues that Schaeffer is ultimately Husserlian in his mode of theorization. Accordingly, because the existence of an ideal, originary object is affirmed as prior to experience, experience can serve to reveal but not sully pure objectivity with vulgar contingencies of history and matter (see Kane's informative discussions in chapters 1–4 of *Sound Unseen*; for the gist of his critique of Schaeffer, see, for instance, pages 17, 34, 60). My disagreement with this reading has to do primarily with the larger, modernist conceptual-aesthetic context in which, as I have been arguing, Schaeffer's work should be situated: Schaeffer is hardly the only theorist or artist to think of art making the way he does. I also believe that boundaries between so-called ideal and concrete objects are often blurred *in practice*. No concrete object can be completely devoid of ideality, and no ideal object can "make sense" without some concrete manifestation. The use and revitalization of myth is an excellent case in point of such indistinction. To give a familiar sonic example, consider the legend of the Sirens. Modern and contemporary adaptations and searches—from James Joyce's use of the nymphs for an episode in his novel *Ulysses* (1922) and Franz Kafka's rendition of them as silent in the short story "The Silence of the Sirens" (1931) to emergency alarm signals deployed in modern cities around the world and the research expedition carried out by contemporary German media experts at the Galli Islands, off the Amalfi Coast in Italy, to verify the location and sources of the Sirens' songs—are worlds apart from the ancient narrative context in which the Sirens first appear. In the historicity of such adaptations and searches—literary, scientific, mediatic, and archaeological—the Sirens as such seem to be both concrete and ideal objects, functioning at once

at the everyday and the metaphysical (or phantasmagorical) levels. For a discussion of the Galli Islands expedition, see the chapter "Resonance of Siren Songs: Experimenting Cultural Sonicity," in Wolfgang Ernst, *Sonic Time Machines: Explicit Sound, Sirenic Voices, and Implicit Sonicity* (Amsterdam: Amsterdam University Press, 2016), 49–69.

35. For an authoritative study, see Jonathan Sterne, *The Audible Past: Cultural Origins of Sound Reproduction* (Durham, NC: Duke University Press, 2003).

36. For related interest, see Ani Maitra and Rey Chow, "What's 'In'? Disaggregating Asia Through New Media Actants," in *The Routledge Handbook on New Media in Asia*, ed. Larissa Hjort and Olivia Khoo (New York: Routledge, 2016, 17–27), in particular the section "From Gulf to Gulf to Gulf," which discusses the ephemeral, low-res digital music videos circulated among sailors trafficking in the oceans around India, the Middle East, and Africa. The fragmentary networks generated in the process are excellent instances of the contemporaneity of acousmaticity in both special and generalized senses.

37. Nancy, *Listening*, 10.

38. For an argument for liberating sound altogether from the time domain still bound to the human sensorium, see Ernst, *Sonic Time Machines,* in particular the chapter "Rescued from the Archive: Archaeonautics of Sound" (113–27). Instead of the human ear, Ernst advocates what he calls the "media-archaeological ear," and instead of acousmatic or reduced listening he advocates "diagrammatic listening" based on computer algorithms (116).

39. Roland Barthes, "The Grain of the Voice," in *Image-Music-Text*, essays selected by and trans. Stephen Heath (Glasgow: Fontana/Collins, 1977), 182 (Barthes's emphasis), 185, 188 (emphasis added).

40. Nancy, *Listening*, 16, 21–22.

41. Nancy, *Listening*, 41. For a fascinating exploration of the status of sound and listening in relation to pregnancy, see Jairo Moreno and Gavin Steingo, "The Alluring Objecthood of the Heartbeat," in *Sound Objects*, ed. Steintrager and Chow, 167–84.

42. For a discussion of shifters and pronouns in relation to the arrival of new sound technologies such as the phonograph, see Kane, *Sound Unseen*, 182–86.

43. See Mikhail Bakhtin, *Problems of Dostoyevsky's Poetics*, ed. and trans. Caryl Emerson, with an introduction by Wayne C. Booth (Minneapolis:

University of Minnesota Press, 1984), in particular the detailed analyses of the internal dialogicality of Dostoyevsky's "discourse" in chapter 5 (181–269). As Nancy writes, "*Écrire* in its modern conception—elaborated since Proust, Adorno, and Benjamin, through Blanchot, Barthes, and to Derrida's *archi-écriture*—is nothing other than making sense resound beyond signification, or beyond itself. It is *vocalizing* a sense that, for classical thought, intended to remain deaf and mute" (*Listening*, 34–35, Nancy's emphasis). Although Nancy does not include Dostoyevsky and Bakhtin on his list of modern writers attuned to this sense "beyond signification," his description certainly echoes the Russian authors' notions of double-voicedness and polyphonicity to some extent.

44. Bakhtin, *Problems of Dostoyevsky's Poetics*, 196 and throughout.
45. Quoted in Nancy, *Listening*, 28.
46. For related interest, see the discussion of Russian novels in Valentin Nikolaevich Vološinov, *Marxism and the Philosophy of Language*, trans. Ladislav Matejka and I. R. Titunik (Cambridge, MA: Harvard University Press, 1986), in particular part 3, 107–59.
47. See Franco Moretti's discussion in *The Bourgeois: Between History and Literature* (London: Verso, 2014), 94–100.

5. From the Confessing Animal to the Smartself

1. Michel Foucault, *The History of Sexuality*, vol. 1: *An Introduction*, trans. Robert Hurley (New York: Vintage, 1980), 57; subsequent citations to this volume (abbreviated *HS*) are given parenthetically in the text. The term *confessing animal* in this chapter's title is from Foucault, *History of Sexuality*, 1:59.
2. Michel Foucault, *Discipline and Punish: The Birth of the Prison*, trans. Alan Sheridan (New York: Vintage, 1979).
3. Giorgio Agamben, *What Is an Apparatus? and Other Essays*, trans. David Kishik and Stefan Pedatella (Stanford, CA: Stanford University Press, 2009), 19–20.
4. Max Horkheimer and Theodor W. Adorno, "The Culture Industry: Enlightenment as Mass Deception," in *Dialectic of Enlightenment: Philosophical Fragments* (originally published in German in 1944 and 1947), ed. Gunzelin Schmid Noerr, trans. Edmund Jephcott (Stanford, CA: Stanford University Press, 2007), 94–136.

5. For Foucault's recurrent remarks on population, see *History of Sexuality*, vol. 1, as well as *Discipline and Punish* and his numerous posthumously published Collège de France lectures.
6. For his film, Bertolucci drew on the anecdotal accounts in Reginald Fleming Johnston, *Twilight in the Forbidden City* (reprint, n.p.: Xiaomina, 2007). First published in 1934, Johnston's book was based on his observations of the tumultuous political situation in Beijing while he was serving as a tutor to Pu Yi in the 1920s and 1930s. For a discussion of the cross-cultural visual and nonvisual representational politics around Bertolucci's film, see Rey Chow, *Woman and Chinese Modernity: The Politics of Reading Between West and East* (Minneapolis: University of Minnesota Press, 1991), 3–33. For the internationally well-known narration by Pu Yi of the first half of his life, see *From Emperor to Citizen: The Autobiography of Aisin-Gioro Pu Yi*, English and Chinese ed., trans. W. J. F. Jenner (Beijing: Foreign Languages Press, 1989). For a filmic rendition of Pu Yi's life after he had become an ordinary citizen in Beijing, see Li Hanxiang, dir., 火龍 *Huo Long* (*The Last Emperor*, 1986).
7. William Hinton, *Fanshen: A Documentary of Revolution in a Chinese Village* (New York: Monthly Review Press, 1966), vii. See in particular the two chapters under the title "Self Report, Public Appraisal," 275–79, 593–600.
8. Hinton, *Fanshen*, 277.
9. It would be interesting to juxtapose this device of communism with the controversial definition of the political offered by Carl Schmitt—namely, the political as a type of decision making based on the distinction between the friend and the enemy. See Carl Schmitt, *The Concept of the Political*, exp. ed., trans. and with an introduction by George Schwab, foreword by Tracy B. Strong, and notes by Leo Strauss (Chicago: University of Chicago Press, 2007).
10. For more recent studies of the Chinese Cultural Revolution, see, for instance, Alexander C. Cook, ed., *Mao's Little Red Book: A Global History* (Cambridge: Cambridge University Press, 2014).
11. For discussions of the influence of Maoism on Western and non-Western societies, see, for instance, Richard Wolin, *The Wind from the East: French Intellectuals, the Cultural Revolution, and the Legacy of the 1960s* (Princeton, NJ: Princeton University Press, 2010); Julia Lovell, "The Cultural Revolution and Its Legacies in International

Perspective," *China Quarterly* 227 (2016): 632–52. As Lovell comments toward the end of her historical account of activities in numerous countries, "The impact of the Cultural Revolution (upper-case) is part of a much more diffuse (and often liberalizing) process of cultural revolution (lower-case) that has transformed society, culture and politics since the 1960s, especially in the developed West" (649). For a discussion of Maoism in France, see Julian Bourg, "The Red Guards of Paris: French Student Maoism of the 1960s," *History of European Ideas* 31, no. 4 (2005): 472–90, and "Principally Contradiction: The Flourishing of French Maoism," in *Mao's Little Red Book*, ed. Cook, 225–44.

12. Michel Foucault, *The Birth of Biopolitics: Lectures at the Collège de France 1978–1979*, ed. Michel Senellart, trans. Graham Burchell (New York: Palgrave MacMillan, 2008), 226. For a pertinent study, see Ulrich Bröckling, *The Entrepreneurial Self: Fabricating a New Type of Subjectivity*, trans. Steven Black (London: Sage, 2016).

13. This interview was conducted by Martin Bashir and broadcast on the BBC's *Panorama Programme* on November 20, 1995. For related interest, see Andrew Morton, *Diana: The True Story—in Her Own Words*, rev. ed. (New York: Simon and Schuster, 2013); first published in 1993, the book was based on secret interviews solicited by Diana.

14. Byung-Chul Han, *In the Swarm: Digital Prospects*, trans. Erik Butler (Cambridge, MA: MIT Press, 2017), 1. Walter Benjamin's descriptions of mass-produced images in the age of technological reproducibility, in contrast to traditional, ritual- and place-bound artwork, are precisely about the loss of distance, which he names the "aura"; see Walter Benjamin, "The Work of Art in the Age of Mechanical Reproduction," in *Illuminations*, ed. and with an introduction by Hannah Arendt, trans. Harry Zohn (New York: Schocken, 1969), 217–51. Guy Debord's discussion in *The Society of Spectacle*, rev. ed., trans. Donald Nicholson-Smith (Brooklyn, NY: Zone Books, 1995), clearly remains topical and current.

15. For an interesting historical study of audience attention pertaining to the U.S. context, see Tim Wu, *The Attention Merchants: The Epic Scramble to Get Inside Our Heads* (New York: Vintage, 2016).

16. See Foucault, *Discipline and Punish*, 195–228.

17. For an informative study of how surveillance both produces and capitalizes on modified human behavior in neoliberal times, see Shoshana Zuboff, *The Age of Surveillance Capitalism: The Fight for a*

Human Future at the New Frontier of Power (New York: Public-Affairs, 2019).
18. I borrow the word *autoillumination* from Han, *In the Swarm*, 72.
19. For a helpful essay on this complex topic in the context of Foucault's work, see Paul Veyne, "Foucault Revolutionizes History," trans. Catherine Porter, in *Foucault and His Interlocutors*, ed. Arnold I. Davidson (Chicago: University of Chicago Press, 1997), 146–82.
20. See the chapter "From Subject to Project" in Han, *In the Swarm*, 45–49.
21. Nikolas Rose, *Inventing Ourselves: Psychology, Power, and Personhood* (Cambridge: Cambridge University Press, 1998), 192.
22. See, for instance, the following works by Eva Illouz: *Cold Intimacies: The Making of Emotional Capitalism* (Cambridge: Polity, 2007); *Saving the Modern Soul: Therapy, Emotions, and the Culture of Self-Help* (Berkeley: University of California Press, 2008); and *Why Love Hurts: A Sociological Explanation* (Cambridge: Polity, 2012); as well as Eva Illouz and Edgar Cabanas, *Manufacturing Happy Citizens: How the Science and Industry of Happiness Control Our Lives* (Cambridge: Polity, 2018).
23. Illouz, *Saving the Modern Soul*, 131.
24. Illouz, *Saving the Modern Soul*, 6.
25. Illouz, *Saving the Modern Soul*, 275 n. 104.
26. Illouz, *Saving the Modern Soul*, 173, emphases added; she is referring to Michel Foucault, *The History of Sexuality*, vol. 3: *The Care of the Self* (Chicago: University of Chicago Press, 1992).
27. Eva Illouz, *Oprah Winfrey and the Glamour of Misery: An Essay on Popular Culture* (New York: Columbia University Press, 2003).
28. Illouz, *Saving the Modern Soul*, 179.
29. Wu, *The Attention Merchants*, 230–31.
30. Illouz, *Saving the Modern Soul*, 170; she is borrowing the concept from Peter Galison.
31. Illouz, *Saving the Modern Soul*, 185–86, emphases added.
32. For an analysis of the imperative of choice as an ideology, see Renata Salecl, *The Tyranny of Choice* (London: Profile Books, 2010).
33. Agamben, *What Is an Apparatus?*, 21.
34. Han, *In the Swarm*, 24, 22, 48.
35. For a succinct literary-historical account of such a bourgeois subject, see Franco Moretti, *The Bourgeois: Between History and Literature* (New York: Verso, 2013).

5. From the Confessing Animal to the Smartself

36. I borrow the phrase "ambient screens" from the following collection: Nikos Papastergiadis, ed., *Ambient Screens and Transnational Public Spaces* (Hong Kong: Hong Kong University Press, 2016).
37. Michel Foucault, "Different Spaces," in *Essential Works of Foucault, 1954–1984*, vol. 2: *Aesthetics, Method, and Epistemology*, ed. James D. Faubion, trans. Robert Hurley (New York: New Press, 1998), 175–85. An earlier translation of the essay is "Of Other Spaces: Utopias and Heterotopias," trans. Jay Miskowiec, *diacritics* 16, no. 1 (Spring 1986): 22–27.
38. "Those spaces which are linked with all the others, and yet at variance somehow with all the other emplacements, are of two great types [utopias and heterotopias]" (Foucault, "Different Spaces," 2:178).
39. Foucault, "Different Spaces," 2:177.
40. Jacques Lacan, "The Mirror Stage as Formative of the Function of the I as Revealed in Psychoanalytic Experience," in *Écrits: A Selection*, trans. Alan Sheridan (New York: Norton, 1977), 3.
41. Foucault, "Different Spaces," 2:179, emphasis added.
42. Foucault, "Different Spaces," 2:179, emphasis added.
43. For an illuminating account of the technosocial, technopsychic experiences that involve media contacts and networks, see the introduction in Thomas Lamarre, *The Anime Ecology: A Genealogy of Television, Animation, and Game Media* (Minneapolis: University of Minnesota Press, 2018).
44. For discussions of interpassivity—the delegation of enjoyment to another, usually a machinic device or process—see Robert Pfaller, *Interpassivity: The Aesthetics of Delegated Enjoyment* (Edinburgh: Edinburgh University Press, 2017). For a related discussion of Pfaller's concept, see James A. Steintrager and Rey Chow, "Dispatches to the Dead: Delegation, Consumption, and Mischievous Pleasure (Thinking with Robert Pfaller in the So-called Present)," *boundary 2*, forthcoming.
45. Han, *In the Swarm*, 18–19. According to Han, however, "Thinking necessarily involves negativity: discernment, discrimination, and selection. In other words, thought always proceeds *exclusively*" (60, Han's emphasis).
46. See Foucault's discussion of the "abilities-machine" in *The Birth of Biopolitics*, 225–37.
47. See Peter Sloterdijk, *Critique of Cynical Reason*, trans. Michael Eldred, foreword by Andreas Huyssen (Minneapolis: University of Minnesota Press, 1987), 451.

Coda: Intimations from a Series of Faces Drawn in Sand

1. Kiri Picone, "Intricate Tibetan Sand Paintings Dismantled After Completion," allthatsinteresting.com, March 30, 2015, updated April 7, 2015, https://allthatsinteresting.com/sand-painting.
2. Michel Foucault, *The Order of Things: An Archaeology of the Human Sciences*, trans. Alan Sheridan (London: Tavistock, 1970), 386–87.
3. "Navajo Sand Painting," Astrology.com, n.d., https://artsology.com/navajo-sand-painting.php.

Index

Abnormal (Foucault), 3, 192n31
abnormality, 95, 192n31
academe, 175n47; altruism, 4–5, 11; compensatory atmosphere of, 19–20; critical race studies, 92; cultural studies, 68; globalized corporate university, 27, 29, 41; knee-jerk denigration, 14, 18–19, 22, 27; moral repair enacted through non-Western X's, 22–23, 27–28; neoliberalization of, 28–29, 61; non-Western X's, empowerment of, 22–23, 26; normalizing work in, 26–27; predeterminism in, 22–23; race controversies in, 91–92; selection process, 22–23, 26–27; "shopping," language of, 18; white academy's burden, 20. *See also* area and identity studies; humanistic inquiry
accessibility, 50, 58
accountability, logic of, 8
accounting, 29

acousmaticity, 117–20, 195n10, 196n20, 199n36; bracketing, 117–19; curtain, role of, 118–19; death linked with, 126–27; double-voicedness/polyphonicity, 134–35, 137; emission and reception, 131–37; fragment as knowledge object, 125–29, 133, 137; grammar and listening, 131–32; hearing, 44, 113–15; information dispersion and, 128–29; listening in age of information dispersion, 129–33, 135; literary study applied to, 133–37; post-structuralist theoretical approach, 117; sound receiver's perspective, 127–29, 134–35; subjectless listening, 131. *See also* listening; sound; voice
actor-network-theory, 9–10
addition: accessibility through technological, 50, 58; to critique, 9–12, 16, 20; in digitized-media world, 163; distant reading and, 57; to object, 23, 30

Index

administration, of population, 84
administration, university, 8, 11, 17, 27, 61, 177n56
Adorno, Theodor, 126, 127, 145
Agamben, Giorgio, 144, 159
agency, 26, 130, 158; confession and, 141, 148; of "invisible hand," 63–64
Ahmed, Siraj, 178–79n11
Althusser, Louis, 103
American version of critique, 6, 9–10
anthropological/ethnographic practice, 89, 114–15
anticipatory reading, 12, 13
Apollinaire, Guillaume, 77
apparatus, subjectification and, 144–45, 159
archaeology of knowledge, 20, 33–34, 49, 121
Archaeology of Knowledge, The (Foucault), 49, 120–25, 137
archives, 31–32, 121
area and identity studies, 17, 172n29; aggrandizement of university manager through, 27, 177n56; normalization of, 61; as risk management/damage control, 18–19; service function of, 19, 20, 29. *See also* academe
Aristotelian analogies, 99
"Ars Poetica" (MacLeish), 44
artificial constructs, 56
artworks, 42, 65; as in action, 70, 75; avant-garde and experimental arts, 47; calligram, 77–79, *78*; captions, 80–81; connections in, 72, 79–81, 85; Foucault's painterly descriptions, 75, 77; nude, genre of, 185n30; "outside" in, 32; picture-object, 70, 184n22; Venuses, portrayal of, 71. *See also* Magritte, René; Manet, Édouard; visibilities
Aschoff, Nicole, 3–4
attention, 137, 152, 153
audit cultures and society, 8
Austen, Jane, 15, 16
autoillumination, 154

Bakhtin, Mikhail, 33, 134–35
Balcony, The (Manet), 32, 82
bareness, figure of, 68–69, 71
Barnwell, Ashley, 14
Barthes, Roland, 33, 41, 49, 50–51, 57, 180n22; "The Grain of the Voice," 130–31
Bataille, Georges, 42, 83, 187n52
Beckett, Samuel, 42
Being, crossing-out of, 49
beings, life and, 97–98
Benjamin, Walter, 202n14
Bentham, Jeremy, 143
Berger, John, 73, 185n30
Bertolucci, Bernardo, 146, 201n6
Bezos, Jeff, 3
billionaires, 3–4
binary relationships, 110, 142
biology, 40, 47, 67, 96–100; Cuvier's influence on Foucault, 96–97; ordering function of, 99–100
biopolitics, 84, 145, 193–94n47; birth of, 63; confessional discourse in, 145–46; as extratextual, 40–41; of literary study, 39–40, 59–62; sexuality and race managed through, 101–4
biopower, 104–6, 171n14
bios, 68

208

Birth of Biopolitics, The (Foucault), 34, 39, 151
Birth of the Clinic, The (Foucault), 66
Black Mirror (television series), 197–98n33
Blanchot, Maurice, 21, 126, 127, 133, 177n59
body: *énoncé* and, 121; extremities, 73–75, 79; grain of the voice and, 130–31; population as, 83; social, 103; visibility of, 66
Borges, Jorge Luis, 17–18, 45
Bourriaud, Nicolas, 187–88n55
bracketing, 117–20
Buffett, Warren, 3
bullshit, 8, 170n10
bureaucratization, 61, 99
business leaders, 3, 169n5
Bynum, Caroline Walker, 175n47

cable television metaphor, 18, 28
caesura, 21–22, 104; face in sand image as, 35–36; sound and, 118
calligram, 77–80, *78*
capitalism, 40–41, 182n2; confession in late capitalist society, 149–50; emotional, 157; philanthrocapitalism, 3–4, 11; policing and, 111; Protestantism, mutuality with, 35
captions, 80–81
care: pastoral, 107; therapeutic, 155
categorization, 30
Chan, Priscilla, 3
Chan Zuckerberg Initiative, 3
Charles, duke of Windsor, 152
China, 146–49; Cultural Revolution, 148, 202n11

Chinese encyclopedia (Borges), 17–18, 45
Chion, Michel, 33, 115, 117, 126–27, 195n10
Christianity: confession and, 140–42; cultural practices linked to residual techniques, 110–11; hermeneutics of the self, 112; pastoral power, 34, 107–12
Cixous, Hélène, 183n16
class struggle: Chinese communism and confession, 146–49; racism as, 33, 104–7, 149
Clough, Patricia Ticineto, 105–6
cogito, 126, 127, 133, 183n10
cold war: confession in environment of, 146, 148; funding for area studies, 17
Collège de France lectures (Foucault), 5–6, 63
colonialism, 88, 90–91, 191n19
communist regimes, 146–49
comparative literature, 18, 53–54, 56
comparativism, 58–59
complainant, 27
computational models, 54, 57–60
confession, 34, 139; as art of war, 149; as avowal, 141, 148; bourgeois institutions of, 143–44; Christian, 140–42; in communist states, 146–49; as compulsory extraction of knowledge, 107; external enemies, discourse of, 146–51; externalization of blame, 148, 150; Foucault's unfinished analytic of, 143–46; as freedom, 141, 149; going public, 34–35, 153; as heterotopia, 158–64; as internal ruse, 140–43; in late capitalist

▷ 209

confession (*continued*)
society, 149–50; mediatized afterlife of, 145–46; obedience and, 34, 107–8; as obligatory act of speech, 141–42; self as enterprise/entrepreneur, 151–58; sexuality as, 142, 151; as spectacle, 152, 154, 158; technosocial setting of, 158–59; will to knowledge and, 143, 145, 155. *See also* self

connections, 48–49, 54, 56; in modernist art, 72, 79–81, 85

consensus: to multinational governance, 112; on repression, 23–26

consumption, 151, 157

correlation, 84, 99

Cousins, Mark, 36

creative writing, as discipline, 46, 178n9

Crenshaw, Kimberlé Williams, 173n31

critique: addiction to, 9, 27; additive, 9–12, 16, 20; American, 6, 9–10; of comparativism, 58–59; controversy over, 6–13; critiques of, 14; of French academics, 9; interdisciplinarity and, 11, 16–17; location of within university, 28–29; paranoid mode, 12–13; post-Kantian, post-structuralist direction of, 6–7; practitioners caricatured, 7, 9–10; reflexivity of, 13–14; transatlantic, 9–10; as verb, 28

crowdsourcing, 154

cultural technique, 117

culture industry, 145–46

curtain, 25, 117–19, 129, 136; in *La Décalcomanie*, 75–76, *76*

cut/divide, 21–22, 118, 162. *See also* curtain

Cuvier, Georges, 96–97

Daston, Lorraine, 48

data, infinitization of, 83

death: acousmaticity linked with, 126–27; class struggle of racism and, 33, 104–6; pastoral power and, 108; positivist view, 104–5; racism and, 33, 104–6, 110–11; sexuality, association with, 42; sound-media technologies and, 197–98n33

décalcomanie, 186n38

Décalcomanie (Magritte), 32, 75–77, *76*

deconstruction, 6–7; voice and, 116–18

defamiliarization, 119–20

Deleuze, Gilles, 49, 73, 184–85n25, 186n37; on *énoncé*, 123; on visibilities, 70

demystification, 12–13

denotation, 51–53, 57–59

déraison, 20

Derrida, Jacques, 33, 113–16, 194n47; "dangerous supplement" concept, 20; *sous rature* (under erasure) concept of, 49, 119; Works: *Of Grammatology*, 113; *Voice and Phenomenon*, 113, 115

desubjectification, 145, 159

Diana, Princess, 151–53, 160

differentiation, 47

"Different Spaces" (Foucault), 160–62

digital humanities, 59, 61

disciplinary society, 143–44, 153

Discipline and Punish (Foucault), 6, 24, 85, 90, 142, 153
disconnection, 81–86, 98–99
discourse: development of, 40; as "found object," 120–22; mutation and differentiation, 47; normalization of self-righteous, 26–27; of repression, 25–26, 93; speaker's benefit, 26; Western representation of East, 89–91
discourse theory, 6–7
discursivity, 150, 187–88n55
disjuncture: captions and, 80–81; gaze and, 81–86
distant reading, 31–32, 56–59, 84
diversity and inclusion, 134, 173n34; as corporatist strategy, 5, 27, 169n5; denigration of Western knowledge, 18–19; as extension of New Critical project, 44
divisibility, 67
Dolar, Mladen, 51–52, 114
Dostoyevsky, Fyodor, 134–37, 200n43
douzheng (鬥爭; struggle), 149
DuBois, W. E. B., 87
Duchamp, Marcel, 119–20, 122

economic rationality, 65
Eliot, T. S., 42, 51
ellipsis, 83, 85
emotional capitalism, 157
emplacement, 160–63
"enemies of the people," 146–49
enfoldment, 79
Enlightenment ideals, 17, 66, 142, 145
énoncé (statement), 34, 113, 196n20, 197n30; as agglomerate of discourse relations, 123–25; *déjà énoncé*, 122; fragment as object of knowledge, 125–29, 133, 137; free indirect style, 123–24, 135–37; as function, 123. *See also* acousmaticity; voice
entrepreneurialism, 18; global, 11, 27; going public, 34–35, 153; non-Western disciplines normed by, 28; progressivist, 18; self-entrepreneurialization, 34–35, 151–58, 162; transnational university, 10–11
epistemological indicator, 98
epoché, 118, 196n14
Ernst, Wolfgang, 199n38
etymologies, 49–50
eugenics, 102
Eurocentrism, 9, 32, 88
evicting language, 41–48, 51, 56–57
excellence, 8, 170n12
exclusion, 3, 10, 66, 96, 189n9. *See also* outside
exteriority: invisibility and, 83; methodological, 31–32; of representation, 88
exteriority, relations of, 14–20, 26

Fabian, Johannes, 89
face drawn in sand, image of, 35–36, 67, 166
facial-recognition systems, 85–86
Fanon, Frantz, 94–95
fanshen (翻身; peasants' revolutionary movement), 147
Faubion, James, 121
feminism, psychology and, 155
Fenichel, Otto, 69
fetishes, 7, 10, 170n8
finitude, 35–36, 42, 98, 163

Foucault, Michel, 171n14, 175n45, 178–79n11; on authorship, 124; cogito, view of, 126, 127, 133, 183n10; comparative method of, 45; on dissatisfaction with phenomenology, 68; *énoncé*, concept of, 120–37; as Eurocentric, 32; on exclusion and inclusion, 3; extremities, focus on in art, 73–75, 79; impact of, 5, 29; on internal discourse of institution, 8; on "invisible hand," 63–64; military metaphors for tension between signs, 79–80; oppression, view of, 175n48, 176n54; "outside" in work of, 15, 20–22; positivism, approach to, 25, 30, 104–5; postcolonial inflection of discourse, 88–92; shift in interests, 179n13; structuralism, view of, 177n59; unpublished works, 5–6, 65; visual-reading tactics, 65–66; Works: *Abnormal*, 3, 192n31; *The Archaeology of Knowledge*, 49, 120–25, 137; *The Birth of Biopolitics*, 34, 39, 151; *The Birth of the Clinic*, 66; Collège de France lectures, 5–6, 63; "Different Spaces," 160–62; *Discipline and Punish*, 6, 24, 85, 90, 142, 153; *The History of Madness*, 21, 66; "'Omnes et Singulatim': Toward a Critique of Political Reason," 107–12; "Society Must be Defended," 33, 39, 87, 102–3; *This Is Not a Pipe*, 77–79, 184n19, 186n38, 187n45. *See also History of Sexuality, The*; *Order of Things, The*

fragment, as knowledge object, 125–29, 133, 137, 199n36
Frankfurt School, 145
Fredrickson, George M., 189n9, 193n4
free indirect style, 123–24, 135–37
French language, 42
French theory, 9
Freud, Sigmund, 69, 93, 96; sexual instinct, view of, 96; *Totem and Taboo*, 102–3
funding, 8, 55, 180n26

Galison, Peter, 48
Gates, Bill, 3
Gates, Melinda, 3
gaze, 66; disconnected, 81–86; invisibility, sense of, 82; as light, 72; noncorrespondent, 81–84; surveillance and, 85; voyeuristic, 152; of worldwide audience, 73
Gelles, David, 3–4, 169nn4, 5
genetics, 189n8, 194n47
genocide, 102
gentility, 112, 136, 143, 154
geopolitics, 39, 54, 56–57, 89
German idealist model, 8, 170n12
Germany: Nazi racism, 101–2; population as object of the police, 108–9
Gilroy, Paul, 87
Ginsberg, Benjamin, 8, 177n56
globality, 14–15
global police force, 111–12
going public, 34–35, 153
governance, 6, 39–40, 107, 142–44; consensus to multinational, 112; cruelty as spectator sport, 154; gentility of, 112, 136, 143, 154; neoliberalism as form of, 28, 64,

175n46; quantification and, 39; self-governance, 28, 31, 34. *See also* pastoral power
government, science of, 95
"Grain of the Voice, The" (Barthes), 130–31
grammar, 131–32
grammatology, 114
Graphs, Maps, Trees (Moretti), 56
graphs and diagrams, 48–53, 56, 85
Greco-Roman antiquity, 6
Greimas, A. J., 49
Grusin, Richard, 61

Han, Byung-Chul, 152, 159, 163, 204n45
Harkness, James, 186n38
hegemony, 21–22, 173n34
Heidegger, Martin, 9, 43, 45, 49, 119
hermeneutics of suspicion, 11–12
heterotopia, 22, 24, 88, 204n38; selfhood as, 158–64. *See also* utopia
Hinton, William, 147–49
historicity, 23; of *énoncé*, 127; of life, 97
history: entry of life into, 95–102; literary, 56–57
History of Madness, The (Foucault), 21, 66
History of Sexuality, The (Foucault), 6, 23–26, 39, 93–96, 101–2, 191–92n28; confession in, 34, 141–43; "Right of Death and Power Over Life," 95–96
Hitchcock, Alfred, 73
homo economicus, 64–65, 85, 151–58
homo prostheticus, 164
Horkheimer, Max, 145
human being, as integrated, 68

humanistic inquiry: classical, 19–20, 46; complainant, as normed paradigm, 27; computational models, 54, 57–60; digital humanities, 59, 61; disinterestedness as characteristic of, 17, 19–20; legitimization of, 5, 8, 19, 41; poetic language as a way to reclaim, 44; postcritique, 29. *See also* academe; literary study
Hussain, Athar, 36
Husserl, Edmund, 113–16; bracketing, concept of, 117–19
hypothesis: of race studies, repressive, 92–95, 99; repression as, 23–28, 92–95, 152; as term, 23–24

ideas, discourse of, 46
identity politics, 87, 99, 106
ideology, 49, 103, 160, 180n22
Illouz, Eva, 155–58
"illustrations," 51–52, 80
image: distant reading and, 57–58; "illustration," 51–52, 80; mass-produced, 202n14; rhetoric of, 50–51
imaginary worlds, as indispensable, 40
immanence, 24–26
indexicality, 73, 79, 124, 146
indication, 114
information dispersion, 127–29, 137; listening in age of, 129–33, 135
infrastructural relations, 90–91
interdisciplinarity, 11, 16–17
intersectionality, 17, 80, 173n31
In the Swarm: Digital Prospects (Han), 159

Index

(in)visibilities, 31–32, 63–67, 69, 81–82, 86, 99, 185n26; in collective life, 64; exteriority and, 83; gaze and, 82; unknowability, 64. *See also* visibilities
"invisible hand," 63–65
Islam, 111–12

Jameson, Fredric, 49
Johnston, Reginald Fleming, 201n6
Jones, William "Sanskrit," 178n11

Kahn, Douglas, 116–17
Kane, Brian, 116, 118, 119, 196n14, 198n34
Kant, Immanuel, 9–10
Kjellén, Johan Rudolf, 39
Klein, Melanie, 13
knowledge, 178–79n11; archaeology of, 20, 33–34, 49, 121; as collective, 121; confession, relationship to, 107, 143, 145, 154; distance as form of, 56; fragment as object of, 125–29, 133; mimesis as stain, 126, 127; nonverbal, 47–48, 52; racial, production of, 188n4, 189n8; staging of human perception, 68; as temporal composite with physical remnants, 121–22; will to, 95–99, 101, 103–4, 143, 145
knowledge production, 11, 15, 27, 40, 45, 47–48, 53, 126; network of, 96; norming of, 31

Lacan, Jacques, 49, 51–52, 134, 160–61
language: denotation, 48–53; dispersal of itself, 21; of entrepreneurialism, 18; epistemic void between words and things, 45, 47–48; eviction of, 41–48, 51, 56–57; imaginary worlds created by, 40; as impotent, 42, 46, 47; inability to communicate, 42–43, 46–47; "literary," 45–46; modernity, relation to, 40–42, 45, 47–48, 52; nostalgia for bygone status of, 42–43; as object, 45; postmodernity's relation to, 41; prefabricated quality of, 121–22; scientific discourse, 48; as speaking, naming, calling, 43–44; theorization of, 31
Las Meninas (Velázquez), 35, 69, 73
Last Emperor, The (film, Bertolucci), 146, 201n6
Latour, Bruno, 6–14, 22, 27, 170n8
Lawrence, Amy, 116
Lévi-Strauss, Claude, 49, 115
life, 39–40; being and non-being, 97–98; destructive ontology of, 97; entry of into history, 95–106; natural history v. biological approaches to, 99–100
Life: A Modern Invention (Tarizzo), 98
light, 66, 80; cinematic, 73; disparate systems of, 75; gaze as, 72; systems of, 74–75; "there is" of, 70, 81. *See also* visibilities
limits, 20–23, 28–29; disassembling of, 21; human, 35–36; as neoliberal options, 158; overcoming of, 29
listening. *See* acousmaticity; sound; voice
Listening (Nancy), 130–31
literary form, as personhood, 44
literary object, 54–55, 62

literary study: abstract models for, 56; acousmaticity and, 133–37; biopolitics of, 39–40, 59–62; comparative literature, 18, 53–54, 56; computational models applied to, 54, 57–60; distant reading, 31–32, 56–59, 84; geopolitical considerations, 54, 59; graphs and diagrams in, 48–53, 56, 85; legitimation of, 41; maps, literary, 32, 48–49, 56–58, 181n30; mathematicity in, 49–50; reform, calls for, 59–60; rescuing, 53–62; surface reading, 12, 59; visual manipulations as prosthesis, 50. *See also* humanistic inquiry; New Criticism

literature: comparative, 18, 53–54, 56; as contestation of philology, 46; decline of, 39; estrangement of, 47; as expression of extratextual reality, 40–41; "literary" language, 45–46; as modern object of interest, 40; sacralization of, 47; scanning of, 56; work of as ontologically self-sufficient, 44

lived experience, coercive apparatus and, 144–45

Lorenz, Chris, 8, 29, 170n10

Lovell, Julia, 201–2n11

"Love Song of J. Alfred Prufrock, The" (Eliot), 42, 51

Luncheon on the Grass (Manet), 32, 73–75, *74*

Lyotard, Jean-François, 42

Macherey, Pierre, 24–26, 28, 176n51

MacLeish, Archibald, 44

madness: confinement–production of, 119; *décalcomanie*, 186n38

Magritte, René, 32, 70, 184n19, 187n45; similitude, use of, *76*, 76–77; Works: *Décalcomanie*, 32, 75–77, *76*; *Représentation*, 77; *The Treachery of Images / This Is Not a Pipe*, 32, 77–79, *78*, 187n45

Manet, Édouard, 70, 184n19, 186n56; discursivity of, 187–88n55; noncorrespondent gaze in, 81–84; unpaintability and, 84; work of as epistemic threshold, 75; Works: *The Balcony*, 32, 82; *Luncheon on the Grass*, 32, 73–75, *74*; *Olympia*, 32, *71*, 71–73; *St.-Lazare Station*, 82

Maoism, 201–2n11

Mao Zedong, 148

maps, literary, 32, 48–49, 56–58, 181n30

Marx, Karl, 182n2

materiality: modern art and, 70; of voice, 116–17

mathematics, 34, 69, 180n22

meaning: polarities, coexistence of, 52; predetermination of, 22–23; sound and, 131; verbal explanation required, 58; voice and, 113

media archaeology, 34

media culture, tabloid, 151–53

media theory, 33–34, 68

Merleau-Ponty, Maurice, 68, 183n10

metanarratives, untenability of, 41, 43, 53

metaphysics of sound object, 113–14, 116, 198n34

mirror, image of, 47, 72, 160–64, 175n45

Mladek, Klaus, 111
modernism, 40, 42, 96; antiquity, modern uses of, 118–20; of Nazi racism, 101–2; Schaefferians, 118, 124, 125–26
modernity: gentility of governance, 112, 136, 143, 154; knowledge production processes in, 126; language, relation to, 40–42, 45, 47–48, 52; life's conceptual status in, 98; will to knowledge, 97
moral repair, 19, 22–23, 27–28. *See also* reparation, logics of
Moretti, Franco, 32, 56–58, 136, 180n24, 181nn30, 32; close reading, critique of, 54–55; distant reading, 31–32, 56–59, 84; on heterogeneity of problem and solution, 53, 59
multiplicity: forms of will to knowledge, 98–99; of narratives, 41, 44, 55–56; of voices, 119, 134–37
myth, structures of, 49

naming, 43–44, 45
Nancy, Jean-Luc, 33, 114, 194–95n3, 199–200n43; *Listening*, 130–31
narcissism/narcissification, 159, 161–63
nativistic approach to voice, 114–15, 117, 119, 131
natural history, 99–100
Nazi racism, 101–2
Nealon, Jeffrey T., 100
neoliberalism, 134, 170n10; governance strategies, 28, 64, 175n46; *homo economicus* and, 151; injuries turned into options, 158; invisibility and, 64; Panopticism

in, 153; self-governance, 28, 34; social relations and, 65; suspicion complicit with, 27; in university, 28–29, 61
New Criticism, 44–45, 178n9; as closed-off world, 46–47; close reading, critique of, 54–58; funding of, 55, 180n26. *See also* literary study
Newfield, Christopher, 171n14
New Humanism, 178n9
New Prophets of Capital, The (Aschoff), 3–4
New Public Management, 170n10
New York Times article (Gelles, 2017), 3–4
noncoincidence, 70
noncorrespondence, 81–84
nonverbal knowledge, 47–48, 52
normalization: of area and identity studies, 61; becoming-normed, 24; immanence and, 24–26; institutional/material benefits of, 27; of psychoanalytic discourse of race, 93; racism as tool of, 106; of repression, 25; of self-righteous discourse, 26–27; of surveillance networks, 86
nostalgic mode, 12–13
"Notes from Babel: A Colonial History of Comparative Literature" (Ahmed), 178–79n11
novels: as archives, 31–32; graphs, maps, and trees in, 57

object: addition to, 23, 30; art as, 81; concrete and ideal, 198–99n34; decimation of, 7; fear of, 170n8; as fetish, 7, 170n8; fragment as knowledge object, 125–29, 133, 137; Husserlian theory of, 196n14; language as, 45; literary, 54–55, 62; proliferation of, 30; quantification and, 180n24; sound as, 116, 196n14, 198n34; visualization and, 32, 53; voice as, 118

Of Grammatology (Derrida), 113

Oksala, Johanna, 107

Olympia (Manet), 32, *71*, 71–73

"'Omnes et Singulatim': Toward a Critique of Political Reason" (Foucault), 107–12

Open Society Foundations, 3

oppression, 93, 173n31, 175n48, 176n54; colonial as psychic, 94–95

Oprah Winfrey Talk Show, 156–57

Order of Things, The (Foucault), 17–18, 30, 31, 35, 54, 89, 178n11; discourse formation in, 40, 47; on discursive disconnection, 78–80, 98–99; language's dislocation in, 45; *Las Meninas* discussed in, 35, 69; life and history in, 96–97; parallel constellations of knowledge production in, 67

orientalism, 89–92

Orientalism (Said), 88–92, 110

origination, 35, 43, 68

"outside," 17, 19–28, 160; in artworks, 32; co-optation of, 26; in Foucault's work, 15, 20–22; imputed to non-Western disciplines, 27–28; normed through service burdens, 29; norming of, 23–28; reparative logics and, 22; thinking without transcendental guarantees, 28–31. *See also* exclusion

Panopticism, 67, 143, 153–54, 163

Panopticon, 85, 136, 143, 153–54, 163

paranoid mode, 12–13, 27

"Paranoid Reading and Reparative Reading, or, You're so Paranoid, You Probably Think This Essay Is About You" (Sedgwick), 12–13

partage, 67

pastoral power, 34, 107–12; cultural practices linked to residual, 110–11; as salvation-oriented operation, 107; soul, individualization of, 110; transnational, 111–12

paternalism, 94–95, 102

penitentiary system, 67, 141–42

People's Republic of China, 146–49, 152

personhood, of literary form, 44

phenomenological reduction, 114, 116, 117, 119

phenomenology, 68, 118

Phenomenology of Perception (Merleau-Ponty), 68

philanthrocapitalism, 3–4, 11

philanthropy, 3–4, 62, 169n4

philology, 46, 59, 178n11

philosophy: analytic tradition, 179n15; as ethnographic exercise, 114–15

phonograph/recording machine, 116, 118–19

place, 81, 131–32; mirror as placeless/nonplace, 161–62

place taking, 32

pleasure, 140

pluralistic perspectives, 11, 15, 30

poetry, 43–44

Index

Poetry, Language, Thought (Heidegger), 43
police, 193n42; pastoral power and, 111–12; population as object of, 108–9
police racism, 111
political economy, 18, 40, 47, 67–68, 96, 98, 178n11
Die Polizei (Schiller), 193n42
population, management of, 84–85, 95, 103, 145–46
positivism, 25, 30; graphs and diagrams, 52; numeric approach, 34; police function and, 108–9; racism and, 102, 104–5; visualization and, 58
"possibility of thinking otherwise," 36
postcolonial studies, 91–93
postmodernity, 41, 44
post-structuralist theory, 13, 118
potentiality, unknowing as, 64
power: free indirect style as mechanism of, 136; impotent, 47; of listener to confession, 141, 148; paternalism of, 95; sexuality managed through, 26, 33, 94, 102, 104; subject as channel for, 144
power relations, 26, 33, 93–94
predeterminism, 22–25
problem-solving approach, 4–5, 19, 53, 56, 62, 169n4
progressive politics, 64
pronouns, 132
Protestantism, 35
Proust, Marcel, 13
Psycho (Hitchcock film), 73
psychoanalysis, 102–3, 125
publishing industry, 60, 182n37
punishment, 24

purism, 44
Pu Yi, Aisin-Gioro, 146–48, 201n6
Pythagorean sect, 118, 195n10

quantification, 14, 39, 54, 84, 180n24

race, 32–33, 87–112, 188n4, 189n8; biologization of, 90–91, 101; biopolitics of, 101–4; essentialization and, 91–92; molar notion of, 91, 189n8; normalization of psychoanalytic discourse of, 93, 99; in postcolonial studies, 91–93; racism not equated with, 99; repressive hypothesis of, 92–95, 99; sexuality and will to knowledge nexus, 96–98
race war, 104, 111–12
racism, 193n45; as class struggle, 33, 104–7, 149; death permitted by, 33, 104–6, 110–11; historical usages of term, 189n9; Nazi, emergence of, 101–2; neoracism, 192n31; nineteenth-century heritage, 90–91; paternalism of, 94–95, 102; police, 111; population-oriented, 105–6; positive agenda of, 102, 104–5; post-September 11, 2001, 111–12; psychic understanding of, 94, 106; race separated from, 99; revolution required to counter, 95
Rajchman, John, 70, 184–85n25
rationality, 27, 65, 110–11, 176n51
rationalization, 150, 155
Readings, Bill, 8, 29
Red Guards (People's Republic of China), 148
regard, 82

reparation, logics of, 13–20, 157, 174n37; predeterminism of, 22–23; service function of, 19–20. *See also* moral repair

representation: language's transformed relation to, 42–43, 48; of life, 99–100; of non-Western populations, 28; of Orient, 88–89

Représentation (Magritte), 77

repression, 175n48; consensus on sexual, 23–28, 103; discourse of, 25–26, 93; hypothesis of, 23–28, 92–95, 152; speaker's benefit, 26

resistance, 144

respectability, systematicity of, 49–50

return effect, 162–64

Ricoeur, Paul, 11

Rose, Nikolas, 90–91, 154–55, 189n8, 194n47

Roussel, Raymond, 121

sacred, language and, 35, 47
Said, Edward, 88–92, 110
salvation, 107, 111, 141, 150
Sarfan, Austin, 20
Sartre, Jean-Paul, 82
Saussure, Ferdinand de, 30, 49
Schaeffer, Pierre, 33, 116–19, 120, 196n14, 198n34
Schiller, Friedrich, 193n42
Schmitt, Carl, 201n9
science of state, 84
scientific discourse, 48
scoptophilia, 69
Sedgwick, Eve Kosofsky, 12–14, 19, 22, 27
selection process, 22–23, 26–27, 30

self: auto-affection for, 113–14; as busyness project, 35; Christian hermeneutics of, 112; computational augmentation of, 162–63; confession as mode of relation to, 140, 142, 149–50; as discursive capacity, 150–51; as heterotopia, 158–64; as interiority, 114, 160–61; self-entrepreneurialization, 34–35, 151–58, 162; split model of responsibility for, 157–58; therapeutic relation to, 154–55. *See also* confession

self-care technologies, 35
self-culpabilization, 19, 173–74n36
self-examination, 108
self-governance, 6, 28, 31, 34
self-hearing, 115–16
self-help narrative, 156
self-sufficiency, ontological, 44
September 11, 2001, 111–12
seriality, 73–75, 74; of *énoncé*, 126; serialization of self, 163
Serres, Michel, 32, 69
service function, 19–20, 29
sexuality: *ars erotica*, 140, 141; biopolitics of, 101–4; as confession, 142, 151; co-opted by repression, 26, 93; death, association with, 42; historical place of, 102–3; immanence of norm and, 24–26; monitoring of, 95–96; "outside" imputed to, 26–27; power and, 26, 33, 94, 102, 104; psychoanalytic view, 102–3; *scientia sexualis*, 140
Shapiro, Gary, 82, 85, 186n33
Siegert, Bernhard, 117

signification, 19–20; as archiving, 125; computational, 58–59; dislocation of sign, 15, 27, 30, 45; *énoncé* and, 120–22; language as, 58; structuralist vocabulary of, 30
Sirens, 198–99n34
slave trade, transatlantic, 90
smartphone, 159
smartself, 164
Smith, Adam, 63–64, 178n11
Smith, David Nowell, 187n53
social body, 103
social constructivism, 7
socialism, racism of, 105
social justice, as subsidiary of capitalist enterprise, 4–5
social organization, 23
social relations, neoliberalization of, 65
social responsibility, 29
social sciences, interpretive, 45, 53
"Society Must be Defended" (Foucault), 33, 39, 87, 102–3
Soros, George, 3
soul, 19, 110, 113, 143, 153
sound: as boundless, 118; phonograph/recording machine, 116, 118–19; presence in, 194–95n3; pronouns and, 132; "sense beyond signification," 200n43; sounding, act of, 114; theory, 33–34; timbre, 131; time domain and, 199n38. *See also* acousmaticity; listening; voice
Sound Unseen: Acousmatic Sound in Theory and Practice (Kane), 116
sous rature (under erasure), 49, 119

Soussloff, Catherine M., 184n22
sovereignty, 64, 66, 67, 72, 77, 84, 101
space: confinement–production of madness, 119; curtain, function of, 118–19; Foucault's conceptions of, 22; literary artifact of, 136; organization of, 77; as place taking, 32; serialization of, 73–75, 74; topological illustrations, 51–52. *See also* curtain
speaker's benefit, 26
speaking subject, 123–25
specialization, 45, 47
speciation, 47
spectacle, 53; confession as, 152, 154, 158; in Manet's work, 71, 72–73, 185n27; media, 152, 158, 162–63; media confession as, 152, 158
speech: as calling, 43–44; public, of suffering, 157–58; as response, 44; self-referential, 52
Spinoza, Baruch, 24
Standard Oil, 180n26
Stanford Literary Lab, 57, 181n32
state: I-as-species mission, 104–5; objectification of the reason of, 110–11; police function of, 108–9; science of, 84; will to, 108
State Department, 17
statistics, 39, 84, 85, 103–4
STEM (science-technology-engineering-math), 50
structuralism, 14–15, 30, 68, 177n59
subject: bourgeois, 160; speaking, 123–25
subjectification, 144–45, 159
subjugation, 26

Index

suffering, 94–95, 106, 156–58
suku 訴苦 (voicing bitterness), 152–55
surface reading, 12, 59, 171n24
surveillance: facial-recognition systems, 85–86; gaze and, 85; internalization of, 153; population managed through, 95–96
suspicion, hermeneutics of, 11–12, 27
symbolic logic, 48

Taguieff, Pierre-André, 189n9
Tanke, Joseph, 80, 82, 188n56
Tarizzo, Davide, 98
Tenen, Dennis, 58
therapeutic discourse, 154–56
This Is Not a Pipe (Foucault), 77–79, *78*, 184n19, 186n38, 187n45
Time and the Other: How Anthropology Makes Its Object (Fabian), 89
Titian, 71
Tomkins, Silvan, 13
topological objects, 51–52
totalitarian state, 149–50
Totem and Taboo (Freud), 102–3
tout-faits (readymades), 120, 122
"Towards a Natural History of Norms" (Macherey), 24–26
Trakl, Georg, 43
transcendence, 24, 26, 28–31
transference, 76, 186n38
transnationality, academic curricular, 14–20
Treachery of Images, The / This Is Not a Pipe (Magritte), 32, 77–79, *78*, 187n45
Tristes Tropiques (Lévi-Strauss), 115

truth: extortion of, 141–42, 150; as phenomenal, 25; production network of, 143–44; production of as rationalization process, 150, 155

unhappiness, as prevailing condition, 42
universalization, 33, 44, 52; race and, 103, 107; of voice, 113
unknowable, 64–65
utopia, 160; character of denotation as, 51–52, 57, 59, 68; grammatology as project of, 114; policing and, 85, 109. *See also* heterotopia

Velázquez, Diego, 35, 69, 72
Venus of Urbino (Titian), 71
Veyne, Paul, 35
victimhood, 92–93
virtual technologies, 49–50
visibilities, 81, 184–85n25, 185n26, 187n48; divisibility, 67; historical emergence of, 32; sight, 69–70, 72–73, 80. *See also* artworks; (in)visibilities; light
Visible and the Invisible, The (Merleau-Ponty), 68
vision, as material practice, 69–70
visualization, 32; in disciplines, 48–50; doubling, 75–76, *76*; graphs and diagrams, 48–53, 56, 85; image, rhetoric of, 50–51; as method of structuration, 57–58; positivistic, 58; respectability through optic systematicity, 49–50; seriality of, 73–76, *74*, *76*; virtual technologies, 49–50
Vogl, Joseph, 108–9, 193n42

▷ 221

voice, 113–37; auto-affection and, 113–14; cut off from body by technology, 116–17, 126–27; double-voicedness/polyphonicity, 134–35; grain of, 130–31; idealization of, 113, 115–16; inner, 113–16, 118; materiality of, 116–17; multiplicity of, 119, 134–37; nativistic approach to, 114–15, 117, 119, 131; as object, 118; phenomenological reduction, 114, 116, 117; phonographic, 116, 118–19; self-hearing loop, 113–16. *See also* acousmaticity; énoncé (statement); listening; sound

Voice and Phenomenon (Derrida), 113, 115

voicing bitterness (訴苦 *suku*), 152–55

void, 42, 45, 49, 68–69, 81, 183n14

wars, 7; confession and justification for, 148, 149; race war, 104, 111–12

Wealth of Nations, The (Smith), 63–64

Weber, Max, 35

Weed, Elizabeth, 171n24

West: as cluster of discourses, 89; Eurocentrism, 32, 88; metaphysics of presence, 113; racism of, 193n45; therapeutic discourse and, 155. *See also* academe; humanistic inquiry; literary study

Wheeler, Roxann, 87, 90, 188n4, 190n12

white authors, subject to dispute, 22–23

"white man's burden," 20, 90, 173–74n36

"Why Has Critique Run Out of Steam? From Matters of Fact to Matters of Concern" (Latour), 6–11

will to knowledge, 95–99, 101, 103–4; confession and, 143, 145, 155; multiplicity of forms, 98–99

Winfrey, Oprah, 156–57, 160, 163

"Winter Evening, A" ("Ein Winterabend") (Trakl), 43

world literature, 54, 56, 59

Wu, Tim, 157, 202n15

Yancy, George, 87

zoe, 68

Zuckerberg, Mark, 3

GPSR Authorized Representative: Easy Access System Europe, Mustamäe tee 50, 10621 Tallinn, Estonia, gpsr.requests@easproject.com

www.ingramcontent.com/pod-product-compliance
Lightning Source LLC
Chambersburg PA
CBHW021944290426
44108CB00012B/956